Self-Esteem

In this edited collection, a distinguished set of contributors present a broad overview of psychological research on self-esteem. Each chapter is written by leading experts in the field, and surveys current research on a particular issue concerning self-esteem. Together, the chapters provide a comprehensive overview of one of the most popular topics in psychology.

Each chapter presents an in-depth review of particular issues concerning self-esteem, such as the connection that self-esteem has with the self-concept and psychological adjustment. A number of further topics are covered in the book, including:

- How individuals pursue self-esteem
- The connection that self-esteem has with the self-concept and psychological adjustment
- The developmental changes in feelings of self-worth over the life span
- The existence of multiple forms of high self-esteem
- The role that self-esteem plays as an interpersonal signal
- The protective properties associated with the possession of high self-esteem.

This collection will be of great interest to researchers and academics, and also to graduate and advanced undergraduate students of social psychology.

Virgil Zeigler-Hill is a social-personality psychologist at Oakland University, USA. He conducts research concerning self-esteem, narcissism, the structure of the self-concept, and interpersonal relationships.

Current Issues in Social Psychology
Series Editor: Arjan E. R. Bos

Current Issues in Social Psychology is a series of edited books that reflect the state-of-the-art of current and emerging topics of interest in basic and applied social psychology.

Each volume is tightly focused on a particular topic and consists of seven to ten chapters contributed by international experts. The editors of individual volumes are leading figures in their areas and provide an introductory overview.

Example topics include: self-esteem, evolutionary social psychology, minority groups, social neuroscience, cyberbullying, and social stigma.

Self-Esteem
Edited by Virgil Zeigler-Hill

Self-Esteem

Edited by Virgil Zeigler-Hill

Psychology Press
Taylor & Francis Group

LONDON AND NEW YORK

First published 2013
by Psychology Press
27 Church Road, Hove, East Sussex BN3 2FA

Simultaneously published in the USA and Canada
by Psychology Press
711 Third Avenue, New York NY 10017

Psychology Press is an imprint of the Taylor & Francis Group, an informa business

British Library Cataloguing in Publication Data
A catalogue record for this book is available from the British Library

Library of Congress Cataloging in Publication Data
A catalog record for this book has been requested

ISBN: 978-1-84872-098-5 (hbk)
ISBN: 978-1-84872-144-9 (pbk)
ISBN: 978-0-203-58787-4 (ebk)

Typeset in Times
by Wearset Ltd, Boldon, Tyne and Wear

Printed and bound in Great Britain by
TJ International Ltd, Padstow, Cornwall

This book is dedicated to Jennifer and my family for all of their love and support over the years.

Contents

Contributors

Jessica Cameron, Department of Psychology, University of Manitoba.

Jennifer Crocker, Department of Psychology, Ohio State University.

Tracy DeHart, Department of Psychology, Loyola University Chicago.

Christopher P. Ditzfeld, Department of Psychology, University of Oklahoma.

M. Brent Donnellan, Department of Psychology, Michigan State University.

Christian H. Jordan, Department of Psychology, Wilfrid Lauried University.

Pelin Kesebir, Pyschology Department, University of Colorado at Colorado Springs.

Tracy Kwang, Department of Psychology, University of Texas at Austin.

Jennifer MacGregor, Department of Psychology, University of Waterloo.

Christopher J. Mruk, Department of Psychology, Bowling Green State University.

Edward J. O'Brien, Department of Psychology and Counseling, Marywood University.

Lora E. Park, Department of Psychology, The State University of New York at Buffalo.

Reyna Peña, Department of Psychology, Loyola University Chicago.

Tom Pyszczynski, Psychology Department, University of Colorado at Colorado Springs.

Richard W. Robins, Department of Psychology, University of California.

Carolin J. Showers, Department of Psychology, University of Oklahoma.

Howard Tennen, Department of Community Medicine and Health Care, University of Connecticut Health Center.

Kali H. Trzesniewski, Department of Human Development, University of California.

Virgil Zeigler-Hill, Department of Psychology, Oakland University.

1   The importance of self-esteem

Virgil Zeigler-Hill

Self-esteem is clearly one of the most popular topics in modern psychology, with more than 35,000 publications on the subject of this construct. This exceptionally wide and diverse literature has examined the potential causes, consequences, and correlates of self-esteem. The considerable attention that has been given to self-esteem is most likely due to the fact that self-esteem was once believed to play a causal role in many important life outcomes. Widespread interest in self-esteem began to build during the 1970s as results emerged that linked self-esteem with a variety of social problems including drug abuse, unemployment, academic underachievement, and violence. The so-called *self-esteem movement* was in full swing by the 1980s, as evidenced by the funding of the California Task Force to Promote Self-Esteem and Personal and Social Responsibility (1990). The goal of this Task Force was to raise the self-esteem of Californian citizens with the hope that some of the social problems that were plaguing the state at that time would be reduced if individuals felt better about themselves. Various efforts to raise self-esteem have been implemented but they have not resulted in the societal changes that had been envisioned and, as a result, self-esteem is no longer considered to be the sort of panacea that many once hoped it would be. In fact, there has been considerable debate in recent years concerning the value of self-esteem, with some researchers continuing to argue that self-esteem is a fundamental construct that is associated with a wide array of important life outcomes (e.g., Orth, Robins, & Widaman, 2012; Schimel, Landau, & Hayes, 2008; Swann, Chang-Schneider, & Larsen McClarty, 2007; Trzesniewski et al., 2006), whereas other researchers have adopted a much more negative view of self-esteem and consider it to have – at best – limited value (e.g., Baumeister, Campbell, Krueger, & Vohs, 2003; Boden, Fergusson, & Horwood, 2008; Damon, 1995; Scheff & Fearon, 2004; Seligman, 1993). Most often, those who argue against the utility of self-esteem believe that it is something akin to an epiphenomenon that simply reflects other processes rather than serving as a causal agent. The purpose of the present chapter – as well as this entire volume to some degree – is to provide a relatively concise overview of this expansive and controversial literature in an effort to answer one of the most vital questions in this area of the literature: Does self-esteem play an important role in our lives?

What is self-esteem?

The construct of self-esteem was first described by William James (1890) as capturing the sense of positive self-regard that develops when individuals consistently meet or exceed the important goals in their lives. More than a century later, the definition of self-esteem that was offered by James continues to be relevant such that self-esteem is generally considered to be the evaluative aspect of self-knowledge that reflects the extent to which people like themselves and believe they are competent (e.g., Brown, 1998; Tafarodi & Swann, 1995). High self-esteem refers to a highly favorable view of the self, whereas low self-esteem refers to evaluations of the self that are either uncertain or outright negative (Campbell et al., 1996). Self-esteem is not necessarily accurate or inaccurate. Rather, high levels of self-esteem may be commensurate with an individual's attributes and accomplishments or these feelings of self-worth may have little to do with any sort of objective appraisal of the individual. This is important because self-esteem reflects perception rather than reality.

Self-esteem is considered to be a relatively enduring characteristic that possesses both motivational and cognitive components (Kernis, 2003). Individuals tend to show a desire for high levels of self-esteem and engage in a variety of strategies to maintain or enhance their feelings of self-worth (see Chapter 3 in this volume, by Park and Crocker, for a review). Individuals with different levels of self-esteem tend to adopt different strategies to regulate their feelings of self-worth, such that those with high self-esteem are more likely to focus their efforts on further increasing their feelings of self-worth (i.e., self-enhancement), whereas those with low self-esteem are primarily concerned with not losing the limited self-esteem resources they already possess (i.e., self-protection; e.g., Baumeister Tice, & Hutton, 1989). In contrast to the self-enhancing tendencies exhibited by those with high self-esteem, individuals with low levels of self-esteem are more likely to employ self-protective strategies characterized by a reluctance to call attention to themselves, attempts to prevent their bad qualities from being noticed, and an aversion to risk. In essence, individuals with low self-esteem tend to behave in a manner that is generally cautious and conservative (Josephs, Larrick, Steele, & Nisbett, 1992). It appears that individuals with low self-esteem are reluctant to risk failure or rejection unless doing so is absolutely necessary. In many ways, the risks taken by individuals with low self-esteem appear to have a greater potential cost for them than for those with high self-esteem because those with low self-esteem lack the evaluative resources necessary to buffer themselves from the self-esteem threats that accompany negative experiences such as failure and rejection.

Who has high self-esteem?

It is sometimes assumed that modern society suffers from rampant low self-esteem. This idea served as the foundation of the self-esteem movement in the 1970s even though there is no empirical support for the idea that society suffers from low self-esteem. Rather, the average scores for most self-esteem instruments are well above the midpoint of their response scales (more than one standard deviation in many cases; Baumeister et al., 1989). Generational increases in self-esteem have also been observed (Gentile, Twenge, & Campbell, 2010; Twenge & Campbell, 2001) which are consistent with the increasing cultural importance placed on this construct (e.g., parents and teachers are much more concerned about the self-esteem of children than they have been in past generations). This pattern suggests that rather than suffering from low self-esteem, most individuals are actually likely to experience somewhat high levels of self-esteem such that they view themselves in a positive manner.

Although individuals tend to report high self-esteem, their feelings of self-worth show age-related changes across the life span. More specifically, self-esteem is often relatively high during childhood before dropping precipitously at the beginning of adolescence (Robins, Trzesniewski, Tracy, Gosling, & Potter, 2002). From that point, self-esteem follows a quadratic developmental trajectory such that it increases throughout adolescence, young adulthood, and middle adulthood before reaching its peak around age 60 and then declining in old age (Erol & Orth, 2011; Orth et al., 2012; Orth, Trzesniewski, & Robins, 2010; Robins et al., 2002; Shaw, Liang, & Krause, 2010; see Chapter 4, this volume, by Trzesniewski, Donnellan, and Robins, for a review). These developmental changes in self-esteem do not emerge consistently across groups. For example, girls have self-esteem levels that are comparable to those of boys during childhood but boys begin reporting higher levels of self-esteem than girls during adolescence (Kling, Hyde, Showers, & Buswell, 1999; Major, Barr, Zubek, & Babey, 1999; Twenge & Campbell, 2001). Adolescence is the first time that this gender difference emerges and it is also the period of life when the difference is the largest. Following this divergence, women do not report feelings of self-worth comparable to those of men again until old age, when the self-esteem of men drops dramatically (Robins et al., 2002). The pronounced gender difference in self-esteem during adolescence has led to a great deal of speculation concerning the reason for this pattern (see Zeigler-Hill & Myers, in press, for a review). The most likely reasons for the more pronounced drop in the self-esteem of girls during adolescence include subtle forms of sexism that occur in the classroom (e.g., teachers treating boys and girls differently; Sadker & Sadker, 1994), a decline in girls' attitudes about their appearance with boys tending to maintain relatively positive attitudes about their appearance (Harter, 1993), and prescriptive gender norms concerning female modesty (e.g., Rudman, 1998; Rudman & Glick, 1999, 2001).

The possibility that cultural differences in self-esteem exist has often captured the interest of researchers. A number of articles have compared the self-esteem levels of individuals from collectivistic cultures (e.g., East Asian countries) with those from individualistic cultures (e.g., Western countries). The results of these studies have been mixed with some studies finding that individuals from individualistic cultures report higher levels of self-esteem than those from collectivistic cultures (e.g., Heine, Lehman, Markus, & Kitayama, 1999), whereas others have not found any difference (Cai, Wu, & Brown, 2009). Similar mixed results have emerged for the connection that low self-esteem has with important outcomes such as psychopathology in these cultures (see Cai et al., 2009 for a review).

In addition to these cross-cultural comparisons, researchers have also been interested in self-esteem differences that may exist between majority group and minority group members within the same culture. The reason for this interest is that minority groups often serve as targets for discrimination and prejudice with one notable consequence being that members of these stigmatized groups often report lower levels of self-esteem than majority group members (see Major & O'Brien, 2005, for a review). The fact that individuals from stigmatized groups often report low levels of self-esteem has been observed for various groups including overweight individuals (Miller & Downey, 1999), individuals with physical abnormalities (Van Loey & Van Son, 2003), and individuals with severe mental illnesses (Markowitz, 1998). The most prominent explanation for the low levels of self-esteem reported by individuals who belong to stigmatized groups is that they internalize the negative views of their groups that are held by wider society.

It is important to note, however, that the internalization of stigma explanation does not appear to apply to all stigmatized groups. Perhaps the most notable exceptions to this pattern is that Black individuals (i.e., African Americans of sub-Saharan biological ancestry) report higher levels of self-esteem than any other racial group in the United States including White individuals (i.e., non-Hispanic Caucasians of European heritage; see Gray-Little & Hafdahl, 2000, or Twenge & Crocker, 2002, for meta-analyses concerning this issue). This pattern led to the development of another explanation for the influence that being a member of a stigmatized minority group member may exert on self-perception which is referred to as *stigma as self-protection* (Crocker & Major, 1989). This explanation suggests that membership in a stigmatized group may serve as a buffer against negative experiences because members of devalued groups have the capacity to attribute these events to discrimination or prejudice which may bolster or protect their feelings of self-worth. This explanation is appealing but it is at least somewhat limited because it only appears to apply to the members of very few stigmatized groups, with Black individuals in the United States being among the most prominent. It is generally assumed that the increases in self-esteem reported by Black individuals during recent decades suggest a positive shift in how these individuals view themselves stemming from cultural events such as the Civil Rights movement and the Black Power movement. However, a recent series of studies suggests that these racial differences in self-esteem may be at least somewhat more complicated because the high levels of self-esteem reported by Black individuals appear to be relatively fragile (Zeigler-Hill, Wallace, & Myers, in press) and may sometimes reflect narcissistic tendencies (Foster, Campbell, & Twenge, 2003; Pickard, Barry, Wallace, & Zeigler-Hill, in press; Zeigler-Hill & Wallace, 2011).

Why do individuals want to feel good about themselves?

Self-esteem is often considered to be a fundamental human need (e.g., Allport, 1955). Consistent with this view, individuals show a clear preference for high levels of self-esteem under most conditions (see Swann, Griffin, Predmore, & Gaines, 1987, for an exception) and even prefer self-esteem boosts over other pleasant activities when given a choice (e.g., eating a favorite food, engaging in a favorite sexual activity; Bushman, Moeller, & Crocker, 2011). Further, increases in self-esteem are often considered to be one of the most important elements of the most satisfying events in the lives of individuals (Sheldon, Elliot, Kim, & Kasser, 2001). However, the underlying reasons for this desire to possess high levels of self-esteem have only recently become the subject of serious empirical attention. Two of the possible benefits associated with the possession of high self-esteem are that it may: (1) be a means for transferring information between the individual and the social environment; and (2) serve a protective function that buffers individuals from negative experiences (e.g., social rejection, achievement failure). These potential functions of self-esteem will be reviewed in the following sections. It is important to note that this is by no means intended to be an exhaustive list of the benefits associated with the possession of high self-esteem. Rather, the goal is simply to review two of the commonly identified benefits that accompany high self-esteem.

Transfer of information between the individual and the social environment

One possible explanation for the desire to possess high self-esteem is that feelings of self-worth may play a role in transferring information concerning social status between the individual and the social environment. The most widely studied informational model of self-esteem is the sociometer model developed by Leary and his colleagues (e.g., Leary, Haupt, Strausser, & Chokel, 1998; Leary, Tambor, Terdal, & Downs, 1995). According to the sociometer model, self-esteem has a *status-tracking property* such that the feelings of self-worth possessed by an individual depend on the level of relational value that the individual believes he or she possesses. This model argues that self-esteem is an evolutionary adaptation that allows individuals to monitor the degree to which they believe they are valued by others. In essence, the sociometer model suggests that self-esteem is analogous to a gauge that tracks gains in perceived relational value (accompanied by increases in self-esteem) as well as losses in perceived value (accompanied by decreases in self-esteem). A variety of studies have shown that feelings of self-worth tend to change in accordance with the perception of social acceptance and rejection (e.g., Downie, Mageau, Koestner, & Liodden, 2006; Leary et al., 1995, 1998; Murray, Griffin, Rose, & Bellavia, 2003). However, it is important to note that a recent meta-analysis found that even though individuals are likely to report an increase in self-esteem following social acceptance, they are unlikely to display any evidence of a significant decline in self-esteem following rejection (Blackhart, Nelson, Knowles, & Baumeister, 2009). This is a potentially important finding because it directly conflicts with one of the basic ideas underlying the sociometer model. That is, it has generally been accepted that individuals tend to experience decreases in their self-esteem when they experience social rejection. This is an important issue that we will return to later in the chapter.

Although the sociometer model has been extremely influential, it may provide only a partial representation of the way this information is transferred between the individual and the social environment. That is, status-tracking models of self-esteem have focused exclusively on the influence that perceived standing has on feelings of self-worth (e.g., Does feeling valued by others lead to higher self-esteem?) without addressing the possibility that self-esteem also influences how others perceive the individual (e.g., Are individuals who appear to feel good about themselves more highly valued by others?). The *status-signaling model of self-esteem* (Zeigler-Hill, 2012; Zeigler-Hill, Besser, Myers, Southard, & Malkin, in press) provides a complement to the sociometer model by addressing the possibility that self-esteem influences how individuals present themselves to others and alters how those individuals are perceived by their social environment. According to this model, the feelings of self-worth possessed by individuals may influence how they are perceived by others such that those with higher levels of self-esteem will generally be evaluated more positively than those with lower levels of self-esteem. The existing data has supported this basic idea (e.g., Zeigler-Hill et al., in press; Zeigler-Hill & Myers, 2009, 2011). Cameron, MacGregor, and Kwang (Chapter 8, this volume) provide an extended discussion of the role of self-esteem as an interpersonal signal.

Protective function of self-esteem

Another possible function of self-esteem is that it may serve as a resource that protects individuals from potential threats such as rejection or failure. That is, those with high self-esteem are thought to be less affected by negative experiences and to recover from these sorts of experiences more quickly than individuals with low self-esteem. This basic idea has been referred to using a variety of labels such as the stress-buffering model of high self-esteem and the vulnerability model of low self-esteem (see Zeigler-Hill, 2011, for a review). The underlying rationale of models that emphasize the protective properties of high self-esteem is that negative experiences may be less detrimental for individuals with high self-esteem because of their enhanced coping resources (Arndt & Goldenberg, 2002) and the certainty they have regarding their positive characteristics (Campbell et al., 1996). In essence, the stress-buffering model proposes that self-esteem and stress will interact in such a way that high self-esteem protects individuals from the deleterious consequences of stress, whereas low self-esteem increases their vulnerability to the effects of stress. The stress-buffering model has received support from a large number of studies (e.g., Brown, 2010; Brown, Cai, Oakes, & Deng, 2009; Brown & Dutton, 1995). For example,

Brown (2010) found that individuals with high self-esteem were more resilient than those with low self-esteem when confronted with negative social feedback (i.e., receiving a negative evaluation from a confederate) or negative achievement feedback (i.e., receiving bogus negative feedback about their performance on an intellectual task). A wide array of studies have shown clear and consistent evidence that individuals who report more positive feelings of self-worth are also more emotionally stable and less prone to psychological distress than those who do not feel as good about themselves (e.g., Sedikides, Rudich, Gregg, Kumashiro, & Rusbult, 2004).

Terror Management Theory (Greenberg, Pyszczynski, & Solomon, 1986) offers a more specialized view of the protective function of high self-esteem. Although Terror Management Theory has been used to explain a range of phenomena, it was initially developed to explain the desire that individuals have for possessing high levels of self-esteem. The foundation of this theory is that humans have a unique ability to understand their mortal nature and this recognition that they will eventually die has the potential to cause them extreme and paralyzing terror. It is believed that humans have learned to cope with this existential anxiety by developing an image of themselves as having value as a member of a social system that will never end. In essence, Terror Management Theory argues that an important function of self-esteem is that it serves as a buffer that protects individuals from the existential anxiety that stems from their awareness of their own eventual deaths (e.g., Pyszczynski, Greenberg, Solomon, Arndt, & Schimel, 2004; Schimel et al., 2008). This is a very interesting perspective on the function of self-esteem and Pyszczynski and Kesebir (Chapter 7, this volume) provide an excellent overview of the connection between Terror Management Theory and self-esteem.

Is self-esteem associated with important life outcomes?

The idea that high self-esteem serves as a buffer that protects individuals from negative experiences suggests that self-esteem should be associated with a wide range of positive outcomes. This assumption is most likely the reason for the considerable empirical attention that has been devoted to self-esteem. However, this seemingly straightforward issue has led to considerable controversy, with some researchers arguing that self-esteem is connected with important life outcomes (e.g., Orth et al., 2012; Trzesniewski et al., 2006), whereas others have challenged these connections (e.g., Baumeister et al., 2003). There is little debate that self-esteem is positively associated with outcomes such as self-reported happiness (Furnham & Cheng, 2000) and overall life satisfaction (Diener & Diener, 1995), so the following sections will focus on the connections that self-esteem has with other important life outcomes (e.g., psychopathology, crime).

Psychopathology

The link between self-esteem and psychopathology is evident in the *Diagnostic and Statistical Manual of Mental Disorders* (DSM-IV-TR, American Psychiatric

Association, 2000), which contains numerous references to self-esteem and related terms (e.g., "grandiose sense of self-importance") in diagnostic contexts (O'Brien, Bartoletti, & Leitzel, 2006). Low self-esteem is included as either a diagnostic criterion or an associated feature for a variety of disorders (see Zeigler-Hill, 2011, for a review). A partial list of the forms of psychopathology associated with low self-esteem includes depression, anxiety, social phobia, anorexia, bulimia, body dysmorphic disorder, alcohol abuse, obsessive compulsive disorder, schizophrenia, and borderline personality disorder.

Although there is a clear link between low self-esteem and psychopathology, the reason for this connection remains unclear. The most popular explanation for this association is the vulnerability model of low self-esteem, which suggests that low self-esteem serves as a risk factor for various forms of psychopathology (e.g., Beck, 1967). The clearest illustration of the vulnerability model can be seen for depression. It is believed that low self-esteem may play a causal role in the development of depression through both intrapsychic processes (e.g., ruminative tendencies) and interpersonal strategies (e.g., excessive reassurance seeking; Orth, Robins, & Roberts, 2008). An important extension of the vulnerability model is that low self-esteem may increase the probability of poor psychological adjustment in the wake of stressful experiences because individuals with low self-esteem do not have positive feelings of self-worth to provide a buffer that protects them from the deleterious consequences of negative experiences such as failure or rejection. DeHart, Peña, and Tennen (Chapter 6, this volume) offer an extended review of the connections between self-esteem and psychological adjustment.

Physical health

Self-esteem has been found to be associated with various aspects of physical health (e.g., Mann, Hosman, Schaalma, & de Vries, 2004; Stinson et al., 2008; Trzesniewski et al., 2006). For example, low levels of self-esteem have been shown to be associated with a number of indicators of poor health, including higher body mass (Trzesniewski et al., 2006), cardiovascular problems (Forthofer, Janz, Dodge, & Clark, 2001), smoking (Yang & Schaninger, 2010), and negative consequences of alcohol consumption (Zeigler-Hill, Madson, & Ricedorf, in press). It has been argued that the reason for these connections is that low self-esteem is a psychological risk factor that leaves individuals vulnerable to health problems or concerns, whereas high self-esteem is a psychological resource that protects individuals from these potential problems and supports good health (Stinson et al., 2008). There are various avenues by which high self-esteem may offer health-related protection including better health maintenance behaviors (Conn, Taylor, & Hayes, 1992) and improved social relationships (Stinson et al., 2008). It is also important to note that the protective properties of high self-esteem may be associated with physiological mechanisms. For example, research has found self-esteem to be connected with cortisol reactivity following stress (Seeman, Berkman, Gulanski, & Robbins, 1995), failure (Pruessner, Hellhammer, & Kirschbaum, 1999), and rejection (Ford & Collins,

2010), as well as cardiovascular responses to performance feedback (Seery, Blascovich, Weisbuch, & Vick, 2004) and general heart rate variability (Schwerdtfeger & Scheel, 2012). Taken together, these results suggest that high self-esteem may produce health benefits by protecting individuals from the deleterious effects of negative experiences by affecting the neuroendocrine system as well as the sympathetic and parasympathetic branches of the autonomic nervous system.

Interpersonal relationships

The connection between self-esteem and interpersonal experiences can be traced back to the earliest thinking about the nature of the self (e.g., James, 1890). An important example of this connection is that interpersonal experiences are generally thought to have a profound impact on self-esteem such that individuals who feel valued and accepted by others generally experience higher levels of self-esteem than those who do not (e.g., Leary et al., 1995). However, a recent meta-analysis found that even though individuals are likely to report an increase in self-esteem following experiences that denote social acceptance, they are unlikely to display any evidence of a significant decline in self-esteem following social rejection (Blackhart et al., 2009). One potential explanation for the confusion in the literature concerning how self-esteem changes in the aftermath of social rejection is that the manner in which individuals respond to rejection may depend to some extent on the feelings of self-worth they possessed prior to the rejection. That is, individuals with low and high levels of self-esteem may process information about rejection quite differently, which is consistent with the protective properties of high self-esteem. These differences in the response to rejection may begin to emerge quite early in the processing of these experiences such that individuals with low self-esteem are more likely than those with high self-esteem to anticipate rejection (Downey & Feldman, 1996), devote more attentional resources to potential rejection cues (Dandeneau & Baldwin, 2004, 2009; Li, Zeigler-Hill, Yang, Luo, & Zhang, in press; Li, Zeigler-Hill, Yang, Xiao, Luo, & Zhang, in press), fail to engage in strategies to prevent rejection (Sommer & Baumeister, 2002), and react more strongly when rejection actually occurs in terms of self-reported responses (Murray, Rose, Bellavia, Holmes, & Kusche, 2002) and physiological reactions (Gyurak & Ayduk, 2007; Somerville, Kelley, & Heatherton, 2010). In addition, the degree to which individuals with low self-esteem feel accepted or rejected is highly contingent on current cues, and their heightened sensitivity to rejection interferes with their ability to form and maintain fulfilling interpersonal relationships, which may perpetuate their feelings of low self-esteem (see Murray, 2006, for a review).

Academic outcomes

The educational system in the United States has focused a great deal on self-esteem due to the belief that high levels of self-esteem contribute to academic achievement. There are good reasons to suspect that individuals with high self-esteem will do well with regard to academic concerns because they may exert more effort and persist in the face of failure. This is important because high self-esteem may protect individuals from the negative consequences of failure, which are very common during the early stages of the learning process. Consistent with this possibility, a number of studies have found that self-esteem is positively correlated with academic performance (e.g., Wylie, 1979). Although there is a clear association between self-esteem and academic achievement, some researchers have argued that the relationship is weaker than it should be given the value that society places on academic achievement, and that self-esteem may actually be a consequence of academic achievement rather than one of its causes (e.g., Baumeister et al., 2003).

Crime

It has often been assumed that low self-esteem is associated with crime, but research concerning this connection has produced mixed results. A number of studies have found clear connections between low self-esteem and various criminal behaviors, including the use of illegal substances (Kaplan, Martin, & Robbins, 1984), delinquent behavior (Donnellan, Trzesniewski, Robins, Moffitt, & Caspi, 2005), sexual offenses (Marshall & Barbaree, 1990), and violence (Sutherland & Shepard, 2002; Trzesniewski et al., 2006). However, other studies have failed to find a consistent association between self-esteem and criminal behaviors (see Baumeister et al., 2003, for a review). This inconsistency has led many criminal justice researchers to question whether self-esteem is a significant predictor of crime and to suggest that low self-esteem should not be a target for correctional treatment programs (Latessa, Cullen, & Gendreau, 2002). An interesting study by Hubbard (2006) found that self-esteem was not associated with recidivism but that the reason for this lack of a main effect was that it was moderated by race, such that self-esteem was positively associated with recidivism for Black individuals and negatively associated with recidivism for White individuals. This suggests that a more nuanced approach to the connection between self-esteem and important life outcomes is important.

Where should self-esteem research go from here?

The self-esteem literature is vast and this construct has been shown to have connections with a wide array of other constructs, demonstrating that self-esteem plays a role in health-related outcomes, the decisions that individuals make about their lives, the goals that individuals develop for themselves, and how individuals interact with others. Despite the strengths of the existing research, it is also clear that there are certainly areas for improvement in future research concerning self-esteem. The areas that I will review include: (1) the improved measurement of self-esteem; (2) less reliance on self-reported outcomes; and (3) the use of appropriate research designs.

Improved measurement of self-esteem

Self-esteem is usually assessed through self-report instruments that directly ask individuals to rate how they feel about themselves, using items such as "I feel that I'm a person of worth, at least on an equal plane with others." This direct approach is certainly reasonable considering that self-esteem is a subjective evaluation of the self, but this measurement strategy is based on two underlying assumptions: (1) that individuals actually know how they feel about themselves; and (2) that individuals will honestly report how they feel about themselves (see Zeigler-Hill & Jordan, 2010, for a review). These assumptions are problematic because they may often be violated. For example, Myers and Zeigler-Hill (2012) found that narcissistic individuals appear to inflate their feelings of self-worth under normal conditions but report lower levels of self-esteem when they believe that others will know if they are lying. That is, narcissistic individuals appear to distort their self-reported self-esteem intentionally, and it is unlikely that narcissistic individuals are the only ones engaging in this general practice. It is important that researchers carefully consider the meaning of responses to self-report instruments – including those that are intended to capture self-esteem – rather than simply assuming that these self-reports are accurate.

Another issue related to the measurement of self-esteem is the fact that the vast majority of studies in this area have focused exclusively on the level of global self-esteem without considering domain-specific feelings of self-worth or other features of self-esteem (e.g., self-esteem instability). This is problematic because there is far more to self-esteem than simply whether global self-esteem is high or low (Kernis, 2003). The use of specificity matching may improve the predictive capacity of self-esteem in the same way that this approach has increased the correspondence between attitudes and behavior (Swann et al., 2007). That is, researchers who are interested in outcomes in a specific area (e.g., academic performance) should consider selecting a self-esteem instrument that has a similar level of specificity (e.g., academic self-esteem) rather than utilizing a global measure of self-esteem.

It is also vital that researchers attend more carefully to aspects of self-esteem other than its level. This is important because individuals with high levels of self-esteem appear to be a heterogeneous group consisting of those with secure high self-esteem and those with fragile high self-esteem (see Chapter 5, this volume, by Jordan and Zeigler-Hill, for a review). Those with secure and fragile forms of high self-esteem are indistinguishable in their responses to direct self-report measures of self-esteem level. The important differences between these two groups of individuals who report feeling good about themselves become evident only when other features of self-esteem (e.g., self-esteem instability, contingent self-esteem, low implicit self-esteem) are taken into account. A rapidly growing body of literature illustrates that these markers of fragility moderate the connections that self-esteem level has with important life outcomes. For example, markers of fragility have recently been found to moderate the connections that self-esteem level has with a range of outcomes, including psychological adjustment (Zeigler-Hill &

Wallace, in press), interpersonal style (Zeigler-Hill, Clark, & Beckman, 2011), the appraisal of romantic relationships (Zeigler-Hill, Fulton, & McLemore, 2011), the use of mate retention strategies (Zeigler-Hill, Fulton, & McLemore, in press), and anticipated reactions to negative events (Zeigler-Hill, Besser, & King, 2011). It is important that future research concerning self-esteem more regularly distinguishes between secure and fragile forms of high self-esteem.

Less reliance on self-reported outcomes

Many studies concerning the links between self-esteem and important life outcomes have relied on self-reported outcomes (e.g., self-reported psychological distress). This is problematic because self-reports may not always be perfectly aligned with reality. For example, discrepancies tend to emerge between self-reported grade point averages (GPAs) and school-record GPAs, such that students systematically overreport their GPAs (Zimmerman, Caldwell, & Bernat, 2002). This is an especially important problem for self-esteem research because it is likely that individuals who intentionally dissemble on other self-report measures (e.g., GPA) may also be likely to inflate their feelings of self-worth on direct self-esteem instruments. As a result, it is important that self-esteem research move away from its reliance on self-reported outcome measures when examining the factors that may be associated with self-esteem. That is, more attention should be given to how individuals actually behave in various situations rather than focusing as much attention on what they claim to have done or believe they would do in hypothetical situations (see Baumeister, Vohs, & Funder, 2007, for a similar argument about all research in social and personality psychology).

It may also be beneficial for researchers to explore the connections between self-esteem and physiological processes more fully. Researchers have already shown connections between self-esteem and activity in specific brain regions (e.g., Eisenberger, Inagaki, Muscatell, Byrne Haltom, & Leary, 2011), cardiovascular reactivity (Lupien, Seery, & Almonte, 2012; Martens et al., 2010; Seery et al., 2004), hormonal activity (e.g., testosterone levels among men; Johnson, Burk, & Kirkpatrick, 2007), and genetic influences (e.g., Neiss, Stevenson, Legrand, Iacono, & Sedikides, 2009). Further, individuals with low self-esteem have been found to demonstrate different physiological responses to social rejection cues, including startle eye-blink responses (Gyurak & Ayduk, 2007), activity in the ventral anterior cingulate cortex and the medial prefrontal cortex (Somerville, Kelley, & Heatherton, 2010), activity in the rostral anterior cingulate cortex (Gyurak et al., 2012), and event-related brain potentials (ERPs; Li, Zeigler-Hill, Yang, Luo, & Zhang, in press; Li, Zeigler-Hill, Yang, Xiao, et al., in press). Taken together, these initial studies concerning the connections between self-esteem and physiological processes suggest that this is an exciting area for future consideration.

The use of appropriate research designs

One of the most important issues in this area of the literature is the extent to which self-esteem causes important life outcomes. Unfortunately, many self-esteem studies are not designed in a way that allows them to address causal processes adequately. One approach would be experimentally to manipulate self-esteem levels more often. For example, Fein and Spencer (1997) found that participants were more likely to engage in stereotyping and prejudice toward members of a stigmatized group following a threat to their self-esteem. Studies of this sort have the advantage of being able to address the causal role of self-esteem in these processes. However, it is important to note that experimental manipulations of self-esteem are far from perfect because these approaches have their primary impact on state self-esteem rather than trait self-esteem.

It would be helpful if longitudinal designs were used more frequently so that researchers could gain a better understanding of the extent to which self-esteem predicts later outcomes. These studies provide extremely valuable information about the predictive utility of self-esteem. For example, Trzesniewski et al. (2006) found that low self-esteem during adolescence predicted poor mental health, poor physical health, worse economic prospects, and more criminal behavior during adulthood. Similarly, Orth et al. (2012) found that self-esteem predicted affect, depression, relationship satisfaction, and job satisfaction across a 12-year period. Results such as these provide evidence that self-esteem may play a causal role in important life outcomes rather than merely being a consequence of these events or an epiphenomenon.

Conclusion

The self-esteem literature is vast and diverse. This body of work has also led to considerable debate about the utility of this construct. Despite the many criticisms of the self-esteem research, there is compelling evidence that self-esteem is an important construct that is associated with outcomes in a wide array of life domains. Self-esteem appears to serve at least two basic functions: (1) it is involved in the transfer of information between the individual and the social environment; and (2) it offers a protective function that buffers individuals from negative experiences. Although the self-esteem literature has made important contributions to the field of psychology, there are clearly a number of areas for improvement in future research, such as refining the measurement strategies used to capture self-esteem and assessing the actual behavioral outcomes that are believed to be associated with self-esteem rather than relying on self-reported behaviors.

References

Allport, G. W. (1955). *Becoming: Basic considerations for a psychology of personality*. New Haven, CT: Yale University Press.

American Psychiatric Association. (2000). *Diagnostic and statistical manual of mental disorders* (4th edn, Text Revision). Washington, DC: American Psychiatric Association.

Arndt, J., & Goldenberg, J. L. (2002). From threat to sweat: The role of physiological arousal in the motivation to maintain self-esteem. In A. Tesser, D. A. Stapel, & J. V. Wood (eds.), *Self and motivation: Emerging psychological perspectives* (pp. 43–69). Washington, DC: American Psychological Association.

Baumeister, R. F., Campbell, J. D., Krueger, J. I., & Vohs, K. D. (2003). Does high self-esteem cause better performance, interpersonal success, happiness, or healthier life-styles? *Psychological Science in the Public Interest, 4*, 1–44.

Baumeister, R. F., Tice, D. M., & Hutton, D. G. (1989). Self-presentational motivations and personality differences in self-esteem. *Journal of Personality, 57*, 547–579.

Baumeister, R. F., Vohs, K. D., & Funder, D. C. (2007). Psychology as the science of self-reports and finger movements: Whatever happened to actual behavior? *Perspectives on Psychological Science, 2*, 396–403.

Beck, A. T. (1967). *Depression: Clinical experimental and theoretical aspects*. New York, NY: Harper and Row.

Blackhart, G. C., Nelson, B. C., Knowles, M. L., & Baumeister, R. F. (2009). Rejection elicits emotional reactions but neither causes immediate distress nor lowers self-esteem: A meta-analytic review of 192 studies on social exclusion. *Personality and Social Psychology Review, 13*, 269–309.

Boden, J. M., Fergusson, D. M., & Horwood, L. J. (2008). Does adolescent self-esteem predict later life outcomes? A test of the causal role of self-esteem. *Development and Psychopathology, 20*, 319–339.

Brown, J. D. (1998). *The self*. New York, NY: McGraw-Hill.

Brown, J. D. (2010). High self-esteem buffers negative feedback: Once more with feeling. *Cognition and Emotion, 24*, 1389–1404.

Brown, J. D., Cai, H., Oakes, M. A., & Deng, C. (2009). Cultural similarities in self-esteem functioning: East is East and West is West, but sometimes the twain do meet. *Journal of Cross-Cultural Psychology, 40*, 140–157.

Brown, J. D., & Dutton, K. A. (1995). Truth and consequences: The costs and benefits of accurate self-knowledge. *Personality and Social Psychology Bulletin, 21*, 1288–1296.

Bushman, B. J., Moeller, S. J., & Crocker, J. (2011). Sweets, sex, or self-esteem? Comparing the value of self-esteem boosts with other pleasant rewards. *Journal of Personality, 79*, 993–1012.

Cai, H., Wu, Q., & Brown, J. D. (2009). Is self-esteem a universal need? Evidence from the People's Republic of China. *Asian Journal of Social Psychology, 12*, 104–120.

California Task Force to Promote Self-Esteem and Personal and Social Responsibility. (1990). *Toward a state of self-esteem*. Sacramento, CA: California State Department of Education.

Campbell, J. D., Trapnell, P. D., Heine, S. J., Katz, I. M., Lavallee, L. F., & Lehman, D. R. (1996). Self-concept clarity: Measurement, personality correlates, and cultural boundaries. *Journal of Personality and Social Psychology, 70*, 141–156.

Conn, V. S., Taylor, S. G., & Hayes, V. (1992). Social support, self-esteem, and self-care after myocardial infarction. *Health Values: The Journal of Health Behavior, Education, and Promotion, 16*, 25–31.

Crocker, J., & Major, B. (1989). Social stigma and self-esteem: The self-protective properties of stigma. *Psychological Review, 96*, 608–630.

Damon, W. (1995). *Greater expectations: Overcoming the culture of indulgence in America's homes and schools*. New York, NY: Free Press.

Dandeneau, S. D., & Baldwin, M. W. (2004). The inhibition of socially rejecting information among people with high versus low self-esteem: The role of attentional bias and the effects of bias reduction training. *Journal of Personality and Social Psychology, 23*, 584–603.

Dandeneau, S. D., & Baldwin, M. W. (2009). The buffering effects of rejection-inhibiting attentional training on social and performance threat among adult students. *Contemporary Educational Psychology, 34*, 42–50.

Diener, E., & Diener, M. (1995). Cross-cultural correlates of life satisfaction and self-esteem. *Journal of Personality and Social Psychology, 68*, 653–663.

Donnellan, M. B., Trzesniewski, K. H., Robins, R. W., Moffitt, T. E., & Caspi, A. (2005). Low self-esteem is related to aggression, antisocial behavior, and delinquency. *Psychological Science, 16*, 328–335.

Downey, G., & Feldman, S. I. (1996). Implications of rejection sensitivity for intimate relationships. *Journal of Personality and Social Psychology, 70*, 1327–1343.

Downie, M., Mageau, G. A., Koestner, R., & Liodden, T. (2006). On the risk of being a cultural chameleon: Variations in collective self-esteem across social interactions. *Cultural Diversity and Ethnic Minority Psychology, 12*, 527–540.

Eisenberger, N. I., Inagaki, T. K., Muscatell, K. A., Byrne Haltom, K. E., & Leary, M. R. (2011). The neural sociometer: Brain mechanisms underlying state self-esteem. *Journal of Cognitive Neuroscience, 23*, 3448–3455.

Erol, R. Y., & Orth, U. (2011). Self-esteem development from age 14 to 30 years: A longitudinal study. *Journal of Personality and Social Psychology, 101*, 607–619.

Fein, S., & Spencer, S. J. (1997). Prejudice as self-image maintenance. *Journal of Personality and Social Psychology, 73*, 31–44.

Ford, M. B., & Collins, N. L. (2010). Self-esteem moderates neuroendocrine and psychological responses to interpersonal rejection. *Journal of Personality and Social Psychology, 98*, 405–419.

Forthofer, M. S., Janz, N. K., Dodge, J. A., & Clark, N. M. (2001). Gender differences in the associations of self-esteem, stress, and social support with functional health status among older adults with heart disease. *Journal of Women and Aging, 13*, 19–36.

Foster, J. D., Campbell, W. K., & Twenge, J. M. (2003). Individual differences in narcissism: Inflated self-views across the lifespan and around the world. *Journal of Research in Personality, 37*, 469–486.

Furnham, A. A., & Cheng, H. H. (2000). Perceived parental behaviour, self-esteem and happiness. *Social Psychiatry and Psychiatric Epidemiology, 35*, 463–470.

Gentile, B., Twenge, J. M., & Campbell, W. K. (2010). Birth cohort differences in self-esteem, 1988–2008: A cross-temporal meta-analysis. *Review of General Psychology, 14*, 261–268.

Gray-Little, B., & Hafdahl, A. R. (2000). Factors influencing racial comparisons of self-esteem: A quantitative review. *Psychological Bulletin, 126*, 26–54.

Greenberg, J., Pyszczynski, T., & Solomon, S. (1986). The causes and consequences of a need for self-esteem: A terror management theory. In R. F. Baumeister (ed.), *Public self and private self* (pp. 189–212). New York, NY: Springer-Verlag.

Gyurak, A., & Ayduk, Ö. (2007). Defensive physiological reactions to rejection. *Psychological Science, 18*, 886–892.

Gyurak, A., Hooker, C. I., Miyakawa, A., Verosky, S., Luerssen, A., & Ayduk, Ö. N. (2012). Individual differences in neural responses to social rejection: The joint effect of self-esteem and attentional control. *Social Cognitive and Affective Neuroscience, 7*, 322–331.

Harter, S. (1993). Causes and consequences of low self-esteem in children and adolescents. In R. Baumeister (ed.), *Self-esteem: The puzzle of low self-regard* (pp. 87–111). New York, NY: Plenum Press.

Heine, S. J., Lehman, D. R., Markus, H. R., & Kitayama, S. (1999). Is there a universal need for positive self-regard? *Psychological Review, 106*, 766–794.

Hubbard, D. J. (2006). Should we be targeting self-esteem in treatment for offenders: Do gender and race matter in whether self-esteem matters? *Journal of Offender Rehabilitation, 44*, 39–57.

James, W. (1890). *The principles of psychology*. Cambridge, MA: Harvard University Press.

Johnson, R. T., Burk, J. A., & Kirkpatrick, L. A. (2007). Dominance and prestige as differential predictors of aggression and testosterone levels in men. *Evolution and Human Behavior, 28*, 345–351.

Josephs, R. A., Larrick, R. P., Steele, C. M., & Nisbett, R. E. (1992). Protecting the self from the negative consequences of risky decisions. *Journal of Personality and Social Psychology, 62*, 26–37.

Kaplan, H. B., Martin, S. S., & Robbins, C. (1984). Pathways to adolescent drug use: Self-derogation, peer influence, weakening of social controls, and early substance use. *Journal of Health and Social Behavior, 25*, 270–289.

Kernis, M. H. (2003). Toward a conceptualization of optimal self-esteem. *Psychological Inquiry, 14*, 1–26.

Kling, K. C., Hyde, J. S., Showers, C. J., & Buswell, B. N. (1999). Gender differences in self-esteem: A meta-analysis. *Psychological Bulletin, 125*, 470–500.

Latessa, E., Cullen, F., & Gendreau, P. (2002). Beyond correctional quackery: Professionalism and the possibility of effective treatment. *Federal Probation, 66*, 43–49.

Leary, M. R., Haupt, A., Strausser, K., & Chokel, J. (1998). Calibrating the sociometer: The relationship between interpersonal appraisals and state self-esteem. *Journal of Personality and Social Psychology, 74*, 1290–1299.

Leary, M. R., Tambor, E., Terdal, S., & Downs, D. L. (1995). Self-esteem as an interpersonal monitor: The sociometer hypothesis. *Journal of Personality and Social Psychology, 68*, 518–530.

Li, H., Zeigler-Hill, V., Yang, J., Luo, J., & Zhang, Q. (in press). Self-esteem modulates attentional responses to rejection: Evidence from event-related brain potentials. *Journal of Research in Personality*.

Li, H., Zeigler-Hill, V., Yang, J., Xiao, J. X., Luo, J., & Zhang, Q. (in press). Low self-esteem and the neural basis of attentional bias for social rejection cues: Evidence from the N2pc ERP component. *Personality and Individual Differences*.

Lupien, S. P., Seery, M. D., & Almonte, J. L. (2012). Unstable high self-esteem and the eliciting conditions of self-doubt. *Journal of Experimental Social Psychology, 48*, 762–765.

Major, B., Barr, L., Zubek, J., & Babey, S. H. (1999). Gender and self-esteem: A meta-analysis. In W. B. Swann Jr., J. H. Langlois, & L. A. Gilbert (eds.), *Sexism and stereotypes in modern society: The gender science of Janet Taylor Spence* (pp. 223–253). Washington, DC: American Psychological Association.

Major, B., & O'Brien, L. T. (2005). The social psychology of stigma. *Annual Review of Psychology, 56*, 393–422.

Mann, M., Hosman, C. M. H., Schaalma, H. P., & de Vries, N. K. (2004). Self-esteem in a broad-spectrum approach for mental health promotion. *Health Education Research, 19*, 357–372.

Markowitz, F. E. (1998). The effects of stigma on the psychological well-being and life satisfaction of persons with mental illness. *Journal of Health and Social Behavior, 39*, 335–347.

Marshall, W., & Barbaree, H. (1990). An integrated theory of sexual offending. In W. Marshall, D. Laws, & H. Barbaree (eds.), *Handbook of sexual assault: Issues, theories, and treatment of the offenders* (pp. 257–275). New York, NY: Plenum.

Martens, A., Greenberg, J., Allen, J. J. B., Hayes, J., Schimel, J., & Johns, M. (2010). Self-esteem and autonomic physiology: Self-esteem levels predict cardiac vagal tone. *Journal of Research in Personality, 44*, 573–584.

Miller, C. T., & Downey, K. T. (1999). A meta-analysis of heavy weight and self-esteem. *Personality and Social Psychology Review, 3*, 68–84.

Murray, S. L. (2006). Self-esteem: Its relational contingencies and consequences. In M. H. Kernis (ed.), *Self-esteem issues and answers: A source book of current perspectives* (pp. 350–358). New York, NY: Psychology Press.

Murray, S. L., Griffin, D. W., Rose, P., & Bellavia, G. M. (2003). Calibrating the sociometer: The relational contingencies of self-esteem. *Journal of Personality and Social Psychology, 85*, 63–84.

Murray, S. L., Rose, P., Bellavia, G. M., Holmes, J. G., & Kusche, A. G. (2002). When rejection stings: How self-esteem constrains relationship-enhancement processes. *Journal of Personality and Social Psychology, 83*, 556–573.

Myers, E. M., & Zeigler-Hill, V. (2012). How much do narcissists really like themselves? Using the bogus pipeline procedure to better understand the self-esteem of narcissists. *Journal of Research in Personality, 46*, 102–105.

Neiss, M. B., Stevenson, J., Legrand, L. N., Iacono, W. G., & Sedikides, C. (2009). Self-esteem, negative emotionality, and depression as a common temperamental core: A study of mid-adolescent twin girls. *Journal of Personality, 77*, 327–346.

O'Brien, E. J., Bartoletti, M., & Leitzel, J. D. (2006). Self-esteem, psychopathology, and psychotherapy. In M. H. Kernis (ed.), *Self-esteem issues and answers: A sourcebook of current perspectives* (pp. 306–315). New York, NY: Psychology Press.

Orth, U., Robins, R. W., & Roberts, B. W. (2008). Low self-esteem prospectively predicts depression in adolescence and young adulthood. *Journal of Personality and Social Psychology, 95*, 695–708.

Orth, U., Robins, R. W., & Widaman, K. F. (2012). Life-span development of self-esteem and its effects on important life outcomes. *Journal of Personality and Social Psychology, 102*, 1271–1288.

Orth, U., Trzesniewski, K. H., & Robins, R. W. (2010). Self-esteem development from young adulthood to old age: A cohort-sequential longitudinal study. *Journal of Personality and Social Psychology, 98*, 645–658.

Pickard, J. D., Barry, C. T., Wallace, M. T., & Zeigler-Hill, V. (in press). Ethnicity, ethnic identity, and adolescent narcissism. *Self and Identity*.

Pruessner, J. C., Hellhammer, D. H., & Kirschbaum, C. (1999). Low self-esteem, induced failure and the adrenocortical stress response. *Personality and Individual Differences, 27*, 477–489.

Pyszczynski, T., Greenberg, J., Solomon, S., Arndt, J., & Schimel, J. (2004). Why do people need self-esteem? A theoretical and empirical review. *Psychological Bulletin, 130*, 435–468.

Robins, R. W., Trzesniewski, K. H., Tracy, J. L., Gosling, S. D., & Potter, J. (2002). Global self-esteem across the life span. *Psychology and Aging, 17*, 423–434.

Rudman, L. A. (1998). Self-promotion as a risk factor for women: The costs and benefits of counterstereotypical impression management. *Journal of Personality and Social Psychology, 74*, 629–645.

Rudman, L. A., & Glick, P. (1999). Feminized management and backlash toward agentic women: The hidden costs to women of a kinder, gentler image of middle managers. *Journal of Personality and Social Psychology, 77*, 1004–1010.

Rudman, L.A., & Glick, P. (2001). Prescriptive gender stereotypes and backlash toward agentic women. *Journal of Social Issues, 57*, 743–762.

Sadker, M., & Sadker, D. (1994). *Failing at fairness: How our schools cheat girls.* New York, NY: Touchstone.

Scheff, T. J., & Fearon, D. S. (2004). Cognition and emotion? The dead end in self-esteem research. *Journal for the Theory of Social Behaviour, 34*, 73–90.

Schimel, J., Landau, M., & Hayes, J. (2008). Self-esteem: A human solution to the problem of death. *Social and Personality Psychology Compass, 2*, 1218–1234.

Schwerdtfeger, A. R., & Scheel, S. (2012). Self-esteem fluctuations and cardiac vagal control in everyday life. *International Journal of Psychophysiology, 83*, 328–335.

Sedikides, C., Rudich, E. A., Gregg, A. P., Kumashiro, M., & Rusbult, C. (2004). Are normal narcissists psychologically healthy? Self-esteem matters. *Journal of Personality and Social Psychology, 87*, 400–416.

Seeman, T. E., Berkman, L. F., Gulanski, B. I., & Robbins, R. J. (1995). Self-esteem and neuroendocrine response to challenge: MacArthur studies of successful aging. *Journal of Psychosomatic Research, 39*, 69–84.

Seery, M. D., Blascovich, J., Weisbuch, M., & Vick, S. B. (2004). The relationship between self-esteem level, self-esteem stability, and cardiovascular reactions to performance feedback. *Journal of Personality and Social Psychology, 87*, 133–145.

Seligman, M. E. R (1993). *What you can change and what you can't: The complete guide to successful self-improvement.* New York, NY: Fawcett.

Shaw, B. A., Liang, J., & Krause, N. (2010). Age and race differences in the trajectories of self-esteem. *Psychology and Aging, 25*, 84–94.

Sheldon, K. M., Elliot, A. J., Kim, Y., & Kasser, T. (2001). What is satisfying about satisfying events? Testing 10 candidate psychological needs. *Journal of Personality and Social Psychology, 80*, 325–339.

Somerville, L. H., Kelley, W. M., & Heatherton, T. F. (2010). Self-esteem modulates medial prefrontal cortical responses to evaluative social feedback. *Cerebral Cortex, 20*, 3005–3013.

Sommer, K. L., & Baumeister, R. F. (2002). Self-evaluation, persistence, and performance following implicit rejection: The role of trait self-esteem. *Personality and Social Psychology Bulletin, 28*, 926–938.

Stinson, D. A., Logel, C., Zanna, M. P., Holmes, J. G., Cameron, J. J., Wood, J. V., & Spencer, S. J. (2008). The cost of lower self-esteem: Testing a self- and social-bonds model of health. *Journal of Personality and Social Psychology, 94*, 412–428.

Sutherland, I., & Shepard, J. (2002). A personality-based model of adolescent violence. *British Journal of Criminology, 42*, 433–441.

Swann, W. B., Chang-Schneider, C., & Larsen McClarty, K. (2007). Do people's self-views matter? Self-concept and self-esteem in everyday life. *American Psychologist, 62*, 84–94.

Swann, W. B. Jr, Griffin, J. J. Jr, Predmore, S. C., & Gaines, B. (1987). The cognitive-affective crossfire: When self-consistency confronts self-enhancement. *Journal of Personality and Social Psychology, 52*, 881–889.

Tafarodi, R. W., & Swann, W. B. Jr. (1995). Self-liking and self-competence as dimensions of global self-esteem: Initial validation of a measure. *Journal of Personality Assessment, 65*, 322–342.

Trzesniewski, K. H., Donnellan, M. B., Moffitt, T. E., Robins, R. W., Poulton, R., &

Caspi, A. (2006). Low self-esteem during adolescence predicts poor health, criminal behavior, and limited economic prospects during adulthood. *Developmental Psychology, 42*, 381–390.

Twenge, J. M., & Campbell, W. K. (2001). Age and birth cohort differences in self-esteem: A cross-temporal meta-analysis. *Personality and Social Psychology Review, 5*, 321–344.

Twenge, J. M., & Crocker, J. (2002). Race and self-esteem: Meta-analyses comparing Whites, Blacks, Hispanics, Asians, and American Indians and comment on Gray-Little and Hafdahl (2000). *Psychological Bulletin, 128*, 371–408.

Van Loey, N. E. E., & Van Son, M. J. M. (2003). Psychopathology and psychological problems in patients with burn scars. *American Journal of Clinical Dermatology, 4*, 245–272.

Wylie, R. C. (1979). *The self-concept: Vol. 2. Theory and research on selected topics*. Lincoln, NE: University of Nebraska Press.

Yang, Z., & Schaninger, C. M. (2010). The impact of parenting strategies on child smoking behavior: The role of child self-esteem trajectory. *Journal of Public Policy and Marketing, 29*, 232–247.

Zeigler-Hill, V. (2011). The connections between self-esteem and psychopathology. *Journal of Contemporary Psychotherapy, 41*, 157–164.

Zeigler-Hill, V. (2012). The extended informational model of self-esteem. In S. De Wals & K. Meszaros (eds.), *Handbook on psychology of self-esteem* (pp. 211–226). Hauppauge, NY: Nova.

Zeigler-Hill, V., Besser, A., & King, K. (2011). Contingent self-esteem and anticipated reactions to interpersonal rejection and achievement failure. *Journal of Social and Clinical Psychology, 30*, 1069–1096.

Zeigler-Hill, V., Besser, A., Myers, E. M., Southard, A. C., & Malkin, M. L. (in press). The status-signaling property of self-esteem: The role of self-reported self-esteem and perceived self-esteem in personality judgments. *Journal of Personality*.

Zeigler-Hill, V., Clark, C. B., & Beckman, T. E. (2011). Fragile self-esteem and the interpersonal circumplex: Are feelings of self-worth associated with interpersonal style? *Self and Identity, 10*, 509–536.

Zeigler-Hill, V., Fulton, J. J., & McLemore, C. (2011). The role of unstable self-esteem in the appraisal of romantic relationships. *Personality and Individual Differences, 51*, 51–56.

Zeigler-Hill, V., Fulton, J. J., & McLemore, C. (in press). Discrepancies between explicit and implicit self-esteem: Implications for mate retention strategies and likelihood of future infidelity. *Journal of Social Psychology*.

Zeigler-Hill, V., & Jordan, C. H. (2010). Two faces of self-esteem: Implicit and explicit forms of self-esteem. In B. Gawronski & B. K. Payne (eds.), *Handbook of implicit social cognition: Measurement, theory, and applications* (pp. 392–407). New York, NY: Guilford Press.

Zeigler-Hill, V., Madson, M. B., & Ricedorf, A. (in press). Does self-esteem moderate the associations between protective behavioral strategies and negative outcomes associated with alcohol consumption? *Journal of Drug Education*.

Zeigler-Hill, V., & Myers, E. M. (2009). Is high self-esteem a path to the White House? The implicit theory of self-esteem and the willingness to vote for presidential candidates. *Personality and Individual Differences, 46*, 14–19.

Zeigler-Hill, V., & Myers, E. M. (2011). An implicit theory of self-esteem: The consequences of perceived self-esteem for romantic desirability. *Evolutionary Psychology, 9*, 147–180.

Zeigler-Hill, V., & Myers, E. M. (in press). A review of gender differences in self-esteem. In S. P. McGeown (ed.), *Psychology of Gender Differences*. Hauppauge, NY: Nova.

Zeigler-Hill, V., & Wallace, M. T. (in press). Self-esteem instability and psychological adjustment. *Self and Identity*.

Zeigler-Hill, V., & Wallace, M. T. (2011). Racial differences in narcissistic tendencies. *Journal of Research in Personality, 45*, 456–467.

Zeigler-Hill, V., Wallace, M. T., & Myers, E. M. (in press). Racial differences in self-esteem revisited: The role of impression management in the Black self-esteem advantage. *Personality and Individual Differences*.

Zimmerman, M. A., Caldwell, C. H., & Bernat, D. H. (2002). Discrepancy between self-reported and school-reported grade point average: Correlates with psychosocial outcomes among African American adolescents. *Journal of Applied Social Psychology, 32*, 86–109.

2 Self-structure

The social and emotional contexts of self-esteem

Christopher P. Ditzfeld and Carolin J. Showers

People wear many different hats in their everyday lives, shifting among multiple selves across diverse social contexts. The "core" self, once conceptualized as a static component of the self-concept that drives behavior across situations (cf. Allport, 1955; Rogers, 1961), has been supplanted by the multidimensional and flexible "working" self (Markus & Wurf, 1987). This self interacts *reciprocally* with context, from one situation to the next, in order to meet intrapsychic and interpersonal demands. It functions as both product and producer of situations (Canevello & Crocker, 2010; Kihlstom & Cantor, 1984). Although Bandura (1977, 1982) initiated a view of a self-concept that is sculpted through social processes, Markus and Wurf (1987) highlighted multiple self-aspects (traits, domains, states) and self-beliefs (attributes) that are linked to the self with different associative strengths, and that change over time and situations in response to social and emotional demands. This perspective on the self subsumes actual, ideal, and possible selves (Schlenker, 1985; Higgins, 1987); motives, needs, and goals (Cantor & Kihlstrom, 1987; Carver & Scheier, 1998; Higgins, 1997); and strategies such as self-enhancement and self-verification (Tesser, 1986, 1988; Swann, 1983). Individual differences in the variation of self-concept content across contexts may drive variations in self-esteem (Kernis & Goldman, 2003). The present contextualized perspective on the self links the structure of self-concept beliefs to the dynamics (e.g., level and stability) of self-esteem.

This shift of perspectives to the dynamic self parallels the general debate as to how individual differences in personality should be conceptualized. The contextualized trait x state conceptualization parallels Mischel and Shoda's (1995) cognitive-affective personality system, the *if-then* contingency model of behavior, wherein specific aspects of personality (e.g., neuroticism) emerge only in certain emotional contexts (e.g., self-threat). Just as people may display neuroticism either across a diverse set of situations (trait consistent) or only in a few (trait inconsistent), so goes self-esteem. Hence, there has been a focus on trait differences in the stability of self-esteem that has influenced self-esteem research greatly for the past 25 years: namely, whether a person's generally high trait self-esteem remains high across states (for reviews, Kernis, 2003, 2005; Leary & Baumeister, 2000). Despite this progress, research on self-esteem stability speaks broadly to qualities across situation, such as general sensitivity to rejection, instead of looking more directly at which contexts are actually encountered in a person's daily life, such as how often rejection actually is salient. To do the latter, we look for a more sophisticated model of the self, one that more precisely approaches the notion of the cognitive-affective self.

Despite the theoretical appeal of Mischel and Shoda's (1995) model, measurement and application has been problematic because trait measures of *trait inconsistencies* (variability due to context), by their nature, are difficult to specify and are statistically noisy. However, they are paramount to more complete models of self and behavior. The evaluative organization model that is the focus of this chapter provides an important middle-ground operationalization of the self in context, highlighting processes that connect contextualized self-aspects to global attitudes such as self-esteem.

The model of evaluative self-organization measures the distribution of positively and negatively valenced self-beliefs across self-aspects (i.e., contexts). This model highlights individual differences in the organization of positive and negative beliefs into same- *or* mixed-valenced self-aspects, labeled *compartmentalization* and *integration*, respectively. Although this model is cognitive in that it measures the ways people think about the self within particular self-aspects, we emphasize an affective component that underlies that cognitive content (Ditzfeld & Showers, 2011, 2012a, 2012b), namely the extent to which people's selves are guided by strong emotional reactions. In this way, this model fits well with the cognitive-affective personality system and actually begins to wed that system with models of self-esteem stability.

Before moving forward, imagine the following prototypes for the cognitive-affective self-system. *If* Erin (high affective reactivity) is in a first-date situation with Mike, *then* she has access primarily to negative self-beliefs because she has a strong negative, anxious response to new dating situations; however, *if* Erin is out for a night with her friends, *then* she feels particularly good about herself (access to many positive self-beliefs) because of a strong positive response to being around friends. On the other hand, it does not matter to Mike (low affective reactivity) *if* he is on the date or spending time with friends, because he *then* has comparatively weaker affective responses and has access to positive and negative self-beliefs in both contexts, even if both of those situations are equally as important to him as they are to Erin. Accordingly, Erin's self-esteem is more context-dependent: her global self-esteem reflects her situation-specific self-esteem. Mike's self-esteem remains fairly consistent: his global self-esteem is unwavering. Hence, self-concept structure and affective reactions are linked closely, so closely that both the cognitive and affective systems activate each other in a backward and forward process.

Evaluative organization: selves in and out of context

As mentioned, the basic model outlines two types of self-organizations: Evaluative compartmentalization, wherein individuals separate their positive and negative self-beliefs into distinct self-aspects, and evaluative integration, wherein individuals intermix positive and negative self-beliefs in each of their multiple self-aspects (Showers, 1992a). Each self-aspect is represented as its own cognitive category, containing its own set of associated self-beliefs; that is, the self-aspects represent people's selves in different mental and social contexts. In compartmentalization the content of each self-aspect category appears to be guided by positive or negative valence, and in integration it is not.

Evaluative compartmentalization

Erin's affective reactivity lends itself to compartmentalized self-organization. When she thinks about herself on dates, she has access to negative self-beliefs (*insecure, indecisive, disorganized*); when thinking about herself with friends, she has access to positive self-beliefs (*happy, friendly, optimistic*). If we asked her for other important self-aspects, she might think of herself when teaching (which she enjoys thoroughly), when visiting with her father (who has unrealistically high expectations), and when she is at home drinking wine during her "me time." All these contexts contain almost exclusively positive or negative self-beliefs, with corresponding emotional experiences. Compartmentalized selves are highly differentiated. As such, one might imagine Erin precariously navigating these contexts, like a captain navigating a ship on testy waters, emotionally rising to the crest of the wave and then dropping when the wave bottoms out. This suggests that compartmentalized individuals have *affect intensity* (Larsen & Diener, 1987), often experiencing strong positive or negative emotions, which contribute to difficulties in emotion regulation and self-control (i.e., self-esteem is highly influenced by situational context). Hence, global trait self-esteem may be difficult to estimate, perhaps reflecting the average time spent in good contexts minus times when not, or the relative accessibility of positive and negative self-beliefs. At any rate, state self-esteem is suspected to have a tenuous relationship with global self-esteem when the affective qualities of the situation mismatch a person's general beliefs about the self.

Evaluative integration

Mike has evaluatively integrative self-organization. The affective qualities of his self-beliefs remain fairly constant regardless of whether he's on a date (*confident, immature, needed, indecisive*) or with friends (*needed, disorganized, self-centered, comfortable*). These same patterns likely exist across most of his self-aspects. Integrative selves are less differentiated and appear to support emotional stability. The particular self-beliefs that Mike has about himself across contexts seem to have little to do with his feelings in those states. Whereas Erin seems only modestly in control of her emotions and cognitions, Mike's structure is well suited for emotion regulation and self-control. This seems handy, particularly in times when negative emotions impose themselves. Emotional waves do not crash as violently for Mike. However, Mike also likely does not experience the highly positive emotions that come at the crest of that wave. Hence, with evaluative integration, there appears to be lower affective intensity. Trait self-esteem is gauged less heavily on affect, but more by cognitive features. Integratives possibly weigh their positive and negative beliefs by more objective standards, such as overall social position. Moreover, state self-esteem is often consistent with trait self-esteem because the situation does not often change the qualities of self-beliefs (such individuals do not feel completely "good" or "bad" about the self, regardless of the situation).

We can apply many themes from existing literature on the self to the model of evaluative self-organization. Compartmentalization is a form of evaluative self-differentiation (self-aspects are distinct from one another; Showers & Ryff, 1996), in a kind of "good-me" versus "bad-me" fashion (e.g., Sullivan, 1953). With this differentiation of the self, it appears that all selves are not created equal. Some selves are more authentic than others. For example, Erin might consider her friends-self more important than her date-self, whereas Mike does not differentiate their importance. When selves are not universally authentic, they are not universally self-determined (Deci & Ryan, 1995), opening the door for self-esteem fluctuations when a person activates inauthentic or false selves (Harter, 1999; Kernis, Paradise, Whitaker, Wheatman, & Goldman, 2000; Sheldon, Ryan, Rawsthorne, & Ilardi, 1997). This instability, at least in part, extends from greater self-worth contingencies (see Crocker & Wolfe, 2001). Compartmentalized individuals' feelings about the self should be contingent on the feedback they receive from situations (e.g., social acceptance); hence self-esteem flows inward from the situation rather than outward from a stable, confidently held self-concept. In this way, compartmentalized individuals' self-concepts may display lower self-clarity, which is associated with unstable, fragile self-esteem (Campbell, 1990; Kernis & Goldman, 2003). Such uncertainty may lend itself to self-enhancement (Steele, 1988) and, ultimately, potentially destructive self-maintenance strategies (Tesser, 1988). In contrast, integration appears to converge with what Kernis (2003) considered "optimal" self-esteem.

Evaluative organization: moderators and correlates

A second important feature of evaluative self-organization is differential importance (see Pelham & Swann, 1989). Some selves are considered subjectively more important than others and, naturally, these important selves weigh heavily in self-esteem judgments. For example, even though Erin may see her dating-self negatively, she may believe that this role is relatively unimportant in comparison to her friends-self and her other selves. This may keep her global self-esteem at healthy levels because, generally, she does not define herself by her negative selves. Moreover, it helps buffer her state self-esteem when she is involved in a less positive context. Despite being dating-challenged, she does not lose complete faith in her worthiness to be in a relationship when on dates.

Overall, differential importance captures the relative strengths with which self-aspects are attached to the core self, at least at that moment in the person's life. Data from our lab indicate that compartmentalized individuals tend to differentiate self-aspects (rate some aspects more important than others) more so than do integratives (who tend to rate self-aspects equally important). Thus, it seems that particular self-aspects are more impactful for people with compartmentalized organizations, so it is especially important that aspects most strongly related to the core self be positive. Hence, global self-esteem is often associated with the positivity or negativity of self-aspects most closely associated with the core self, particularly in compartmentalization (Showers, 1992a).

A third important feature of evaluative self-organization is the amount of negative content in the self-concept. Although how one organizes the self is key to issues such as emotional responding and self-regulation, no matter how one arranges them, rarely is having many negative self-beliefs a good thing. High negative self-content is associated with dysphoria (Showers, 1992a) and broadly indexes negative trait affect (Ditzfeld & Showers, 2012b). Moreover, negative content has particularly important consequences in integration because this variable is associated with an inability to suppress, or fully "integrate," negative self-beliefs, that pervades the self-concept across contexts and therefore is related to low global self-esteem (Showers, Zeigler-Hill, & Limke, 2006).

Individuals whose positive self-aspects are more important than their negatives (differential importance) are referred to as *positively compartmentalized* or *positively integrative*; and those whose negative selves are most important are referred to as *negatively compartmentalized* or *negative integrative*. Alternatively, people with relatively more positive than negative content in their self-concept (proportion of negative attributes) have been referred to as positively (negatively) compartmentalized and integrative as well. However, there are some qualitative differences between differential importance and proportion of negative self-beliefs that should have unique contributions to global and state self-esteem, which we speak to in this chapter.

Support for the model of evaluative organization is robust. Compartmentalization is associated with especially high (or especially low) global, trait self-esteem, depending on whether people's important (most salient) self-aspects are perceived to be more positive than they are negative; accordingly, integration is associated with more modest levels of global self-esteem (Showers, 1992a, 1992b, 2000, 2002). Compartmentalization is associated with slower recovery from sad mood than is integration (Showers & Kling, 1996) and integration is associated with better coping in stressful circumstances, such as students' first year of college (Showers, Abramson, & Hogan, 1998). Compartmentalization is also associated with vulnerable self-esteem. Zeigler-Hill and Showers (2007) showed that compartmentalized individuals were more reactive to both negative (state self-esteem spikes) and positive (state self-esteem peaks) events in their daily lives (via diary entries) and compartmentalized individuals with high trait self-esteem reported greater fluctuation of self-esteem following a computerized social rejection task (i.e., Cyberball; see Williams, Cheung, & Choi, 2000).

Methodology, analysis, and assumptions

Evaluative organization

The most common way to measure evaluative organization is a card-sorting task. In this task, individuals sort through 40 cards, each containing a potentially self-descriptive positive or negative self-belief (20 each). People then self-generate their important or salient self-aspects and place into those aspects the self-beliefs that they feel fit most appropriately. They can use as many or as few of the self-beliefs as they choose and self-beliefs can be used in multiple self-aspects. Evaluative organization is scored by calculating a measure of *phi* for each person's card sort (Cramer's V; see Cramer, 1945/1974). Phi indexes the tendency for positive and negative content to be either segregated or mixed across self-aspects. Conceptually, a fully mixed-valence card sort is equivalent to a completely random organization; hence, scores range from 0 (completely mixed = perfectly integrative) to 1 (completely ordered = perfectly compartmentalized). Most people fall on a relative continuum from integrative to compartmentalized. Table 2.1 presents two sample card sorts and their phi scores. For more detail on the card-sorting task, see Showers and Kevlyn (1999); for additional measures of evaluative organization, see Showers (2002).

Differential importance and negativity of selves

Following the card sort, participants rate the positivity, negativity, and importance of each self-aspect group. A measure of differential importance (Pelham & Swann, 1989) is calculated by taking the correlation between positivity (positivity minus negativity) and importance across self-aspects for each participant. Hence, scores range from −1 (negative aspects most important) to +1 (positive aspects most important). In addition, the overall negativity of people's self-concepts is measured by simply calculating the proportion of negative self-beliefs in their card sorts.

Typically, self-esteem and/or mood outcomes are the criterion variables regressed onto measures of evaluative organization, differential importance, and the proportion of negative self-beliefs using a hierarchical multiple regression procedure. That is, the unique main effect terms for compartmentalization/integration, differential importance, and negative content are entered on Step 1 of the regression, followed by tests of the two-way interactions (Step 2) and the three-way interaction of all three variables (Step 3). Although we primarily focus on the evaluative organization variable, they are often moderated by these other measures (e.g., Showers & Zeigler-Hill, 2012).

Assumptions

If the working self-concept changes with context, then how meaningful is a single global measure of the self-concept like self-esteem? This is what makes

Table 2.1 Examples of compartmentalized and integrative self-organization

Compartmentalized Organization

On Good Days	On Bad Days	General Characteristics	Shortcomings	Insecurities	Securities
Happy	– Not the "real me"	Capable	– Weary	– Inferior	Organized
Successful	– Lazy	Friendly	– Indecisive	– Isolated	Hardworking
Communicative	– Disorganized	Optimistic	– Isolated	– Immature	Intelligent
Independent	– Indecisive	Interested	– Tense	– Self-centered	Capable
Optimistic	– Immature	Capable	– Lazy	– Incompetent	Lovable
Outgoing	– Like a failure	Comfortable	– Uncomfortable	– Disorganized	Optimistic
Intelligent	– Tense	Intelligent		– Tense	Interested
Energetic	– Irritable	Mature			Happy
Confident		Fun and entertaining			Independent

Integrative Organization

In School	In my Relationship	Me Most of the Time	With Roommate	In my Family
Organized	Energetic	– Indecisive	– Irritable	Needed
Hardworking	Lovable	Happy	– Indecisive	Lovable
Friendly	Fun and entertaining	Communicative	– Tense	– Indecisive
– Tense	– Insecure	Energetic	Hardworking	Energetic
Successful	– Weary	Friendly	Friendly	
– Not the "real me"	– Self-centered	Optimistic		
	Communicative			
	Needed			
	– Immature			
	– Irritable			
	Happy			
	Comfortable			
	Outgoing			

Notes

Examples of actual participants' compartmentalized (phi = 1.0; differential importance = 0.76; proportion of negative self-beliefs = 0.44) and integrative (phi = 0.27; differential importance = 0.44; proportion of negative self-beliefs = 0.35) card sorts.

The negative sign (–) indicates negative factors.

the evaluative self-model particularly versatile and unique. We consider people's representations of self in the card sort to reflect different self-structural "styles," which are stable over time and consistent across contexts, even though the content of their beliefs may change. Because compartmentalization highlights the valence of self-beliefs in self-aspects (segregated versus mixed), it captures the underlying affective qualities of people's *responses* to selves in context. This means that a person's self-concept content need not be entirely stable (importance of self-aspects likely change over time), complete (no one has access to the full self-repertoire at any one time), or even accurate (whether aspects are true, imagined, or biased makes little difference). The critical measure is the *kinds* of feelings and self-beliefs people have when thinking about selves that are currently accessible in the working self-concept. Hence, the model emphasizes affect and cognition simultaneously, such that we can predict people's responses in a wide range of contexts, from feelings (affect) to thoughts (self-beliefs) to their current evaluation of the self (self-esteem).

Cognitive-affective self

Considerable research on evaluative self-organization suggests that self-content organization and emotions are intimately linked. However, it is difficult to know the directionality of these processes. That is, do people's cognitive structures aid or hinder the ability to self-regulate emotions? Or, do underlying affective responses contribute to the differentiation of these cognitive structures? Models of emotional regulation seem to support the former (e.g., Gross, 2008). Strong emotions are the result of: (1) placing oneself into an emotional context (accepting a date); (2) failing to modify the situation (*it's only a date, what is the big deal?*); (3) attending to one's emotions (*why am I so nervous?*) without an ability to downplay those cognitions (e.g., emotional suppression or distraction); (4) failing to down-regulate the emotion via cognitive reappraisal (*don't be nervous – you should be happy that you're out on a date doing something fun*); and (5) response modulation (attempts to manipulate physiological responses of emotion; e.g., smile despite your nervousness). Potential differences in the strength of an affective response seem contingent on a chain of events – a chain of events that can be stalled by cognitive control strategies, with the end result, when cognitions fail, being a full-blown physiological emotional reaction. Hence, differences in affective intensities do not lie in the initial response to emotional events, but rather in the ability to control those responses before they intensify.

In a similar fashion, previous research on evaluative self-organization has emphasized the role of cognitive structure in controlling emotional responses, particularly to negative situations. In other words, one of the important differences between compartmentalization and integration is that these individuals use alternative ways of coping with negative self-beliefs. In compartmentalization, people may isolate their negatives into particular categories because that way they can ignore them when not in those contexts ("sweep them under the rug").

This strategy is effective if negatives generally are inaccessible, avoidable, and considered unimportant to overall self-concept. In integration, negatives are not ignored. Instead, the impact of negative beliefs seems subdued by a cognitive reframing process. They acknowledge their negative qualities, but mitigate their influence by considering their positive qualities as well ("I'm a shy but loyal friend"). This strategy is effective when positive self-beliefs outweigh negatives across important self-aspects.

Recently, however, we have reconsidered the role of affect in the cognitive organization of the self. Although cognitive control is crucial in regulating emotions, we argue that it is not appropriate to assume that individuals are predisposed to the same initial affective reactions. Stronger emotional reactions should increase accessibility of positive (or negative) self-beliefs that grab attention (Bower, 1981; Bower & Forgas, 2001) and add to the challenge of emotion regulation. Consistent with Zajonc's (1980, 1984) view of affect preceding cognition, we suggest that the process of "compartmentalizing" versus "integrating" may be rooted in an emotional process, wherein compartmentalization is the strong affective response to the self in particular contexts; hence, a particular self-aspect has all positive self-beliefs because that self-aspect arouses a positive affective response. Integration, on the other hand, may be rooted in a subdued affective response, making available a mixture of valenced self-beliefs across self-aspects.

Evaluative organization and emotional reactivity

Recent findings link the cognitive structures of compartmentalized and integrative selves to affective processes. These studies point to an emotional reactivity that underlies compartmentalization but that seems absent in integration. Ditzfeld and Showers (2011) found that compartmentalization was associated with emotional response categorization (Niedenthal, Halberstadt, & Innes-Ker, 1999). Emotional response categorization refers to a phenomenon in which emotional qualities of stimuli become more salient when people are in emotional states. For example, Niedenthal and colleagues found that individuals categorized *puppy* as more similar to *parade* (emotion link) than to *beetle* (semantic link) when in happy or sad moods. In our study, we showed that compartmentalization was associated with emotion-based categorization independent of the influence of mood. This suggests that compartmentalization is associated with affective responses that guide the cognitive categorization of emotional concepts, which were not explicitly self-relevant. This was most robustly true for sad concepts. Emotional response categorization for happy and fear concepts was contingent on the compartmentalized individuals' current level of life stress. Compartmentalized individuals responded to happy concepts when life stress was low (and did not do so when stress was high) and responded to fear concepts when life stress was high (and did not do so when stress was low). Overall, compartmentalized individuals appear sensitive to the emotional qualities of concepts, to which they respond under appropriate emotional conditions, and this response guides their cognition.

Emotional response categorization can also be demonstrated in the processing of non-verbal stimuli, namely facial expressions (Halberstadt & Niedenthal, 1997; Niedenthal et al., 1999). People in emotional states rely more heavily on the emotional expressions of faces, smiles and frowns, in making judgments of similarity. Hence, in a follow-up study we examined the association between compartmentalization and emotional response categorization for faces (Ditzfeld & Showers, 2012a). Participants rated the similarity of face pairs, each of which displayed either a happy, sad, or neutral expression. Each participant saw seven male and seven female actors that were paired only once with each other (91 trials); for each actor pair, a participant only saw one of a number of possible expression combinations (randomly assigned). Scores were computed for each participant's ratings for faces that shared emotional expressions (happy-happy, sad-sad, neutral-neutral) and faces with different expressions (happy-sad, happy-neutral, sad-neutral), in order to examine the tendency for people to rate same-emotion faces as more similar. As predicted, compartmentalization was associated with greater reliance on emotional expression for judgments of emotional state; integratives with primarily positive self-concepts rated these faces as more similar than did those who were compartmentalized or than did integratives with relatively negative self-concepts. Consistent with previous research (Showers et al., 2006), negative-integratives may be struggling to override their emotional reactions to emotionally disparate faces in an ongoing process that is not yet resolved.

If the underlying mechanism for these effects is compartmentalized individuals' high affective reactivity to emotional stimuli, then one would suspect that this reactivity should predispose compartmentalized individuals to greater high-arousal trait affect and integratives to greater low-arousal trait affect. Several findings support this suspicion (Ditzfeld & Showers, 2012b). In Study 1, compartmentalized individuals self-reported experiencing more high-arousal positive (e.g., excitement) than low-arousal positive (e.g., calm) trait affect, whereas integration was associated with the opposite result. Moreover, integratives' negative trait affect tended to be that of the low-arousal variety (e.g., feeling dull), whereas compartmentalized individuals were more likely to experience nervousness and sadness. We were also interested in how much people valued high and low arousal affect (*affect valuation*; Tsai, Knutson, & Fung, 2006), hypothesizing that compartmentalized (integrative) individuals would *prefer* high-arousal (low-arousal) affect that was consistent with their dispositional arousal. As predicted, compartmentalization was associated with preferring high-arousal to low-arousal positive affect; that is, prefer excitement to calm. Integration was associated with a preference for low-arousal positive affect, but only for individuals with relatively negative self-concepts (Figure 2.1). Interestingly, even high-arousal positive states may make salient irresolvable negative self-beliefs in negative-integratives, thus making those states somewhat aversive, a problem to which positive-integratives are mostly immune. Taken together, these findings suggest that compartmentalization and integration differ at their *affective cores* (e.g., Russell & Barrett, 1999), which influence the ways that individuals

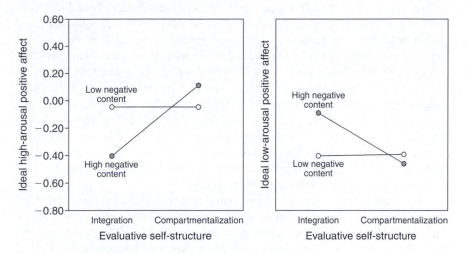

Figure 2.1 Predicted values for the interaction of evaluative self-structure (phi) and proportion of negative content for ideal high-arousal positive affect (left) and
ideal low-arousal positive affect (right), at values 1 standard deviation above
and below the means (Ditzfeld & Showers, 2012b). Ideal affect scores were
ipsatized (standardized within persons); i.e., people's scores are relative to
their own ratings for all other ideal positive affect states.

respond to emotional stimuli (see above) and motivate them toward somewhat
different ideal affect states (Tsai, 2007).

   Ditzfeld and Showers (2012b) also examined the emotional granularity of compartmentalized and integrative individuals' affective experience. As defined by
Feldman (1995, Feldman Barrett 2004), low emotional granularity involves self-
reporting multiple affect states at the same time (e.g., sadness, nervousness, and
loneliness), whereas high emotional granularity refers to self-reporting feelings
that are narrowed down to specific states (e.g., only anger), under everyday emotional circumstances. Overall, a low-granular person usually feels "good" or "bad,"
which is their summation of an assortment of same-valence affect states. Hence,
low granularity is associated with emotions that can be unclear and difficult to
control, such as intense affect in everyday experiences (Feldman Barrett, 2006;
Pietromonaco & Feldman Barrett, 2009) and even bipolar disorder (Suvak et al.,
2011). In our studies, compartmentalization was associated with low granularity of
experienced affect ratings (Study 1B). Compartmentalized individuals self-
reported experiencing same-valence affect states (e.g., sadness and nervousness)
relatively equally, whereas integratives reported discrete states (loneliness but not
nervousness). In a follow-up study, we tested whether granularity differences stem
from distinct cognitive representations of affect states. That is, do compartmentalized individuals actually *see* affect states differently than do integratives? Participants made similarity judgments among 16 affect states, which were used to create
cognitive maps of their affect representations using multidimensional scaling

techniques (see Barrett, 2004). Compartmentalized individuals did not differ from integratives in their semantic representations of valenced states. Although compartmentalization was associated with experiencing states such as sadness and nervousness equally, it was not associated with seeing those states as any less distinct semantically. Interestingly, compartmentalization was associated with different semantic representations of arousal states. Compartmentalized individuals judged high-arousal states as especially distinct from low-arousal states and also lumped low-arousal states (e.g., *inactive*) into "bad feelings" categories. Taken together, compartmentalized individuals appear to experience high-arousal positive and negative emotions that elicit an assortment of same-valence affect states; although these strong, undifferentiated emotions may be difficult to control, high-arousal states still are viewed favorably overall.

With this kind of research, a more complete model of the *processes* underlying evaluative self-organizations is coming into focus, which offers implications for cognitive-affective self-processing. In this working model, evaluative compartmentalization's high emotional reactivity makes individuals with this kind of self-organization more responsive to the emotional qualities of situations, from the mundane (e.g., seeing a puppy or being passed by a funeral procession while driving) to the more highly self-relevant (e.g., a potentially negative work evaluation or anticipating an upcoming visit from a loved one). Although any context may set off a full-blown emotional event, we presume that the strongest emotions often coincide with the contexts in which the self is most salient and most subjectively important, particularly for compartmentalized individuals. Therefore, when individuals reveal their self-aspects in the card-sorting task, they give us insight into the typical kinds of feelings they experience in those situations. This may allow for precise predictions about how often, and under which circumstances, in particular, people will experience the kinds of strong emotional reactions that evoke cognitive attention to one's affect, albeit conscious or outside of awareness. With greater affective reactivity comes a greater *potential* for strong emotions and emotion-based cognitive processing. Figure 2.2 is a schematic representation of these processes at work in selves across contexts.

By the time compartmentalized individuals find themselves in emotional states, regulating their emotions is likely not simply a matter of cognition. Because the affective experience may in fact be stronger, individuals with compartmentalized self-organizations are often fighting levels of physiological arousal, and a corresponding influx of positive/negative cognitive content, that is not existent in highly integrative people. During strong emotional events, people should have heightened self-focus (Carver & Scheier, 1998), greater access to positive or negative content (depending on the valence of the emotion), and possibly a mixture of discrete affective states (commonly of similar valence, e.g., sad and nervous, but also at times of mixed valence, e.g., happy but also sad; Larsen & McGraw, 2011). Affect therefore makes cognitive control more difficult and commonly is the true culprit of poor self-regulation.

To be clear, this model shares features of traditional personality theories (e.g., Eysenck, 1967; Gray, 1981, 1990) and, particularly, affect intensity (Larsen &

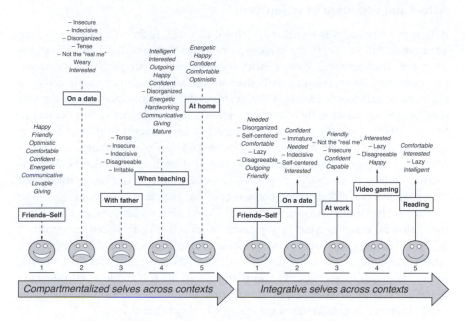

Figure 2.2 Compartmentalized and evaluative self-structures across contexts. Facial expressions represent strength of affect state. Arrow length shows perceived importance of each self-aspect. Downward arrows represent top-down self-esteem processes; upward arrows represent bottom-up self-esteem processes.

Note: The negative sign (−) indicates negative factors.

Diener, 1987), but diverges in at least four of its assumptions. First, compartmentalization reflects the potential for intense affect, but this does not imply that compartmentalized people's everyday emotions are necessarily labile. The potential for fluctuating affect may lie dormant in people with particularly positive or negative dispositions or environments. Second, greater sensitivity to negative or positive emotional qualities of stimuli does not mean that a person is destined to experience the corresponding emotions more frequently. In fact, greater sensitivity to negatives may be a means by which many compartmentalized individuals successfully avoid negative emotions (see the first step of Gross' model of emotion regulation). Third, strong affect does not equal poor cognitive control of emotions or self-control. We propose that strong affect makes cognitive control more difficult, but that does not mean that some reactive people are not adept at down-regulating even powerful emotions. Fourth, having the lower affective reactivity and the weaker emotional experiences associated with integrative organization does not mean that the experience of negative affect is any less severe psychologically. Presumably, if integratives experience a slow and persistent burn of a negative self-concept, this is not better (and it may be worse) than the perpetual blazes and quenches of emotionality in negative compartmentalization.

Affect and cognition in self-esteem

Although self-esteem is sometimes defined as one's feeling about the self (see Tafarodi & Milne, 2002), the affective processes that contribute to self-esteem are not well understood. From a strict social-cognitive perspective, self-esteem processes may be represented as bottom up, meaning that individuals compute an index of self-worth based on the positive and negative qualities of the self (i.e., self-evaluations) in their most important domains (Harter, 1993; Pelham & Swann, 1989). Trait self-esteem is a cognitive summation of self-worth across contexts, whereas state self-esteem is perceived self-worth while a person is embedded in particular contexts (e.g., states, domains, roles; Leary & Baumeister, 2000). In this view, cognitive self-evaluations give rise to affect, and then cognitive and affective components combine to potentiate actions.

Brown (1993; also Brown, Dutton, & Cook, 2001) addresses an alternative psychological order in which self-esteem, at its roots, is an affective, top-down process. That is, people feel either pleasant or unpleasant about the self (affect), which then guides evaluation (cognition), and drives action (behavior). Hence, to have high self-esteem is to *feel* positively about the self and low self-esteem is to have negative, mixed, or indifferent *feelings* about the self, whereas other conceptualizations emphasize the ways one *thinks* about the self.

Instead of debating which of these self-esteem perspectives is better, we outline how either might be the dominant self-esteem process based on individual differences in emotional reactivity. Imagine again two people, one with a highly reactive affective core and the other with a less reactive core. As the reactive compartmentalized individual navigates the social world, emotional processes guide self-relevant thought. Affect guides attention, such that emotions, particularly when they are strong, bring about self-beliefs that are accessible in a particular situation. Although global or central self-beliefs may be accessible across many contexts, and overall there might be considerable self-consistency, reactive individuals likely have self-esteem that is more contingent on the qualities of the situation: a top-down process. Less reactive integrative people cannot rely on an emotional compass to guide self-esteem, so they may rely more heavily on objective qualities of the self in context; how they think they are doing, not how they feel they are doing. Hence, they calculate roughly the positive minus the negative qualities of the self and then make judgments relevant to self-esteem: a bottom-up process.

One point of divergence in the self-esteem processes of reactive compartmentalization and the less reactive integration is in terms of stability of self-esteem (e.g., Zeigler-Hill & Showers, 2007). Perhaps the most important role of emotion is that it guides self-regulatory processes (e.g., Carver, 2004). Potential threats to one's social goals (e.g., a need to belong) should trigger negative emotions, and alert a person's cognitive system to the need for a solution. Presumably, these are the times when people are acutely self-aware and the initial self-beliefs accessible from the self-concept are likely to be negative (Mead, 1913; Ryan & Brown, 2003). Recovery systems may initiate very quickly, but resolution may take seconds, minutes, hours, or longer, depending on the effectiveness of a particular emotional regulation process for a given circumstance. Compartmentalized and integrative self-concepts represent two distinctive responses to self-threat. Compartmentalized individuals are liable to become mired in a flood of negative beliefs about the self, and may take a long time to recover from self-threat. In accordance with this, they may develop defensive strategies that help them avoid the experience of threat and its intense and inescapable companion affect (Grundy & Showers, 2012). In contrast, integratives may be relatively more willing to confront self-threats, in part because they are able to return self-esteem to baseline relatively quickly. Indeed, reactions to negative self-views have long been a main ingredient in the evaluative self-organizational model (Showers & Kling, 1996).

Although the literature has painted a particularly negative picture of unstable self-esteem (and reasonably so; e.g., Kernis, 2003; Kernis et al., 2000), we argue that there are some potential benefits in unstable responding that may have been overlooked. It is true that a compartmentalized organization does appear constructed on a tenuous foundation and that high explicit self-esteem may mask a fragile core self that is exposed when negative events occur (e.g., Rhodewalt, Madrian & Cheney, 1998; Zeigler-Hill & Showers, 2007). However, compartmentalized individuals may be especially motivated to minimize self-threat in their everyday lives, in part because they are sensitive to threats when they occur. For example, they may be highly motivated to remain in their own, and others', good graces, aiding in successful social navigation by avoiding negative outcomes before they manifest. Hence, although positively compartmentalized individuals may have contingent self-esteem, they may often live up to their contingencies. In contrast, with positive integration may come a more peaceful mode of life, characterized by more unconditional positive regard, but this may be at the cost of less emotional flavor. These individuals may not get to experience the same emotional "ups" as do those with positive compartmentalization. Remember, individual differences in core affect predict the kinds of emotionality people prefer, wherein integratives prefer low-arousal positive (e.g., calm) over high-arousal positive (e.g., elation) emotions (Ditzfeld & Showers, 2012b).

Consider also that stability is not always a good thing. Integratives with negative self-concepts may have even-keeled emotionality and self-esteem – they may always think somewhat negatively of the self, regardless of the circumstances (i.e., consistent negative self-regard). If negative compartmentalization implies occasional bursts of positive self-feelings, it may offer the potential for feeling better. Despite their current depths of despair, these individuals may recognize the potential for feeling good about the self. However, waiting for one's ship to come in at times might be worse than knowing for certain that the ship has ready passed one by. In these ways, integratives may come to feel *defeated* by their awareness of their perpetual weaknesses, whereas compartmentalized individuals may *despair* of what might have been.

Social selves: authenticity and consistency of the self

Applying the *sociometer* perspective, that a person's self-esteem is guided by perceived relational value across social contexts (i.e., how well they are satisfying their need to belong; Baumeister & Leary, 1995; Leary & Baumeister, 2000), the affective reactivity model suggests important implications for sensitivity to others' approval. Compartmentalized individuals should be particularly sensitive to potential disapproval and, perhaps to a lesser extent, potential approval (high contingencies). Integrative individuals' self-esteem should be bound by the same need, but their reactions to others should be less extreme (low contingencies). Self-esteem is then the *intra*personal calculation of how well one is living up to one's personal standards for need to belong, both globally (across situations) and currently (state self-esteem).

Evidence for this hypothesis is found in three studies reported by Zeigler-Hill, Ditzfeld, & Showers (2012). First, compartmentalization was associated with higher contingencies of self-worth (Crocker & Wolfe, 2001), particularly in individuals with positive self-concepts. Overall, compartmentalized individuals reported basing their self-esteem on belongingness-related domains, such as *others' approval*, *family support*, and *virtue*. Second, a measure of authenticity of the self (Sheldon et al., 1997) showed that people with more overall positive self-concepts saw their multiple selves as more authentic than did those with more negative self-concepts. Further, in individuals with positive self-concepts, integration was associated with more authentic selves than was compartmentalization. Hence, positive integratives saw their self-aspects as highly *self-determined* (i.e., not driven by external forces such as other people; see Ryan & Deci, 2000). Third, in people with negative self-concepts, integration was associated with highly accessible self-esteem beliefs (i.e., tendencies to report their responses on the Rosenberg (1965) self-esteem scale quickly; see DeMarree, Petty, & Strunk, 2010). That is, negative integratives were particularly fast to respond with their negative self-esteem beliefs, whereas negative compartmentalized individuals were relatively slow. This suggests that the self-evaluations of negative integratives are more secure and strongly held than they are for people with negative compartmentalization (as if they would like to override their negative responses and see the self more positively). Because the self-evaluations of negative integratives are more consistent across contexts, their self-beliefs are more accessible.

Taken together, these findings point to a dynamic relationship between self and others, wherein compartmentalized selves are more reflexive and integrative selves are more static in social situations. Despite their generally high self-esteem, positively compartmentalized individuals most likely walk into social contexts with concerns about social acceptance. They take steps to ensure success in those domains and satisfy their contingencies. Interestingly, acceptance motives may make them particularly receptive to others, which increases relationship quality, and maintains and improves self-esteem (see Canevello & Crocker, 2010). Positive integratives appear to have fewer concerns about their impressions, perhaps because their overall feelings of acceptance buffer the occasional bad impression they make on others or criticisms they receive. For compartmentalized individuals, difficulties in obtaining acceptance give rise to a self-concept that is inauthentic and high in negative beliefs about the self. Both negatively compartmentalized and integrative individuals feel as though acceptance from others is beyond their control, but their reactions and approaches to life may differ dramatically. Presumably, negatively compartmentalized individuals strive to obtain belongingness in much the same way as their positively compartmentalized counterparts, but they fail in their efforts to live up to contingencies. This likely makes social acceptance particularly desirable and the inability to achieve it all the more frustrating, culminating in a despairing form of low self-esteem (a judgment they might arrive at reluctantly). On the other hand, negative integratives' response to rejection seems more accepting, as if they can simply conclude that they are not worthy of acceptance and concede that their needs are unlikely ever to be met: a defeated form of low self-esteem.

Whether compartmentalized or integrative predispositions more greatly facilitate positive adjustment should depend on the affective disposition of the person. Indeed, evidence for self-change, particularly in individuals who were emotionally maltreated in childhood, suggests that sometimes it is best for people to compartmentalize their negative relationships and at other times it is better to integrate (Limke & Showers, 2010; Showers et al., 2006; Showers & Zeigler-Hill, 2006). Here, we suggest that the main contributor to positive well-being is a high perceived level of social belongingness. However, perception must be met with a level of accuracy; that is, belongingness must be met in an absolute sense. Artificially inflating one's relational value will leave self-esteem hollow and highly vulnerable to spikes: an inauthentic self. When this need is met, compartmentalization confers potential vulnerability and, with integration, consistency; however, compartmentalization also appears to accompany high self-esteem and positive emotionality most of the time.

When belongingness needs are not met, compartmentalization actually may have particular advantages for self-change. First, it appears that compartmentalized people desperately want to be liked by others (and themselves), so they may actively look for, or even naturally respond to, positive feedback (but also negative feedback). As their social worlds improve, they may more easily move from feeling negatively most of the time to feeling positively, and with this change comes a more positive self-concept and higher self-esteem. Further, they may then compartmentalize their previous self as distinct from the newer self, thereby moving, at least for the time being, to positive compartmentalization. Successful transition from negative integration to positive integration may result in more stable and resilient self-change, but the transition may be more difficult to initiate. Because negative integratives are already having difficulty coping with their negative self-beliefs (Showers et al., 2006), they may have difficulty summoning up the social efficacy needed to improve their current circumstances (i.e., they feel defeated). Also, they may have difficulty accepting the positive responses of others, disallowing positive beliefs from others to seep into the self-concept.

Hence, integration's consistency, never feeling particularly awful or particularly great about the self, aids resiliency – for better *or worse*.

Naturally, these self-changes are an oversimplification of a complicated social and developmental process. Overall, we suggest a temperament-based theory of cognitive-affective processing, but these processes do not develop outside of the social context. Presumably, variables such as attachment and childhood situational factors influence strongly the kinds of circumstances in which people find themselves in adulthood (e.g., the kinds of relationships they form) and the ways that people deal with adversity (e.g., emotion regulation). On top of good-to-poor life circumstances are differences in the ability to deal with such circumstances, in people's feeling control over the things they can control, and not ruminating on the things they cannot. Recently we have begun to examine the role of self-determination and attachment as possible moderators of evaluative organizations (cf. La Guardia, Ryan, Couchman, & Deci, 2000; Ryan & Deci, 2000).

Conclusions

Evaluative self-organization has been shown to predict individual differences in trait and state self-esteem (Showers, 2000; Zeigler-Hill & Showers, 2007), but recent research focuses on the cognitive-affective components that may underlie such tendencies (Ditzfeld & Showers, 2011, 2012b). We suggest that individual differences in self-organization reflect distinct affective cores, such that compartmentalized individuals show greater affective reactivity to emotional stimuli than do integrative individuals, which sets in motion distinct cognitive processes. Compartmentalized individuals' strong emotional reactions give access to primarily positive or negative self-beliefs, whereas integrative individuals' weaker reactions give access to a mixture of valenced self-beliefs. Here, we highlight the implications of these processes for self-esteem, such that compartmentalization is associated with self-esteem instability, whereas integration fosters self-esteem stability. Interestingly, both modes of self-esteem processing are seen as adaptive, given the individual differences at the affective core. They result in distinctive strategies to regulate the quality of people's social lives, with the shared goal of achieving perceived belongingness across and within social contexts.

References

Allport, G. W. (1955). *Becoming: Basic considerations for a psychology of personality.* New Haven, CT: Yale University Press.

Bandura, A. (1977). Self-efficacy: Toward a unifying theory of behavioral change. *Psychological Review, 84*, 191–215.

Bandura, A. (1982). Self-efficacy mechanism in human agency. *American Psychologist, 37*, 122–147.

Baumeister, R. F., & Leary, M. R. (1995). The need to belong: Desire for interpersonal attachments as a fundamental human motivation. *Psychological Bulletin, 117*, 497–529.

Bower, G. H. (1981). Mood and memory. *American Psychologist, 36*, 129–148.

Bower, G. H., & Forgas, J. P. (2001). Mood and social memory. In J. P. Forgas (ed.), *Handbook of affect and social cognition* (pp. 95–120). Mahwah, NJ: Erlbaum.

Brown, J. D. (1993). Self-esteem and self-evaluation: Feeling is believing. In J. M. Suls (ed.), *The self in social perspective* (pp. 27–58). Hillsdale, NJ: Erlbaum.

Brown, J. D., Dutton, K. A., & Cook, K. E. (2001). From the top down: Self-esteem and self-evaluation. *Cognition and Emotion, 15*, 615–631.

Campbell, J. D. (1990). Self-esteem and clarity of the self-concept. *Journal of Personality and Social Psychology, 59*, 538–549.

Canevello, A., & Crocker, J. (2010). Creating good relationships: Responsiveness, relationship quality, and interpersonal goals. *Journal of Personality and Social Psychology, 99*, 78–106.

Cantor, N., & Kihlstrom, J. F. (1987). *Personality and social intelligence.* Englewood Cliffs, NJ: Prentice-Hall.

Carver, C. S. (2004). Self-regulation of action and affect. In R. F. Baumeister & K. D. Vohs (eds.), *Handbook of self-regulation: Research, theory, and applications* (pp. 13–39). New York, NY: Guilford Press.

Carver, C. S., & Scheier, M. F. (1998). *On the self-regulation of behavior.* Cambridge, MA: Cambridge University Press.

Cramer, H. (1945/1974). *Mathematical methods of statistics.* Princeton, NJ: Princeton University Press.

Crocker, J., & Wolfe, C. T. (2001). Contingencies of self-worth. *Psychological Review, 108*, 593–623.

Deci, E. L., & Ryan, R. M. (1995). Human autonomy: The basis for true self-esteem. In M. H. Kernis, *Efficacy, agency, and self-esteem* (pp. 31–49). New York, NY: Plenum Press.

DeMarree, K. G., Petty, R. E., & Strunk, D. R. (2010). Self-esteem accessibility as attitude strength: On the durability and impactfulness of accessible self-esteem. *Personality and Social Psychology Bulletin, 36*, 628–641.

Ditzfeld, C. P., & Showers, C. J. (2011). Emotional processing in categorization: Understanding the cognitive structure of the self. *Social Cognition, 29*, 111–124.

Ditzfeld, C. P., & Showers, C. J. (2012a). *Self-structure and emotional response categorization: Who judges a face by its emotional cover?* Manuscript submitted for publication.

Ditzfeld, C. P., & Showers, C. J. (2012b). *Self-structure and emotional experiences.* Manuscript submitted for publication.

Eysenck, H. J. (1967). *The biological basis of personality.* Springfield, IL: Thomas.

Feldman, L. A. (1995). Variations in the circumplex structure of mood. *Personality and Social Psychology Bulletin, 21*, 806–817.

Feldman Barrett, L. (2004). Feelings or words? Understanding the content in self-report ratings of experienced emotion. *Journal of Personality and Social Psychology, 87*, 266–281.

Feldman Barrett, L. (2006). Valence is a basic building block of emotional life. *Journal of Research in Personality, 40*, 35–55.

Gray, J. A. (1981). A critique of Eysenck's theory of personality. In H. J. Eysenck (ed.), *A model for personality* (pp. 246–276). Berlin: Springer-Verlag.

Gray, J. A. (1990). Brain systems that mediate both emotion and cognition. *Cognition and Emotion, 4*, 269–288.

Gross, J. J. (1998). The emerging field of emotion regulation: An integrative review. *Review of General Psychology, 2*, 271–299.

Grundy, C., & Showers, C. J. (2012, January). *Self-concept organization in response to threat and self-affirmation.* Poster presented at the annual meeting of the Society of Personality and Social Psychology, San Diego, CA.

Halberstadt, J. B., & Niedenthal, P. M. (1997). Emotional state and the use of stimulus dimensions in judgment. *Journal of Personality and Social Psychology, 72,* 1017–1033.

Harter, S. (1993). Visions of self: Beyond the me in the mirror. In J. E. Jacobs (ed.), *Nebraska symposium on motivation: Developmental perspectives on motivation* (Vol. 40, pp. 99–144). Lincoln: University of Nebraska Press.

Harter, S. (1999). *The construction of the self: A developmental perspective.* New York, NY: Guilford Press.

Higgins, E. T. (1987). Self-discrepancy: A theory relating self and affect. *Psychological Review, 94,* 319–340.

Higgins, E. T. (1997). Beyond pleasure and pain. *American Psychologist, 52,* 1280–1300.

Kernis, M. H. (2003). Toward a conceptualization of optimal self-esteem. *Psychological Inquiry, 14,* 1–26.

Kernis, M. H. (2005). Measuring self-esteem in context: The importance of stability of self-esteem in psychological functioning. *Journal of Personality, 73,* 1569–1605.

Kernis, M. H., & Goldman, B. M. (2003). Stability and variability in self-concept and self-esteem. In M. H. Kernis & J. P. Tangney (eds.), *Handbook of self and identity* (pp. 106–127). New York, NY: Guilford Press.

Kernis, M. H., Paradise, A. W., Whitaker, D. J., Wheatman, S. R., & Goldman, B. N. (2000). Master of one's psychological domain? Not likely if one's self-esteem is unstable. *Personality and Social Psychology Bulletin, 26,* 1297–1305.

Kihlstrom, J. F., & Cantor, N. (1984). Mental representations of the self. In L. Berkowitz (ed.), *Advances in experimental social psychology* (pp. 1–47). San Diego, CA: Academic Press.

La Guardia, J. G., Ryan, R. M., Couchman, C. E., & Deci, E. L. (2000). Within-person variation in security of attachment: A self-determination theory perspective on attachment, need fulfillment, and well-being. *Journal of Personality and Social Psychology, 79,* 367–384.

Larsen, J. T., & McGraw, A. P. (2011). Further evidence for mixed emotions. *Journal of Personality and Social Psychology, 100,* 1095–1110.

Larsen, R. J., & Diener, E. (1987). Affect intensity as an individual difference characteristic: A review. *Journal of Research in Personality, 21,* 1–39.

Leary, M. R., & Baumeister, R. F. (2000). The nature and function of self-esteem: Sociometer theory. In M. P. Zanna (ed.), *Advances in experimental social psychology* (Vol. 32, pp. 1–62). San Diego, CA: Academic Press.

Limke, A., & Showers, C. J. (2010). Organization of parent knowledge: Compartmentalization and integration in adult child-parent relationships. *Personality and Social Psychology Bulletin, 36,* 1225–1240.

Markus, H., & Wurf, E. (1987). The dynamic self-concept: A social psychological perspective. *Annual Review of Psychology, 38,* 299–337.

Mead, G. H. (1913). The social self. Reprinted in A. J. Reck (ed.) (1964), *Selected writings of George Herbert Mead.* Indianapolis, IN: Bobbs-Merril.

Mischel, W., & Shoda, Y. (1995). A cognitive-affective system theory of personality: Reconceptualizing situations, dispositions, dynamics, and invariance in personality structure. *Psychological Review, 102,* 246–268.

Niedenthal, P. M., Halberstadt, J. B., & Innes-Ker, Å. H. (1999). Emotional response categorization. *Psychological Review, 106,* 337–361.

Pelham, B. W., & Swann, W. B. (1989). From self-conceptions to self-worth: On the sources and structure of global self-esteem. *Journal of Personality and Social Psychology, 57,* 672–680.

Pietromonaco, P. R., & Barrett, L. F. (2009). Valence focus and self-esteem lability: Reacting to hedonic cues in the social environment. *Emotion, 9,* 406–418.

Rhodewalt, F., Madrian, J. C., & Cheney, S. (1998). Narcissism, self-knowledge organization, and emotional reactivity: The effect of daily experiences on self-esteem and affect. *Personality and Social Psychology Bulletin, 24,* 75–87.

Rosenberg, M. (1965). *Society and the adolescent self-image.* Princeton, NJ: Princeton University Press.

Russell, J. A., & Barrett, L. F. (1999). Core affect, prototypical emotional episodes, and other things called emotion: Dissecting the elephant. *Journal of Personality and Social Psychology, 76,* 805–819.

Ryan, R. M., & Brown, K. W. (2003). Why we don't need self-esteem: On fundamental needs, contingent love, and mindfulness. *Psychological Inquiry, 14,* 71–76.

Ryan, R. M., & Deci, E. L. (2000). Self-determination theory and the facilitation of intrinsic motivation, social development, and well-being. *American Psychologist, 55,* 68–78.

Schlenker, B. R. (1985). *The self and social life.* New York, NY: McGraw-Hill.

Sheldon, K. M., Ryan, R. M., Rawsthorne, L. J., & Ilardi, B. (1997). Trait self and true self: Cross-role variation in the big-five personality traits and its relations with psychological authenticity and subjective well-being. *Journal of Personality and Social Psychology, 73,* 1380–1393.

Showers, C. J. (1992a). Compartmentalization of positive and negative self-knowledge: Keeping bad apples out of the bunch. *Journal of Personality and Social Psychology, 62,* 1036–1049.

Showers, C. (1992b). Evaluatively integrative thinking about characteristics of the self. *Personality and Social Psychology Bulletin, 18,* 719–729.

Showers, C. J. (2000). Self-organization in emotional contexts. In J. P. Forgas (ed.), *Feeling and thinking: The role of affect in social cognition* (pp. 283–307). New York, NY: Cambridge University Press.

Showers, C. J. (2002). Integration and compartmentalization: A model of self-structure and self-change. In D. Cervone & W. Mischel (eds.), *Advances in personality science* (pp. 271–291). New York, NY: Guilford Press.

Showers, C. J., Abramson, L. Y., & Hogan, M. E. (1998). The dynamic self: How the content and structure of the self-concept change with mood. *Journal of Personality and Social Psychology, 75,* 478–493.

Showers, C. J., & Kevlyn, S. B. (1999). Organization of knowledge about a relationship partner: Implications for liking and loving. *Journal of Personality and Social Psychology, 76,* 958–971.

Showers, C. J., & Kling, K. C. (1996). Organization of self-knowledge: Implications for recovery from sad mood. *Journal of Personality and Social Psychology, 70,* 578–590.

Showers, C. J., Limke, A., & Zeigler-Hill, V. (2004). Self-structure and self-change: Applications to psychological treatment. *Behavior Therapy, 35,* 167–184.

Showers, C. J., & Ryff, C. D. (1996). Self-differentiation and well-being in a life transition. *Personality and Social Psychology Bulletin, 22,* 448–460.

Showers, C. J., & Zeigler-Hill, V. (2006). Pathways among self-knowledge and self-esteem: How are self-esteem and self-knowledge linked? Are these links direct or indirect? In M. H. Kernis (ed.), *Self-esteem issues and answers: A source book of current perspectives* (pp. 216–223). New York, NY: Psychology Press.

Showers, C. J., & Zeigler-Hill, V. (2012). Organization of self-knowledge: Features, functions, and flexibility. In M. R. Leary & J. Tangney (eds.), *Handbook of self and identity* (2nd edn, pp. 105–123). New York, NY: Guilford.

Showers, C. J., Zeigler-Hill, V., & Limke, A. (2006). Self-structure and childhood maltreatment: Successful compartmentalization and the struggle of integration. *Journal of Social and Clinical Psychology, 25*, 473–507.

Swann, W. B., Jr. (1983). Self-verification: Bringing social reality into harmony with the self. In J. Suls & A. G. Greenwald (eds.), *Psychological perspectives on the self* (Vol. 2, pp. 33–66). Hillsdale, NJ: Erlbaum.

Steele, C. M. (1988). The psychology of self-affirmation: Sustaining the integrity of the self. In L. Berkowitz (ed.), *Advances in experimental social psychology* (Vol. 21, pp. 261–302). New York, NY: Academic Press.

Suvak, M. K., Litz, B. T., Sloan, D. M., Zanarini, M. C., Barrett, L. F., & Hofmann, S. G. (2011). Emotional granularity and borderline personality disorder. *Journal of Abnormal Psychology, 120*, 414–426.

Sullivan, H. S. (1953). *The interpersonal theory of psychiatry*. New York, NY: Norton.

Tafarodi, R. W., & Milne, A. B. (2002). Decomposing global self-esteem. *Journal of Personality, 70*, 443–483.

Tesser, A. (1986). Some effects of self-evaluation maintenance on cognition and action. In R. M. Sorrentino & E. T. Higgins (eds.), *Handbook of motivation and cognition: Foundations of social behavior* (pp. 435–464). New York, NY: Guilford.

Tesser, A. (1988). Toward a self-evaluation maintenance model of social behavior. In L. Berkowitz (ed.), *Advances in experimental social psychology* (pp. 181–227). San Diego, CA: Academic Press.

Tsai, J. L. (2007). Ideal affect: Cultural causes and behavioral consequences. *Perspectives on Psychological Science, 2*, 242–259.

Tsai, J. L., Knutson, B., & Fung, H. H. (2006). Cultural variation in affect valuation. *Journal of Personality and Social Psychology, 90*, 288–307.

Williams, K. D., Cheung, C. K. T., & Choi, W. (2000). Cyberostracism: Effects of being ignored over the internet. *Journal of Personality and Social Psychology, 79*, 748–762.

Zajonc, R. B. (1980). Feeling and thinking: Preferences need no inferences. *American Psychologist, 35*, 151–175.

Zajonc, R. B. (1984). On the primacy of affect. *American Psychologist, 39*, 117–123.

Zeigler-Hill, V., Ditzfeld, C. P., & Showers, C. J. (2012). *Evaluative organization of self-knowledge and self-esteem: Implications of compartmentalization for contingency, accessibility, and authenticity*. Manuscript in preparation.

Zeigler-Hill, V., & Showers, C. J. (2007). Self-structure and self-esteem stability: The hidden vulnerability of compartmentalization. *Personality and Social Psychology Bulletin, 33*, 143–159.

3 Pursuing self-esteem

Implications for self-regulation and relationships

Lora E. Park and Jennifer Crocker

The pursuit of self-esteem – the desire to protect, maintain, and enhance feelings of self-worth – is pervasive in Western societies in which the self and self-esteem are strongly emphasized and valued (Crocker & Park, 2003, 2004). Beginning in the late 1980s, programs were implemented across the United States to boost self-esteem in the hopes of reducing a variety of societal problems, such as academic underachievement, teenage pregnancy, crime, drug use, and alcohol abuse (Dawes, 1994; Mecca, Smelser, & Vasconcellos, 1989; Twenge, 2006). A comprehensive review of the literature, however, revealed limited benefits of high self-esteem, which called into question the utility of the self-esteem movement and the validity of self-esteem as a construct more generally (Baumeister, Campbell, Krueger, & Vohs, 2003). In light of these findings, Baumeister and colleagues suggested that:

> In our view, a crucial issue for both research and policy is the heterogeneity of high self-esteem. Only a few of the many studies we reviewed distinguished carefully between different categories of favorable self-regard, yet these few often found the distinction to be quite powerful ... We recommend that researchers interested in self-esteem begin paying closer attention to narcissism, self-deception, stability of self-esteem, and other distinctions within the broad category of self-esteem.
>
> (Baumeister et al., 2003, p. 38)

Consistent with this idea, a growing body of research has examined distinct aspects of self-esteem (see also Swann, Chang-Schneider, & McClarty, 2007). For example, researchers have distinguished between self-esteem that is secure, stable, or congruent (e.g., having high explicit and high implicit self-esteem) versus self-esteem that is fragile, unstable, narcissistic, contingent, or discrepant (e.g., having high explicit but low implicit self-esteem; Bosson et al. 2008; Campbell, Rudich, & Sedikides, 2002; Jordan, Spencer, Zanna, Hoshino-Browne, & Correll, 2003; Kernis, 2003; Tracy & Robins, 2003; Zeigler-Hill, 2006). Consistent with this literature, we propose that the importance of self-esteem lies not just in whether it is high or low, but in people's *pursuit* of self-esteem as a goal – that is, all the ways in which people seek to protect, maintain, and enhance self-esteem in those areas on which their self-worth is based, or contingent. In particular, contingencies of self-worth (CSWs) reflect the areas in which people are psychologically invested and motivated to prove to themselves (and often, to others) that they possess certain qualities.

In this chapter, we first describe CSW theory and discuss how people's CSWs are tied to the pursuit of self-esteem via the regulation of safety and security concerns. Next, we propose that individuals differ in the strategies they use to pursue self-esteem and feelings of security, such that when self-worth is at stake, people tend to pursue goals that are consistent with, and reinforce, existing self-views and interpersonal expectations. Importantly, these processes often depend on interactions between people's trait level of self-esteem (i.e., whether self-esteem is high or low) and their contingencies of self-worth. Examining the interaction between people's global self-evaluations – in conjunction with their CSWs – can reveal important insights into the motivational dynamics underlying people's responses to threat. By assessing people's CSWs, we can also predict – with greater accuracy and precision – who among those with high self-esteem (HSE) or low self-esteem (LSE) will be most motivated to pursue self-esteem following threat, and in what ways, with implications for self-regulation and interpersonal relationships.

Contingencies of self-worth

Over a century ago, William James (1890) observed that whereas global self-esteem is relatively stable and does not depend on objective circumstances or achievements, state self-esteem fluctuates around people's baseline trait levels of self-esteem in response to positive and negative events. Furthermore, James proposed that individuals differ in the domains on which they base their self-esteem: "Our self-feeling in this world depends entirely on what we *back* ourselves to be and do" (James, 1890, p. 45).

Expanding upon these ideas, Crocker and Wolfe (2001) proposed a model of CSWs that examined affective, cognitive, and motivational consequences of basing self-worth in specific domains. According to the model, individuals differ in the areas on which they base their self-worth, with the original CSWs scale measuring seven domains of contingency: academic competence, physical appearance, virtue, having God's love, having love and support from family, outdoing others in competition, and obtaining others' approval (Crocker, Luhtanen, Cooper, & Bouvrette, 2003).

In recent years, researchers have expanded upon these domains to examine contingent self-worth in other domains, such as friendships (Cambron, Acitelli, & Steinberg, 2010), romantic relationships (Knee, Canavello, Bush, & Cook, 2008; Park, Sanchez, & Bryndilsen, 2011), and body weight (Clabaugh, Karpinski, & Griffin, 2008).

A key prediction of the CSWs model is that the impact of life events on self-esteem and affect depends on the relevance of such events to one's CSWs. That is, self-threats within a particular domain are more emotionally devastating when self-esteem is strongly staked in that domain than when it is not (Crocker & Wolfe, 2001). Indeed, students who strongly based their self-worth on academic competence experienced lower state self-esteem, less positive affect, and more negative affect and depressive symptoms when they performed poorly on academic tasks, received lower-than-expected grades, or were rejected from graduate schools, compared to those whose self-worth was less invested in this domain or did not experience self-threat (Crocker, Karpinski, Quinn, & Chase, 2003; Crocker, Sommers, & Luhtanen, 2002).

Another key feature of the CSWs model is that people are highly motivated to pursue self-esteem in domains on which their self-esteem is based; that is, people seek to obtain boosts in their state self-esteem, over and above their trait levels of self-esteem, and to avoid drops in their state self-esteem, around their trait levels, in areas on which their self-worth is staked. Along these lines, research has shown that CSWs shape the goals that people pursue and the activities they engage in on a daily basis. For example, in a longitudinal study of college freshmen, those who more strongly based their self-worth on having God's love were more likely to join religious organizations, and college women who based their self-worth on being physically attractive were more likely to join sororities (Crocker, Luhtanen, et al., 2003). Even after controlling for participants' gender, race, and socioeconomic status, CSWs assessed prior to entering college significantly predicted how much time students spent in specific activities. For example, students who based their self-worth on academic competence spent more time studying; those who based self-worth on love and support from family spent more time with their families; those who based self-worth on virtue spent more time volunteering and less time partying; and those who based self-worth on their appearance spent more time grooming, exercising, shopping for clothes, socializing, and partying. Thus, CSWs were associated with how people regulated their day-to-day involvement in a variety of activities.

Contingencies of self-worth and regulation of safety and security concerns

CSWs are thought to originate in response to acute events and/or cumulative experiences in which one's sense of safety or security was threatened, such as being abandoned, rejected, teased, or criticized (Crocker & Park, 2004). Resulting from such experiences, people may internalize specific beliefs – in the form of CSWs – about what they need to be or do in order to be a person of worth and value, and in doing so, feel protected from future harm or threat (Park, Crocker, & Vohs, 2006). The conclusions that people draw about what they must do to be a person of value is likely to depend on both intrapersonal and social factors, such as family, neighborhood, and cultural influences. Cumulative, idiosyncratic histories of rewards and punishments may thus contribute to variability in the specific areas in which people come to base their self-worth. The domains in which people base their self-worth are not necessarily the areas that they think they will succeed in, but rather, the areas in which they think that *if* they could succeed, they would feel safe and protected from threats they perceived earlier in their lives. Indeed, CSWs are associated with attachment styles in adulthood, consistent with the idea that insecure attachment relationships can be a source of distressing events that lead people to conclude that their worth depends on being or doing certain things (Park, Crocker, & Mickelson, 2004).

Attachment styles and contingencies of self-worth

The strategies people use to regulate feelings of safety and security in childhood (e.g., adopting specific CSWs) may persist into adulthood, as well. That is, people with different attachment styles may regulate feelings of safety and security in adulthood by pursuing self-esteem in specific domains. According to attachment theory, attachment styles reflect individual differences in prototypical, internal working models of self and others formed in the context of the early caregiver-infant relationship (Bowlby, 1969; Hazan & Shaver, 1987; Mikulincer & Shaver, 2003; Rholes & Simpson, 2004). Working models of the self as worthy or unworthy of love and of others as responsive or unresponsive are thought to guide social interactions and emotion regulation throughout life (Bowlby, 1973, 1979; Collins & Read 1990).

Individuals with a secure attachment style report feeling loved, cared for, and supported by their partners (Shaver & Hazan, 1988) and believe that others will be responsive to their needs in times of stress (Hazan & Shaver, 1987). Given that individuals with a secure attachment style have close, mutually caring relationships with others, they were expected to base their self-esteem on having positive, supportive relations with others (see also Brennan & Bosson, 1998). Indeed, people with a secure attachment style are likely to recall positive perceptions of their early family relationships (Feeney & Noller, 1990), describe their parents as more benevolent and less punitive (Levy, Blatt, & Shaver, 1998), and show better adjustment in adolescence than those with insecure attachment styles (Cooper, Shaver, & Collins, 1998). Consistent with these ideas, we found that people with a secure attachment style were likely to base their self-worth on having love and support from their families (Park et al., 2004). In contrast to those with a secure form of attachment, people with a dismissing-avoidant attachment style regulate interpersonal closeness by basing their self-worth *less* on domains that rely on others for validation or support; this makes sense, given that avoidants feel uncomfortable with closeness and find it difficult to trust and depend on others (Hazan & Shaver, 1987). In our research, dismissing-avoidants were less likely to base self-worth on obtaining others' approval, having love and support from family, or having God's love (Park et al., 2004). Given that dismissing-avoidants are less invested in domains that depend on others, it is not surprising that their relationships with close others are often characterized by high levels of negative affect and low trust, commitment, satisfaction, and interdependence (Collins & Read, 1990; Simpson, 1990).

People with a preoccupied-anxious attachment style seek emotional intimacy, yet worry that other people will not want to be as close to them as they would like (Collins & Read, 1990; Feeney & Noller, 1990; Simpson, Rholes, & Nelligan, 1992). From a developmental perspective, people with an anxious attachment style are likely to have had inconsistent caregivers who were both punitive and benevolent (Levy et al., 1998). As a result of receiving conflicting interpersonal messages, these individuals are thought to internalize a negative mental model of the self and a positive model of others. According to Bartholomew, "preoccupied individuals are preoccupied with attachment needs ... the result is an overly dependent style in which personal validation is sought through gaining others' acceptance and approval" (Bartholomew, 1990, p. 252). Because people with this attachment style doubt their worth and value, they often look to other people for validation and reassurance (Brennan & Bosson, 1998) and their self-esteem fluctuates dramatically in response to perceived acceptance and rejection (Collins & Read, 1990).

Based on these findings, we predicted that people with a preoccupied attachment style would seek to regulate feelings of safety and security by basing self-worth in domains that rely on interpersonal validation and reassurance. Consistent with this hypothesis, having a preoccupied attachment style was related to basing self-worth more on being physically attractive – a domain that depends heavily on interpersonal approval. People with a fearful attachment style – who have a negative mental model of the self and others – were also likely to base self-worth on being physically attractive. Given that a negative model of self underlies both preoccupied and fearful attachment styles, it makes sense that both attachment styles would be related to adopting similar strategies in regulating feelings of security – e.g., by basing self-worth on appearance, which reflects a relatively indirect, less interpersonally risky way of seeking others' acceptance.

In sum, attachment theory describes how early interactions with caregivers shape perceptions of interpersonal safety and security and affect emotional and behavioral self-regulation (Bowlby, 1973). People with a secure attachment style, who likely had warm, responsive caregivers growing up, regulate feelings of safety and security by drawing close to significant others in times of need and deriving self-esteem from their family's love, for example. People with a dismissive-avoidant attachment style, who likely had cold and unresponsive interactions with caregivers, regulate feelings of security by being less emotionally reliant on others (Bartholomew, 1990). Accordingly, they tend not to base self-worth on domains that depend on interpersonal connection and closeness, such as family support, God's love, or others' approval. Finally, people with an anxious attachment style (preoccupieds and fearfuls) are likely to base self-worth on how they appear to others, consistent with the idea that people with negative self-views often look to the external environment for validation of their worth by adhering to cultural standards and ideals. Together, these findings suggest that while the desire to regulate feelings of safety and security is fundamental to the human experience, how people seek to achieve this goal (e.g., the specific domains that people invest or disengage their self-esteem from) depends on their past experiences, perceptions, and attachment histories.

Self-esteem and contingencies of self-worth

In addition to attachment styles, the degree to which people feel favorably about themselves may be tied to specific strategies they adopt to regulate feelings of safety and security. Indeed, a key aspect of attachment styles is the mental model of self, which is similar to having high vs low trait self-esteem, which reflects chronic, global evaluations of the self (Griffin & Bartholomew, 1994). According to sociometer theory, self-esteem functions as a psychological indicator of one's relational value and alerts people to the possibility of relational devaluation (Leary & Baumeister, 2000; Leary, Tambor, Terdal, & Downs, 1995). Having high self-esteem (HSE) implies that one has high relational value; low self-esteem (LSE) implies that one has low relational value and increases sensitivity to the possibility of being rejected (Baldwin & Sinclair, 1996).

People with HSE vs LSE have very different ways of orienting to their social worlds and regulating feelings of safety and security in response to self-esteem threats. HSE people's self-confidence and interpersonal security motivates them to strive for positive end states (e.g., positive affect, social rewards) more than avoiding negative end states (e.g., loss of self-esteem, rejection). For example, following self-esteem threats, HSEs are quicker to access their strengths relative to weaknesses, are likely to dismiss the validity of negative feedback, derogate out-group members, make self-serving biases, and express increased zeal about value-laden opinions and ideologies (Beauregard & Dunning, 1998; Blaine & Crocker, 1993; Crocker, Thompson, McGraw, & Ingerman, 1987; Dodgson & Wood, 1998; McGregor, Gailliot, Vasquez, & Nash, 2007). In short, HSEs become approach-oriented in their general motivational orientation and adoption of regulatory strategies following self-threats (Baumeister, Tice, & Hutton, 1989; Cavallo, Fitzsimons, & Holmes, 2009; Heimpel, Elliot, & Wood, 2006; McGregor et al., 2007; Park, 2010; Tice, 1991). Indeed, even at a neurological level, HSEs show greater activation in the left frontal cortex – a region associated with approach motivation, positive mood, risk-taking, and behavioral activation – following self-threats (Harmon-Jones, Lueck, Fearn, & Harmon-Jones, 2006; McGregor, Nash, & Inzlicht, 2009).

In relational contexts, HSEs often show approach-motivated responses by drawing closer to their relationship partners following threat. For example, Murray and colleagues found that HSEs who recalled their faults or transgressions (Murray, Holmes, MacDonald, & Ellsworth, 1998) or were led to believe that their partners perceived a problem in the relationship (Murray, Rose, Bellavia, Holmes, & Kusche, 2002) affirmed their commitment to their relationship and enhanced perceptions of their partners' love for them, which served to attenuate the effects of threat and bolstered their pre-existing perceptions of perceived regard.

Relative to people with HSE, those with LSE possess less favorable self-evaluations and lack self-clarity and self-confidence (Blaine & Crocker, 1993; Campbell, 1990; Leary & Baumeister, 2000). Whereas HSEs possess an arsenal of tactics to refute self-threats directly, LSEs lack the inner resources and confidence to defend against such threats. For example, Heimpel and colleagues (Heimpel, Wood, Marshall, & Brown, 2002) found that fewer LSEs than HSEs reported the goal to improve their mood following failure in their daily lives. When LSEs fail, they feel ashamed and humiliated (Brown & Dutton, 1995), generalize the failure to other aspects of themselves (Kernis, Brockner, & Frankel, 1989), have difficulty accessing positive thoughts about themselves (Dodgson & Wood, 1998), are less likely to show self-serving biases (Blaine & Crocker, 1993), and are thought to possess fewer positive aspects of their self-image with which to affirm themselves (Spencer, Josephs, & Steele, 1993).

In close relationships, LSEs typically adopt avoidance strategies following threat, such as distancing from their romantic partner and devaluing their relationship (Murray et al., 1998, 2002). LSEs also tend to use the silent treatment – a form of defensive ostracism – to avoid feeling inferior and to buffer themselves against the possibility of future rejection or loss of self-esteem (Sommer, Williams, Ciarocco, & Baumeister, 2001). Such findings support the idea that people who feel relationally devalued prioritize self-protection goals over self-enhancement goals or relationship-promotion goals, especially under conditions of heightened threat or perceived risk (Murray, Holmes, & Collins, 2006; Sommer, 2001).

In sum, people with HSE vs LSE differ in their self-regulatory strategies and interpersonal responses to self-threat. HSEs – who feel confident and accepted by others – actively seek boosts to their self-esteem following threat, reflecting an underlying approach orientation. LSEs – who feel less self-confident and doubtful of their relational value – seek to protect themselves from further loss of self-esteem, reflecting an underlying avoidance orientation. Importantly, though, even among those with HSE or LSE, there may be variability in response to threat, suggesting that self-esteem is more nuanced and interactive with other self-related processes.

Self-esteem, contingencies of self-worth, and self-regulation

Although global self-esteem may be related to the general tendency to approach or avoid positive or negative outcomes, people's reactions to events in their everyday lives depend largely on the degree to which they base their self-worth in specific domains. Along these lines, a strength of the CSWs model is that different predictions can be made depending on the content of the domain. For example, participants who strongly based their self-worth on being virtuous engaged in more volunteering activities than those who based less of their self-worth in this domain (Crocker, Luhtanen et al., 2003). In contrast, CSWs that depend more on external circumstances and feedback, such as having others' approval, being physically attractive, and outdoing others in competitive settings, predict increased symptoms of depression over the first semester of college, whereas more internally based CSWs, such as being a virtuous person, are not associated with depressive symptoms (Sargent, Crocker, & Luhtanen, 2006).

CSWs also matter in predicting how people will respond to self-threats in various domains. In one set of studies, we examined how failing in the domain of academic competence shaped people's subsequent goal pursuits (Park, Crocker, & Kiefer, 2007). We hypothesized that the more HSEs based their self-worth on competence, the more motivated they would be to present an image of themselves to others as competent following threat. Because HSEs are confident in their abilities, we expected them to want to appear competent to others, even in the face of failure. LSEs who base their self-worth on competence may also want to appear competent, but, when faced with failure, may have heightened self-doubts and therefore disengage from the goal to appear competent to others.

Consistent with predictions, HSEs who strongly based their self-worth on being competent and received negative feedback in this domain (i.e., negative test feedback) adopted the self-presentational goal of wanting to appear competent to others. In contrast, LSEs who based their self-worth on academic success and received negative feedback in this domain showed lowered state self-esteem, less positive affect, and less motivation to appear competent to others. Perhaps failure undermined LSEs' already fragile feelings of competence, leading them to disengage from this domain in order to protect themselves from further threat. Indeed, LSEs (but not HSEs) were quicker to associate themselves with words related to failure vs success on an implicit, automatic level, and this was only true for LSEs who strongly based their self-worth on the threatened domain of competence. Together, these findings support the idea that whereas HSEs regulate their responses to threat by defending and maintaining their favorable self-views, LSEs regulate their emotional reactions by withdrawing from the situation (e.g., disengaging from self-presentational goals in the threatened domain) to avoid further loss of self-esteem. Importantly, though, not all HSE and LSE people reacted this way to threat; only those who staked their self-worth in the threatened domain showed such responses, suggesting that the pursuit of self-esteem goals underlied their responses.

Whereas threats to competence led HSEs to become increasingly self-focused, threats to more interpersonally relevant domains that rely on having others' approval may lead to a different set of responses. To examine this idea, Park and Crocker (2008) examined how HSEs and LSEs reacted to negative interpersonal feedback about their likability. In the first part of the study, two same-sex participants interacted with each other and then received no feedback or bogus negative feedback, ostensibly from the other participant, regarding how friendly, outgoing, and interesting they seemed. After receiving this feedback, participants reported their state self-esteem, positive and negative affect, and self-presentation goals – i.e., how much they wanted to be perceived by others in various ways. Results showed that overall, participants who received negative interpersonal feedback reported lower state self-esteem, less positive affect, and more negative affect the more they based their self-worth on having others' approval.

Moreover, HSE and LSE people adopted different self-presentational goals following threat. HSEs who strongly based their self-worth on having others' approval were primarily motivated to appear warm/caring/kind to others following threat. Wanting to appear warm/caring/kind could be viewed as a relatively direct way of restoring one's perceived likability. In contrast, LSEs who strongly based their self-worth on having others' approval and received negative feedback about their likability were concerned with appearing physically attractive to others. Given that physical attractiveness is tied to both feelings of self-esteem and belonging, wanting to appear attractive may be a less interpersonally risky way for LSE people to bolster their sense of self-worth and feelings of belonging following threat, because wanting to appear attractive does not require as much contact or interaction with others as being warm/caring/kind might entail (Park & Crocker, 2008).

Overall, the results of these studies suggest that HSE and LSE people differ in their self-presentational goals following threats to intrapersonal (e.g., competence) vs interpersonally relevant domains (e.g., likability). HSE people wanted to validate their intelligence to others whereas LSE people disengaged from this goal following a threat to competence, but these patterns were observed only among those who strongly based self-worth in the threatened domain. On the other hand, HSE people who based their self-worth on having others' approval and received negative feedback about their likability showed greater desire to validate their interpersonal qualities to others (appear warm/caring/kind), while LSE people showed a similar pattern, although the domain they preferred to validate themselves in was more externally oriented and less interpersonally risky (wanting to appear physically attractive/good-looking/physically fit).

Self-esteem, contingencies of self-worth, and interpersonal relationships

Threats to self-esteem have consequences not only for goal pursuit but for interpersonal processes as well. For example, in one study (Park & Crocker, 2005), we examined HSE and LSE people's responses to others following a threat to academic competence. We hypothesized that people with HSE – who are generally confident and certain of their abilities – would become preoccupied with themselves the more they based their feelings of self-worth on being competent and received negative feedback in this domain, and might therefore come across as less supportive and less focused on another person's personal problem. In contrast, we thought that people with LSE – who are generally less confident and less certain of their abilities – might try to repair self-esteem following failure by deflecting attention away from their threatened sense of self and focusing more on others. Again, though, we thought this would only be the case for those who strongly based their self-worth on the threatened domain, and would therefore be the ones most motivated to repair self-esteem following threat.

To test these ideas, target participants received negative academic test feedback or no feedback and then interacted with another participant (partner) who disclosed a personal problem to them. Afterwards, both targets and partners completed measures assessing how supportive and likable targets were during the interaction. Results showed that following academic threat (vs no threat), HSE targets who strongly based their self-worth on being competent reported feeling less supportive, compassionate, and empathic, and liked partners less. Partners, in turn, rated these targets as being less supportive, empathic, more preoccupied, and less likable. In contrast, LSE people who strongly based their self-worth on being competent and experienced failure showed the opposite pattern – becoming more supportive and likable. Importantly, further analyses revealed that the effects of self-esteem threat were specific to basing self-worth on competence, rather than having contingent self-worth in general or basing self-worth in external versus internal domains.

Whereas participants in the previous study (Park & Crocker, 2005) interacted with a stranger, participants in the next set of studies were examined in the context of existing relationships. In addition, in these studies, we threatened an interpersonally relevant domain of contingent self-worth: physical appearance (Park & Maner, 2009). Given that perceptions of attractiveness are linked to feelings of self-esteem and social acceptance (Dion, Berscheid, & Walster, 1972; Harter, 1993), threats to appearance were expected to activate people's desire to restore their self-esteem and sense of belonging. Because HSE people feel accepted by close others, they may draw upon this social resource following threats to their appearance, but only if they strongly base their self-worth in this area. In contrast, LSE people who base their self-worth on appearance might distance themselves from close others after receiving negative feedback about their looks, because LSE people doubt their relational value and are worried about being rejected. Instead, people with LSE – the more they base self-worth on appearance – might respond to appearance-based threats by seeking alternate routes to repairing self-esteem that are less interpersonally risky than interacting directly with close others, such as striving to appear physically attractive.

To test these hypotheses, we brought unacquainted, opposite-sex pairs of participants into the lab and had them complete measures assessing their trait self-esteem and CSWs (Park & Maner, 2009, Study 3). Next, participants interacted with another participant in a "getting acquainted" paradigm and were then led to separate rooms where they rated the other person's attractiveness or competence. Participants then received bogus negative feedback – ostensibly from the other person – about their attractiveness or competence. Finally, they reported how much they wanted to engage in various activities that involved close others (e.g., talk on the phone with a friend, spend time with a close friend). Results showed that among HSE people who received negative feedback about their appearance (vs their competence), those who more strongly based self-worth on their appearance reported greater desire to be with close others than those who based self-worth less in this domain. Among LSE people who received negative feedback about their appearance, those who more strongly based their self-worth on their appearance reported less desire to affiliate with close others. These effects were not observed, however, among participants who received negative competence feedback, attesting to the importance of matching CSWs with the domain of threat. Thus, it was the combination of trait self-esteem and the degree to which people based their self-worth on appearance that led individuals with HSE vs LSE to respond with different interpersonal preferences following threat.

In a subsequent study (Park & Maner, 2009, Study 4), we examined whether HSE people's desire to turn toward close others following threat was specific to close others or extended to wanting to be with other people more generally. Participants were randomly assigned to write about a time when they felt negatively about their appearance (threat condition) or their commute to school that day (control). Participants were then asked how much they wanted to interact with close others and with people in general (e.g., meet new people, go to a party, play a team sport). Replicating the previous study, people with HSE preferred to interact with close others following an appearance threat, the more they based self-worth on this domain, but this preference did not extend to social contact with people in general. Because people in general are less familiar than close others, they are presumably less likely to be perceived as sources of reassurance and support. People with LSE who based their self-worth on appearance responded to an appearance threat by showing greater desire to avoid others – both close others and others more generally.

If people with LSE who base self-worth on their appearance do not seek to affiliate with close others or with people in general following threats to their appearance, what are they motivated to do? We hypothesized that for people with LSE, interacting directly with others might be perceived as relatively risky, particularly following threat, because of the risk of being relationally devalued. Thus, we predicted that LSE people might prefer to repair their self-esteem in a "safer," less interpersonally risky way, such as wanting to boost their attractiveness to others, which does not require extensive contact or interaction with others, and thus minimizes the possibility of rejection or negative social evaluation. Thus, we expected that people with LSE – but only those who strongly based self-worth on being attractive – would be most motivated to pursue self-esteem in this manner following threat.

Similar to the paradigm used in the previous study (Park & Maner, 2009, Study 4), participants in this study (Park & Maner, 2009, Study 6) received negative or positive feedback about their appearance, ostensibly from their partner, and were then asked to report how much they wanted to engage in various appearance-boosting activities (e.g., shop for clothes that make you look good, read fashion/health magazines). Consistent with predictions, among LSE participants who received negative feedback about their appearance, those who strongly based their self-worth on their looks reported greater desire to engage in appearance-boosting activities. This was not the case, however, when people received positive appearance feedback or if they had HSE.

To clarify the psychological mechanisms underlying people's responses to threat, we conducted a further study (Park & Maner, 2009, Study 2) in which we examined effects of self-affirmation and close relationship priming on interpersonal responses to threat. Given the associations between physical attractiveness and feelings of self-esteem and belonging, we expected that a threat to people's sense of attractiveness would pose a threat to both their sense of self-esteem and belonging. We reasoned that if either one of these needs was satisfied, then responses to threat that might otherwise be observed among people with HSE and LSE would be attenuated.

Specifically, we expected that following a threat to appearance, those who were asked to think of something neutral in their environment (i.e., list an object in the room) would not have their self-esteem or belongingness needs satisfied. In this case, we would expect, as in the previous studies, that people with HSE would want to affiliate with close others, and people with LSE would want to avoid close others the more they based their self-worth on the threatened domain. However, following a self-threat, if people engaged in self-affirmation (i.e., list your greatest strength) or were reminded of a close relationship (i.e., list the initials of someone who loves you unconditionally), then any divergent interpersonal responses between appearance-contingent HSE and LSE people should be attenuated, because the desire for self-esteem and belonging may be temporarily satiated.

Consistent with this hypothesis, we found that after writing about a negative aspect of their appearance, HSE people showed greater desire to affiliate with close others the more they based their self-worth on appearance and thought of a neutral object in the room (which did nothing, presumably, to alleviate the threat). In contrast, LSE people showed less desire to want to be with close others the more they based their self-worth on appearance, experienced a threat to their domain, and thought of a neutral object in the room. These differences were eliminated, however, in the self-affirmation and close relationship prime conditions, suggesting that needs for self-esteem and belonging motivated HSE and LSE people's responses to threat, but again, only among those whose self-worth was strongly staked in the threatened domain.

In sum, whereas people with HSE responded to threatened perceptions of their attractiveness by seeking to affiliate with close others, people with LSE sought to avoid other people following threat and preferred instead to engage in appearance-improving activities. Importantly, these effects were found only among those who strongly based their self-worth on appearance, and thus, were most motivated to repair their damaged self-esteem following threat. For HSE people who strongly based their self-worth on appearance, experiencing a threat to this domain led them to turn toward close others as sources of potential support and reassurance. Seeking contact with close others (rather than others in general) may be one way that HSE people seek to restore self-esteem and feelings of belongingness following threats to interpersonally relevant domains, but this appears to be driven by how much they stake their self-esteem in the domain.

LSE people, who are concerned about the possibility of rejection, were less inclined to seek out other people (both close others and people in general) the more they based their self-worth on appearance and experienced a threat to this domain. Instead, they wanted to engage in activities that would make them feel more attractive to others. Striving to appear attractive may be a less interpersonally risky route to restore self-esteem following threat because it does not require extensive contact or interaction with others, and thus minimizes the potential for future rejection or disapproval. Overall, then, these studies suggest that interpersonally motivated responses – to draw closer or distance from others following threat – depends on one's global level of self-esteem, the degree to which self-worth is invested in a domain, and whether or not one experiences a threat to that domain.

Conclusion

Throughout this chapter, we have emphasized the importance of examining self-esteem not just in terms of its overall level, but in conjunction with more nuanced aspects, such as the domains in which people stake their self-worth. Individuals differ in the degree to which they base their self-worth in specific domains; by taking this factor into account, we can come to a better understanding of how and why people regulate feelings of safety and security in the ways that they do. That is, by examining distinct aspects of self-esteem, and how they work together, we can gain deeper insight into the motivations underlying why people with varying levels of self-regard do what they do.

References

Baldwin, M. W., & Sinclair, L. (1996). Self-esteem and if–then contingencies of interpersonal acceptance. *Journal of Personality and Social Psychology, 71*, 1130–1141.

Bartholomew, K. (1990). Avoidance of Intimacy: An attachment perspective. *Journal of Social and Personal Relationships, 7*, 147–178.

Baumeister, R. F., Campbell, J. D., Krueger, J. I., & Vohs, K. D. (2003). Does high self-esteem cause better performance, interpersonal success, happiness, or healthier life-styles? *Psychological Science in the Public Interest, 4*, 1–44.

Baumeister, R. F., Tice, D. M., & Hutton, D. G. (1989). Self-presentational motivations and personality differences in self-esteem. *Journal of Personality, 57*, 547–579.

Beauregard, K. S., & Dunning, D. (1998). Turning up the contrast: Self-enhancement motives prompt egocentric contrast effects in social judgments. *Journal of Personality and Social Psychology, 74*, 60–621.

Blaine, B., & Crocker, J. (1993). Self-esteem and self-serving biases in reactions to positive and negative events: An integrative review. In R. F. Baumeister (ed.), *Self-esteem: The puzzle of low self-regard* (pp. 55–85). Hillsdale, NJ: Erlbaum.

Bosson, J. K., Lakey, C. E., Campbell, W. K., Zeigler-Hill, V., Jordan, C. H., & Kernis, M. H. (2008). Untangling the links between narcissism and self-esteem: A theoretical and empirical review. *Social and Personaltiy Psychology Compass, 2*, 1415–1439.

Brennan, K. A., & Bosson, J. K. (1998). Attachment-style differences in attitudes toward and reactions to feedback from romantic partners: An exploration of the relational bases of self-esteem. *Personality and Social Psychology Bulletin, 24*, 699–714.

Bowlby, J. (1969). *Attachment and loss: Vol. 1. Attachment.* New York, NY: Basic Books.

Bowlby, J. (1973). *Attachment and loss: Vol. 2. Separation: Anxiety and anger.* New York, NY: Basic Books.

Bowlby, J. (1979). *The making and breaking of affectional bonds.* London: Tavistock.

Brennan, K. A., & Bosson, J. K. (1998). Attachment-style differences in attitudes toward and reactions to feedback from romantic partners: An exploration of the relational bases of self-esteem. *Personality and Social Psychology Bulletin, 24*, 699–714.

Brown, J. D., & Dutton, K. A. (1995). The thrill of victory, the complexity of defeat: Self-esteem and people's emotional reactions to success and failure. *Journal of Personality and Social Psychology, 68*, 712–722.

Cambron, M. J., Acitelli, L. K., & Steinberg, L. (2010). When friends make you blue: The role of friendship contingent self-esteem in predicting self-esteem and depressive symptoms. *Personality and Social Psychology Bulletin, 36*, 384–397.

Campbell, J. D. (1990). Self-esteem and clarity of the self-concept. *Journal of Personality and Social Psychology, 59*, 538–549.

Campbell, W. K., Rudich, E. A., & Sedikides, C. (2002). Narcissism, self-esteem, and the positivity of self-views: Two portraits of self-love. *Personality and Social Psychology Bulletin, 28*, 358–368.

Cavallo, J. V., Fitzsimons, G. M., & Holmes, J. G. (2009). Taking chances in the face of threat: Romantic risk regulation and approach motivation. *Personality and Social Psychology Bulletin, 35*, 737–751.

Clabaugh, A., Karpinski, A., & Griffin, K. (2008). Body weight contingency of self-worth. *Self and Identity, 7*, 337–357.

Collins, N. L., & Read, S. J. (1990). Adult attachment, working models and relationship quality in dating couples. *Journal of Personality and Social Psychology, 58*, 644–663.

Cooper, M. L., Shaver, P. R., & Collins, N. L. (1998). Attachment styles, emotion regulation, and adjustment in adolescence. *Journal of Personality and Social Psychology, 74*, 1380–1397.

Crocker, J., Karpinski, A., Quinn, D. M., & Chase, S. (2003). When grades determine self-worth: Consequences of contingent self-worth for male and female engineering and psychology majors. *Journal of Personality and Social Psychology, 85*, 507–516.

Crocker, J., Luhtanen, R. K., Cooper, M. L., & Bouvrette, S. (2003). Contingencies of self-worth in college students: Theory and measurement. *Journal of Personality and Social Psychology, 85*, 894–908.

Crocker, J., & Park, L. E. (2003). Seeking self-esteem: Construction, maintenance, and protection of self-worth. In M. Leary & J. Tangney (eds.), *Handbook of Self and Identity* (pp. 291–313). New York, NY: Guilford Press.

Crocker, J., & Park, L. E. (2004). The costly pursuit of self-esteem. *Psychological Bulletin, 130*, 392–414.

Crocker, J., Sommers, S. R., & Luhtanen, R. K. (2002). Hopes dashed and dreams fulfilled: Contingencies of self-worth and admissions to graduate school. *Personality and Social Psychology Bulletin, 28*, 1275–1286.

Crocker, J., Thompson, L. L., McGraw, K. M., & Ingerman, C. (1987). Downward comparison, prejudice, and evaluations of others: Effects of self-esteem and threat. *Journal of Personality and Social Psychology, 52*, 907–917.

Crocker, J., & Wolfe, C. T. (2001). Contingencies of self-worth. *Psychological Review, 108*, 593–623.

Dawes, R. M. (1994). *House of cards: Psychology and psychotherapy built on myth.* New York, NY: Free Press.

Dion, K. K., Berscheid, E., & Walster, E. (1972). What is beautiful is good. *Journal of Personality and Social Psychology, 24*, 285–290.

Dodgson, P. G., & Wood, J. V. (1998). Self-esteem and the cognitive accessibility of strengths and weaknesses after failure. *Journal of Personality and Social Psychology, 75*, 178–197.

Downey, G., & Feldman, S. (1996). Implications of rejection sensitivity for intimate relationships. *Journal of Personality and Social Psychology, 70*, 1327–1343.

Feeney, J. A., & Noller, P. (1990). Attachment style as a predictor of adult romantic relationships. *Journal of Personality and Social Psychology, 58*, 281–291.

Griffin, D., & Bartholomew, K. (1994). Models of self and other: Fundamental dimensions underlying measures of adult attachment. *Journal of Personality and Social Psychology, 67*, 430–445.

Harmon-Jones, E., Lueck, L., Fearn, M., & Harmon-Jones, C. (2006). The effect of personal relevance and approach-related action expectation on relative left frontal cortical activity. *Psychological Science, 17*, 434–440.

Harter, S. (1993). Causes and consequences of low self-esteem in children and adolescents. In R. F. Baumeister (ed.), *Self-esteem: The puzzle of low self-regard* (pp. 87–116). New York, NY: Plenum.

Hazan, C., & Shaver, P. R. (1987). Romantic love conceptualized as an attachment process. *Journal of Personality and Social Psychology, 52*, 511–524.

Heimpel, S. A., Elliot, A. J., & Wood, J. V. (2006). Basic personality dimensions, self-esteem, and personal goals: An approach-avoidance analysis. *Journal of Personality, 74*, 1293–1320.

Heimpel, S. A., Wood, J. V., Marshall, M. A., & Brown, J. D. (2002). Do people with low self-esteem really want to feel better? Self-esteem differences in motivation to repair negative moods. *Journal of Personality and Social Psychology, 82*, 128–147.

James, W. (1890). *The principles of psychology, Vol. 1*. Cambridge, MA: Harvard University Press.

Jordan, C. H., Spencer, S. J., Zanna, M. P., Hoshino-Brown, E., & Correll, J. (2003). Secure and defensive self-esteem. *Journal of Personality and Social Psychology, 85*, 385–405.

Kernis, M. H. (2003). Toward a conceptualization of optimal self-esteem. *Psychological Inquiry, 14*, 1–26.

Kernis, M. H., Brockner, J., & Frankel, B. S. (1989). Self-esteem and reactions to failure: The mediating role of overgeneralization. *Journal of Personality and Social Psychology, 57*, 707–714.

Knee, R. C., Canevello, A., Bush, A. L., & Cook, A. (2008). Relationship-contingent self-esteem and the ups and downs of romantic relationships. *Journal of Personality and Social Psychology, 95*, 608–627.

Leary, M. R., & Baumeister, R. F. (2000). The nature and function of self-esteem: Sociometer theory. In M. Zanna (ed.), *Advances in Experimental Social Psychology* (Vol. 32, pp. 1–62). San Diego, CA: Academic Press.

Leary, M. R., Tambor, E. S., Terdal, S. K., & Downs, D. L. (1995). Self-esteem as an interpersonal monitor: The sociometer hypothesis. *Journal of Personality and Social Psychology, 68*, 518–530.

Levy, K. N., Blatt, S. J., & Shaver, P. R. (1998). Attachment styles and parental representations. *Journal of Personality and Social Psychology, 74*, 407–419.

McGregor, I., Gailliot, M. T., Vasquez, N., & Nash, K. A. (2007). Ideological and personal zeal reactions to threat among people with high self-esteem: Motivated promotion focus. *Personality and Social Psychology Bulletin, 33*, 1587–1599.

McGregor, I., Nash, K., & Inzlicht, M. (2009). Threat, high self-esteem, and reactive approach motivation: Electroencephalographic evidence. *Journal of Experimental Social Psychology, 45*, 1003–1007.

Mecca, A. M., Smelser, N. J., & Vasconcellos, J. (1989). *The social importance of self-esteem*. Berkeley, CA: University of California Press.

Mikulincer, M., & Shaver, P. R. (2003). The attachment behavioral system in adulthood: Activation, psychodynamics, and interpersonal processes. In M. P. Zanna (ed.), *Advances in experimental social psychology* (pp. 53–152). New York, NY: Academic Press.

Murray, S. L., Holmes, J. G., & Collins, N. L. (2006). Optimizing assurance: The risk regulation system in relationships. *Psychological Bulletin, 132*, 641–666.

Murray, S. L., Holmes, J. G., MacDonald, G., & Ellsworth, P. C. (1998). Through the looking glass darkly? When self-doubt turns into relationship insecurities. *Journal of Personality and Social Psychology, 75*, 1459–1480.

Murray, S. L., Rose, P., Bellavia, G. M., Holmes, J. G., & Kusche, A. G. (2002). When rejection stings: How self-esteem constrains relationship-enhancement processes. *Journal of Personality and Social Psychology, 83*, 556–573.

Park, L. E. (2010). Responses to self-threat: Linking self and relational constructs with approach and avoidance motivation. *Social and Personality Psychology Compass, 4*, 201–221.

Park, L. E., & Crocker, J. (2005). Interpersonal consequences of seeking self-esteem. *Personality and Social Psychology Bulletin, 11*, 1587–1598.

Park, L. E., & Crocker, J. (2008). Contingencies of self-worth and responses to negative interpersonal feedback. *Self and Identity, 7*, 184–203.

Park, L. E., Crocker, J., & Kiefer, A. K. (2007). Contingencies of self-worth, academic failure, and goal pursuit. *Personality and Social Psychology Bulletin, 33*, 1503–1517.

Park, L. E., Crocker, J., & Mickelson, K. D. (2004). Attachment styles and contingencies of self-worth. *Personality and Social Psychology Bulletin, 30*, 1243–1254.

Park, L. E., Crocker, J., & Vohs, K. D. (2006). Contingencies of self-worth and self-validation goals: Implications for close relationships. In K. D. Vohs & E. J. Finkel (eds.), *Self and relationships: Connecting intrapersonal and interpersonal processes* (pp. 84–103). New York, NY: Guilford Press.

Park, L. E., & Maner, J. K. (2009). Does self-threat promote social connection? The role of self-esteem and contingencies of self-worth. *Journal of Personality and Social Psychology, 96*, 203–217.

Park, L. E., Sanchez, D. T., & Bryndilsen, K. (2011). Maladaptive responses to relationship dissolution: The role of relationship contingent self-worth. *Journal of Applied Social Psychology, 14*, 1749–1773.

Rholes, S. W., & Simpson, J. A. (2004). Attachment theory: Basic concepts and contemporary questions. In S. W. Rholes & J. A. Simpson (eds.), *Adult attachment: Theory, research, and clinical implications* (pp. 3–17). New York, NY: Guilford Press.

Sargent, J. T., Crocker, J., & Luhtanen, R. K. (2006). Contingencies of self-worth and symptoms of depression in college students. *Journal of Social and Clinical Psychology, 25*, 628–646.

Shaver, P. R., & Hazan, C. (1988). A biased overview of the study of love. *Journal of Social and Personal Relationships, 5*, 473–501.

Simpson, J. A. (1990). Influence of attachment styles on romantic relationships. *Journal of Personality and Social Psychology, 59*, 971–981.

Simpson, J. A., Rholes, W. S., & Nelligan, J. S. (1992). Support seeking and support giving within couples in an anxiety-provoking situation: The role of attachment styles. *Journal of Personality and Social Psychology, 62*, 434–446.

Sommer, K. L. (2001). Coping with rejection: Ego-defensive strategies, self-esteem, and interpersonal relationships. In M. Leary (ed.), *Interpersonal rejection* (pp. 167–188). New York, NY: Oxford University Press.

Sommer, K. L., Williams, K. D., Ciarocco, N. J., & Baumeister, R. F. (2001). When silence speaks louder than words: Explorations into the interpersonal and intrapsychic consequences of social ostracism. *Basic and Applied Social Psychology, 23*, 227–245.

Spencer, S. J., Josephs, R. A., & Steele, C. M. (1993). Low self-esteem: The uphill struggle for self-integrity. In R. F. Baumeister (ed.), *Self-esteem: The puzzle of low self-regard* (pp. 21–36). New York, NY: Plenum Press.

Swann, W. B., Jr., Chang-Schneider, C., & McClarty, K. L. (2007). Do people's self-views matter? Self-concept and self-esteem in everyday life. *American Psychologist, 62*, 84–94.

Tice, D. M. (1991). Esteem protection or enhancement? Self-handicapping motives and attributions differ by trait self-esteem. *Journal of Personality and Social Psychology, 60*, 711–725.

Tracy, J. L., & Robins, R. W. (2003). Death of a (narcissistic) salesman: An integrative model of fragile self-esteem. *Psychological Inquiry, 14*, 57–62.

Twenge, J. M. (2006). *Generation me: Why today's young Americans are more confident, assertive, entitled – and more miserable than ever before.* New York, NY: Free Press.

Zeigler-Hill, V. (2006). Discrepancies between implicit and explicit self-esteem: Implications for narcissism and self-esteem instability. *Journal of Personality, 74*, 119–143.

4 Development of self-esteem

Kali H. Trzesniewski, M. Brent Donnellan, and Richard W. Robins

Self-esteem is one of the most widely studied constructs in the social sciences and interest in self-esteem unites clinical, developmental, personality, and social psychology. In the last decade, researchers have focused increasingly on the development of self-esteem and are working to achieve consensus about the degree to which self-esteem changes over the life course. The existing evidence indicates that self-esteem shows remarkable rank-order consistency over time, despite the vast array of experiences that impinge upon a lived life. At the same time, average self-esteem levels show systematic and psychologically meaningful changes from one phase of development to the next. In this chapter we review evidence about the development of self-esteem by drawing on recent large-scale studies and meta-analytic findings. We also discuss potential mechanisms underlying patterns of stability and change, and briefly consider intervention and prevention efforts that aim deliberately to change self-esteem.

What is self-esteem?

Self-esteem is one of the oldest constructs in psychology; historically, it has been conceptualized in terms of an individual's phenomenological experience. We define self-esteem as an individual's *subjective* evaluation of her or his worth as a person. If a person believes that she is a person of worth and value, then she has high self-esteem, regardless of whether her self-evaluation is validated by others or corroborated by external criteria. Researchers often distinguish between global and domain-specific self-evaluations, the former referring to an individual's overall evaluation of his or her worth as a person and the latter referring to an evaluation of a specific domain or facet of the self, such as academic competence or physical appearance. In this chapter we will focus on global self-esteem, a construct that seems to have important affective, motivational, and behavioral consequences (see Brown, 2010; Ford & Collins, 2010; Orth, Robins, & Widaman, 2012; Swann, Chang-Scheider, & McClarty, 2007; Trzesniewski et al., 2006).

Current conceptions of global self-esteem can be traced to the seminal work of William James (1890/1983), who defined self-esteem as the match between people's accomplishments and their goals and aspirations. Specifically, he proposed that global self-esteem is "determined by the ratio of *our actualities* to *our supposed potentialities*" (James, 1890/1983, p. 54, italics added). It is important to emphasize that James took an explicitly phenomenological perspective on self-esteem and noted that "our self-feeling in this world depends entirely on what we *back* ourselves to be and do" (James, 1890/1983, p. 54, italics added). Morris Rosenberg (the developer of one of the most widely used measures of global self-esteem) and colleagues added that self-esteem involves feelings of self-respect and self-acceptance:

> When we speak of high self-esteem, then, we shall simply mean that the individual respects himself, considers himself worthy; he does not necessarily consider himself better than others, but he definitely does not consider himself worse; he does not feel that he is the ultimate in perfection but, on the contrary, recognizes his limitations and expects to grow and improve. Low self-esteem, on the other hand, implies self-rejection, self-dissatisfaction, self-contempt. The individual lacks respect for the self he observes.
>
> (Rosenberg, 1965, p. 31)

Some authors have attempted to reconceptualize self-esteem in a way that potentially conflicts with its roots in phenomenology by focusing on accuracy when defining self-esteem (e.g., Baumeister, Campbell, Krueger, & Vohs, 2003). Such authors often dicuss the idea of valid versus inflated appraisals of the self in the context of defining self-esteem (e.g. Baumeister, Smart, & Boden, 1996). This approach has led to a consideration of the potential benefits of "accurate" self-esteem and the idea that it might be worthwhile to lower self-esteem rather than raise it in certain contexts (Baumeister et al., 2003). The problem with moving the defintion of self-esteem in this direction is that it requires the existence of an "external yardstick" that serves as a criterion to judge the accuracy of judgments about the self (e.g. Robins & John, 1997; Tangney & Leary, 2003). This approach can then lead to thorny questions involving the imposition of a set of values used to judge the self. Tangney and Leary raised this concern when they posed this question: "Is the suggestion here that the average college freshman, unemployed person, or mentally retarded individual *shouldn't* on the whole take a positive attitude toward themselves?" (Tangney & Leary, 2003, p. 670; italics in original).

Given the difficulty of objectively assessing an individual's overall worth as a person, we favor the explicitly phenomenological perspective on self-esteem offered by William James, Morris Rosenberg, and others. If Sam likes himself and sees himself as a worthy person, then Sam has high self-esteem regardless of his actual abilities, traits, or level of social acceptance. There are other important questions that can be asked about Sam's self-evaluations but these often refer to different constructs. If someone were concerned with the possibility that Sam has an overly positive assessment of his actual likability or intellectual capability, then they would be interested in self-enhancement rather than self-esteem. If someone wondered if Sam were arrogant, egotistical, or had a grandiose sense of self, they would be interested in narcissism and related constructs. It might be interesting to evaluate how self-esteem is related to self-enhancement and narcissism, but self-esteem is conceptually distinct from these constructs.

Indeed, this phenomenological perspective makes it easier to draw conceptual distinctions between high self-esteem and narcissism. As we have noted elsewhere, Rosenberg made it clear that high self-esteem is not synonymous with egotism (e.g. Donnellan, Trzesniewski, Robins, Moffitt, & Caspi, 2005; Maxwell, Donnellan, Hopwood, & Ackerman, 2011; Trzesniewski, Donnellan, & Robins, 2008). Self-esteem tends to be only moderately correlated with global measures of narcissism (e.g., Trzesniewski et al., 2008) and it is either unrelated or negatively correlated with measures of narcissistic entitlement, depending on how the construct is measured (Ackerman & Donnellan, 2011; Trzesniewski et al., 2008; see also Hill & Roberts, in press). Blurring the distinction between self-esteem and narcissism has generated unnecessary concerns about the potential dark side of self-esteem (e.g., Baumeister, Boden, & Smart, 1996). As it stands, much of this "dark side" discussion applies to narcissism and not self-esteem (reviewed in Donnellan, Trzesniewski, & Robins, 2011; see also Tangney & Leary, 2003). It is also possible that the presumed "dark side" of self-esteem concerns the fragility, not the level, of one's self-esteem. Indeed, individuals with fragile self-esteem (assessed by within-person variability in self-esteem from moment to moment and day to day) tend to be more angry and hostile, even when their self-esteem is high (Kernis, Grannemann, & Barclay, 1989). However, there are methodological complexities involved in this kind of research (Baird, Le, & Lucas, 2006). Regardless of these issues, it is possible that instability (rather than level) of self-esteem might be related to psychosocial problems.

The consistency of self-esteem across the life span

We now consider the consistency of self-esteem from childhood through adulthood. We define consistency in this chapter as rank-order stability, which is typically assessed using test-retest correlations (i.e., the correlation between self-esteem scores obtained at two points in time). Rank-order stability reflects the degree to which the relative ordering of individuals is maintained over time. That is, to what extent do individuals who are high (or low) in self-esteem relative to others at Time 1 remain high (or low) relative to others at Time 2.

A high degree of rank-order stability indicates *either* that (a) individuals did not change much over time *or* that (b) individuals changed over time, but in more or less the same way (i.e., everyone increased or decreased to the same extent). A low level of rank-order stability indicates *both* that (a) individuals changed over time *and* that (b) there were individual differences in the direction of change (i.e., some individuals increased while others decreased). Low stability can occur when non-normative developmental events occur, for example, if some individuals experience parental divorce and decline in self-esteem, whereas others do not experience parental divorce and maintain their self-esteem. Low stability can also occur when the factors that influence the construct are normative but individuals have unique reactions to these events, for example, if puberty causes some individuals to increase in self-esteem but causes others to decrease in self-esteem. It is important to note that low stability can also be found when a high degree of measurement error attenuates test-retest correlations.

The degree of rank-order stability is an important consideration when evaluating whether the construct of self-esteem is more state- or trait-like (Trzesniewski, Donnellan, & Robins, 2003). Psychological traits such as the Big Five typically exhibit high stability over time, whereas mood and other states tend to exhibit lower levels of stability (Asendorpf, 1992; Conley, 1984; Kenny & Zautra, 2001; Roberts & DelVecchio, 2000). Although debate persists (Conley, 1984; Donnellan, Kenny, et al., 2011), we believe that the evidence now supports the conclusion that self-esteem is best conceptualized as a stable trait. Most notably, Trzesniewski and colleagues (2003) examined the rank-order stability of self-esteem using data from 50 published articles ($N=29{,}839$). They found that test-retest correlations are moderate in magnitude and comparable to those found for personality traits; across all age groups, the median correlation was .47 ($r=.64$, corrected for measurement error).

The rank-order stability of self-esteem showed a robust curvilinear trend: stability (uncorrected for measurement error) was relatively low during early childhood (.40), increased throughout adolescence (.51) and early adulthood (.55 during the college years and .65 during people's twenties), and then declined during midlife (.55) and old age (.48). This curvilinear trend could not be explained by age differences in the reliability of self-esteem measures and generally replicated across different self-esteem scales, gender, ethnicity (Caucasian vs African American), nationality (US vs non-US), and the year the study was conducted. Recent studies have replicated the curvilinear trend for the Big Five personality domains (Lucas & Donnellan, 2011; Wortman, Lucas, & Donnellan, in press), suggesting that the pattern observed for self-esteem may reflect a more general developmental process.

The increasing consistency of self-esteem from childhood to mid-life conforms well to the *cumulative continuity* principle (see Caspi, Roberts, & Shiner, 2005), which states that psychological traits become more consistent as individuals mature into adulthood. Nonetheless, these descriptive findings for self-esteem require explanation. Specifically, why does the longitudinal consistency of self-esteem increase for much of the life span, and then decrease in the later stages of life?

Consistency is expected to be highest during those periods of the life span when the individual can exercise agency and is not generally subject to maturational and environmental change. Such a characterization aptly describes large portions of adulthood. In contrast, the transitions from childhood to adulthood and from adulthood to old age involve substantial changes in the social, cognitive, and biological domains, changes that are assumed to reduce stability (Alsaker & Olweus, 1992; Donnellan, Trzesniewski, & Robins, 2006; Lucas & Donnellan, 2011; Trzesniewski et al., 2003).

The adolescent period is marked by pronounced social and maturational changes associated with puberty, as well as significant changes in the educational context. Family relationships are also transformed as the individual moves beyond the family of origin to form intimate relationships with peers and, in many cases, romantic partners. These challenges may impact individuals in different ways, thereby shifting the relative ordering of individual differences. The changes that occur during the transition to adulthood also have an interesting parallel with the end phases of the life span. Development past mid-life often involves declines in health and cognitive functioning as well as changes in social roles and family relationships. Individuals retire and sometimes become grandparents. Many individuals endure the loss of spouses. Similar to the adolescent period, this plethora of changes may impact individuals in different ways and at different times, thus accounting for the observed decline in the consistency of self-esteem at the end of the life span.

In summary, an accumulating body of evidence suggests that self-esteem shows high stability across the life span, with the level of stability approaching that of basic personality traits. Self-esteem is most stable during mid-life but it shows an appreciable degree of consistency at all phases of the life span from adolescence to old age. In general, individuals with relatively high (or low) self-esteem at one phase of their life tend to have relatively high (or low) self-esteem at subsequent phases of life. Such evidence supports the conclusion that self-esteem is a trait-like construct, not an ephemeral state that varies dramatically from situation to situation.

Changes in average levels of self-esteem across the life course

Are there periods in life when self-esteem levels tend to be particularly high or low? Such *mean-level changes* are conceptually and empirically distinct from rank-order stability. For example, adolescents could show large increases in self-esteem as they enter adulthood but the rank ordering of individuals would be maintained if everyone increased by the same amount. Conversely, the rank ordering of individuals could change substantially over time without producing any aggregate increases or decreases in self-esteem (e.g., if the number of people who decreased offset the number of people who increased).

Mean-level change can be investigated using a variety of methods, including cross-sectional studies that compare the mean self-esteem levels of different age groups (e.g., do adolescents have higher or lower self-esteem than young adults? See Robins, Trzesniewski, Tracy, Gosling, & Potter, 2002), longitudinal studies that track changes over time in the mean self-esteem level of a specific age cohort (e.g., do adolescents increase or decrease in self-esteem as they become young adults?), and cohort-sequential designs that combine these two methods by tracking changes over time in the mean self-esteem levels of multiple age cohorts (e.g., Erol & Orth, 2011; Orth et al., 2012; Orth, Trzesniewski, & Robins, 2010).

Cohort-sequential designs allow researchers to distinguish between age and cohort effects when understanding the development of self-esteem. An age effect is attributable to maturational changes or to common life experiences that characterize different developmental periods (e.g., moving away from home in late adolescence/early adulthood). A cohort effect is attributable to the unique socio-cultural factors that impact people differently based on when they were born (e.g., growing up during the Great Depression or the Cultural Revolution in China). Age and cohort are confounded in cross-sectional studies because older participants were born at an earlier point in history than younger participants, and thus experienced different socio-cultural factors. Consequently, any observed differences could be attributable to maturational differences or cohort differences between age groups. In a cohort-sequential study, separate age trajectories can be examined for people of different cohorts. If the age trajectory of self-esteem is similar for all participants, regardless of when they were born, then cohort effects are not a major factor. This pattern tends to be what is observed when cohort-sequential designs are used (Orth et al., 2012; Orth et al., 2010; see also Trzesniewski & Donnellan, 2010). Thus, cohort-sequential studies provide the most powerful method to evaluate mean-level changes in self-esteem.

After decades of contentious debate (e.g., Demo, 1992; McCarthy & Hoge, 1982; O'Malley & Bachman, 1983; Twenge & Campbell, 2001), research accumulating over the past several years suggests that there are reliable age differences in self-esteem across the life span (see Huang, 2010 for a recent meta-analysis). A broad generalization is that levels of self-esteem decline from childhood to adolescence, increase during the transition to adulthood, reach a peak sometime in middle adulthood, and decrease in old age (e.g., Galambos, Barker, & Krahn, 2006; Orth et al., 2010). Orth and colleagues (2010; see also Shaw, Liang, & Krause, 2010) conducted one of the most extensive cohort-sequential analyses of mean levels of self-esteem across the life span and found that such a quadratic trend of increasing and then decreasing self-esteem was a reasonable approximation of the age trend from ages 25 to 104. This study was based on the Americans' Changing Lives study (House, 1986), which used probability-based sampling methods, a design feature that addresses concerns about the use of convenience samples in this literature (Pullmann, Allik, & Realo, 2009). Orth and colleagues (2012) also found a similar trajectory for self-esteem across the life span in a second large dataset spanning multiple generations.

The Orth and colleagues (2010) results are not entirely consistent with those of the meta-analysis conducted by Huang (2010), which found no evidence that self-esteem declines in old age. However, the meta-analysis included few studies with older participants, prompting Huang to note that "caution is necessary in interpreting the mean-level change in self-esteem beyond the college years as the data points are not sufficiently large" (Huang, 2010, p. 256). Thus, additional research is needed to determine the trajectory of self-esteem during the latter phases of the life span; however, the size and nature of the Orth and colleagues (2010, 2012) samples point to the possibility of a late-life decline in self-esteem.

Decreasing self-esteem from childhood to adolescence

It appears that average levels of self-esteem decline during the transition from childhood to adolescence (Robins et al., 2002; Wigfield, Eccles, Mac Iver, Reuman, & Midgley, 1991; except see Hirsch & Rapkin, 1987). However, this finding is difficult to interpret because there are debates about whether global self-esteem can be validly assessed in younger children, due to their cognitive limitations (Davis-Kean & Sandler, 2001; Harter, 1999; Marsh, Craven, & Debus, 1991; Marsh, Ellis, & Craven, 2002; Trzesniewski, Kinal, & Donnellan, 2010). For instance, Harter (2006) argues that the changes in self-esteem from childhood to adolescence stem from underlying cognitive changes that cause self-evaluations to be based more strongly on external criteria (e.g., academic performance) and tied more closely to social comparison processes (see also Cole, Maxwell, Martin, Peeke, Serocyznski, & Tram, 2001). From this perspective, it is possible that adolescents do not actually feel worse about themselves than children do, but simply change the way they formulate their global self-views, and therefore the way they respond to items on a self-esteem scale. Resolving debates about the validity of self-esteem measures with children and generally establishing longitudinal measurement invariance for common assessments of self-esteem (Chen, 2008) is an important area for future research.

Increasing self-esteem from adolescence to adulthood

Although adolescence may not be a time of storm and stress, as it has often been characterized in classic accounts (e.g., Hall, 1904), it might still be a *relatively* difficult period in a person's life (see Arnett, 1999, for a review). For much of adolescence, individuals are reproductively and cognitively mature, but they are given fairly limited opportunities to express their maturity. Adolescents do not have clearly defined roles in society. This so-called maturity gap was identified by Moffitt (1993) as an explanation for why many youths engage in transitory antisocial behavior during adolescence. The elimination of the maturity gap that happens during adulthood may facilitate increases in self-esteem because individuals are able to select environments in accordance with their individual attributes and gradually assume meaningful roles. This process may end up promoting psychological health and maturity, as illustrated by the increase in self-esteem.

This general trend for increasing mean-levels of self-esteem during the transition to adulthood is broadly consistent with the *maturity principle* of personality development (Caspi et al., 2005) or the idea that individuals become more emotionally stable, confident, and capable during adulthood. Huang concluded that "self-esteem matures during the first decade of adulthood" (Huang, 2010, p. 257) and Gove, Ortega, & Style (1989) noted that "during the productive adult years, when persons are engaged in a full set of instrumental and social roles, their sense of self will reflect the fullness of this role repertoire [...] levels of life satisfaction and self-esteem will also be high" (Gove et al, 1989, p. 1122). All in all, increases in self-esteem that accompany the transition to adulthood might be part of a suite of psychological changes that occur at this time in the life span, related to changes in agency, opportunities, and social roles.

Mid-life peak in self-esteem

The last life-span trend that deserves comment is the finding that self-esteem peaks sometime around the 50s or 60s, and subsequently declines (e.g., Orth et al., 2010, 2012). Erikson (1968), Jung (1958), Neugarten (1967), Levinson (1978), and others have all theorized that mid-life is characterized by a focus on activity, achievement, power, and control. For example, Erikson suggested that the maturity and superior functioning associated with mid-life is linked to the "generativity" stage. This is a period in which individuals tend to be increasingly productive and creative at work and concerned with promoting and guiding the next generation. Similarly, Mitchell and Helson (1990) described the latter part of mid-life as a period characterized by higher levels of psychological maturity and adjustment, and noted that during the post-parental period "the energy that went to children is redirected to the partner, work, the community, or self-development" (Mitchell & Helson, 1990, p. 453). Role theories of aging suggest that over the course of adulthood individuals increasingly occupy positions of power and status, which might confer a sense of self-worth (Dannefer, 1984; Helson, Mitchell, & Moane, 1984; Hogan & Roberts, 2004; Sarbin, 1964).

In contrast to the prime of adulthood, the period of development past the sixties may, on average, involve a number of changes that can contribute to declines in self-esteem. These include loss of a spouse, decreased social support, declining physical health, cognitive impairments, and a downward shift in socio-economic status. Indeed, Orth et al. (2010) found that changes in health and economic conditions explained the decline in self-esteem. Thus, some of the less pleasant aspects of aging may account for why self-esteem levels tend to decline late in life. We should emphasize again that research about declines in self-esteem toward the end of the life span are based on only a few studies. More work is needed on the phase of life beyond age 60 to improve the understanding of how and why average levels of self-esteem may decline in old age.

The role of nature and nurture in shaping the development of self-esteem

Many classic developmental accounts emphasize the role of environmental factors such as relationships with parents and peers as important contributors to self-esteem (e.g., Harter, 2006). However, there is also a biological component to self-esteem that is being increasingly recognized. Twin studies indicated that genetic factors account for about 40% of the observed variability in self-esteem (Neiss, Sedikides, & Stevenson, 2002). The relatively high heritability of self-esteem, which approaches that found for basic personality traits, is not inconsistent with developmental accounts that assume a central role for socializing agents such as parents and peers. Self-esteem no doubt emerges from complex transactions between a person's genetic make-up and his or her family, social, and cultural context. For example, genetically influenced differences in temperament, intelligence, physical attractiveness, health, and so on will shape social interactions: which social contexts individuals seek out; the reactions they elicit from parents, peers, relationship partners, and other important figures in their lives; and their capacity to attain success in work and relationship contexts. Collectively these interpersonal processes and environmental influences may in turn shape the individual's level of self-esteem.

It is important to emphasize that no one claims there is a single gene that codes for high (or low) self-esteem; it is much more likely that a vast number of genes contribute to self-esteem. However, researchers are beginning to develop a list of which genetic factors are most relevant. For example, recent research suggests that self-esteem is influenced by the oxytocin receptor gene (Saphire-Bernstein, Way, Kim, Sherman, & Taylor, 2011). Past research has linked this oxytocin receptor gene to how individuals deal with stress and to their social skills. Thus, the pathway from genes to environment to self-esteem is beginning to be explored.

Processes of self-esteem development

An important objective of developmental research is to specify and investigate the mechanisms that account for stability and change in self-esteem across the life span. Which processes promote consistency and which promote change? A critical insight from the developmental literature is that separate processes may be responsible for consistency as opposed to change (e.g., Caspi & Roberts, 2001; Caspi et al., 2005; Roberts, Donnellan, & Hill, in press; Shiner & Caspi, 2003). Researchers and practitioners interested in intervening to improve self-esteem may take advantage of the processes that facilitate change and consider how to disrupt the processes that promote consistency. The mechanisms that may create changes in self-esteem include the process whereby self-esteem is responsive to environmental contingencies and the notion that levels of self-esteem might change in response to self-reflection or changes in perceptions by significant others. The mechanisms that promote consistency include the processes whereby different levels of self-esteem evoke specific environmental reactions, shape individualized interpretations of situations, and motivate individuals to seek out specific environments that are consistent with their levels of self-esteem.

Mechanisms that promote change in self-esteem

Responding to contingencies

Individuals are responsive to environmental feedback, which has been demonstrated through social psychology experiments to impact self-esteem in the short term (e.g., Dandeneau & Baldwin, 2004). In everyday life, many contingencies are implicitly associated with particular social roles. For example, children and adolescents are rewarded and punished for certain behaviors at school and at home. These different contingencies may help shape self-esteem. For example, a child who frequently fails at key developmental tasks may internalize that feedback and develop a negative self-image. It is also likely that non-normative shifts in family roles could shape self-esteem. For example, following a parental divorce an adolescent may have to assume greater responsibility for the care of younger siblings. This could lead to an increase in feelings of mastery. Similarly, as individuals mature and settle into established roles as parents and workers, they likely experience more mastery experiences and more stable social support. These normative contingencies may account for the normative increase in self-esteem found during adulthood.[1]

Self-reflection

Self-reflection can be one avenue of self-esteem change. As children and adolescents mature, cognitive changes lead to greater self-reflective abilities. These self-reflective abilities can provide the tools to change their own self-esteem. One avenue for changing self-esteem suggested by the classic Jamesian formulation is to bring one's pretensions to closer in line with one's performance. James suggested that giving up pretensions "is as blessed relief as to get them gratified" (James, 1890/1983, p. 54). Even so, it is not clear how easy it is willfully to change one's self-esteem through this mechanism.

Reflected appraisals

Perceptions by others may shape self-esteem and these reflected appraisals have long been implicated in self-esteem development (Cooley, 1902; Rosenberg, Schooler, & Schoenbach, 1989). For example, according to dependency model developed by Murray, Holmes, & Griffin (2000), feelings about the self are regulated by individuals' perceptions of their partners' feelings about them. That is, perceiving one's partner as supportive and loving leads to greater self-esteem over time, and perceiving a partner to view one less positively leads to diminished self-esteem over time. Similarly, being viewed as competent and liked by peers may promote self-esteem, whereas being viewed as incompetent and disliked by peers may diminish self-esteem (Fenzel, 2000; Wade, Thompson, Tashakkori, & Valente, 1989). One complicated issue (see below) is that self-esteem may actually shape how individuals perceive the world (e.g., Shrauger & Schoeneman, 1979). Individuals with low self-esteem may perceive peer rejection and negativity even when peers do not actually harbor such perspectives. These self-perceptions – whether true or not – may reinforce levels of self-esteem.

Mechanisms that promote continuity

Environmental elicitation

An emerging body of evidence suggests that people with low self-esteem elicit particular responses from the social environment. This notion is similar to the notion of evocative genotype-environment interactions (Scarr & McCartney, 1983), the process of evocation outlined by Buss (1987), and the general idea that the individual plays an active role in shaping his or her own development (e.g., Lerner & Busch-Rossnagel, 1981). For example, people report being more interested in voting for presidential candidates that are perceived as having higher self-esteem and people perceived as having higher self-esteem are thought to make more desirable relationship partners, particularly when the high self-esteem target is male (Zeigler-Hill & Myers, 2009, 2011). This high self-esteem is linked with confidence and social potency. This is consistent with the idea that individuals high in self-esteem are more approach-oriented than individuals low in self-esteem (Heimpel, Elliot, & Wood, 2006). Confident adults (presumably those high in self-esteem) may be given more difficult tasks at work and therefore have more opportunities to succeed (Judge & Bono, 2001). Consider as a different example that adolescents lower in self-esteem may evoke peer victimization, possibly because they are perceived as having less desirable characteristics and are viewed as easy targets (Egan & Perry, 1998).

In many cases, the environmental stimuli evoked by self-esteem seems to follow the "corresponsive principle" (Caspi et al., 2005) of personality development, the idea that life experiences accentuate the characteristics that were initially responsible for the environmental experiences in the first place. For instance, when low self-esteem invites victimization, it is likely that peer victimization will further depress self-esteem. Similarly, Holmes and Wood (2009) found that individuals with low self-esteem are less disclosing in interpersonal settings, which tends to hamper the development of close relationships. As they note, "the avoidance of risk is self-defeating, resulting in lost social opportunities, the very lack of close connection that [individuals with low self-esteem] fear, and the perpetuation of their low self-esteem" (Holmes & Wood, 2009, p. 250).

Environmental construal

Traits shape how individuals perceive and construe social situations. For example, a child with low self-esteem may expect that she will not be good at a new sport. This construal will likely affect how her lessons are experienced, how much effort she expends learning a new sport, and how setbacks and initial difficulties are interpreted. The upshot is that individual differences in self-esteem affect how individuals perceive and ultimately experience situations. This process is likely to maintain individual differences in self-esteem according to the correspondsive principle such that environmental construals will likely strengthen the traits that gave rise to the perceptions in the first place.

The risk-rejection model provides an apt example of how these processes play out in intimate relationships. According to this model, individuals with low self-esteem are particularly sensitive to interpersonal rejection and more likely to interpret ambiguous stimuli as evidence of rejection (Dandeneau & Baldwin, 2004; Holmes & Wood, 2009). A recent study by Ford and Collins (2010) provides support for this idea. Participants read about a potential interaction partner's attributes and were led to believe that a potential partner was learning about their attributes. Some participants were told that the potential partner became ill whereas others were told that the potential partner elected to stop the experiment (the rejection condition). Individuals with low self-esteem blamed themselves for the rejection and derogated their potential partners by providing more negative evaluations of the individual. Participants with low self-esteem also showed more physiological stress in response to the rejection.

Research, however, has shown that this pattern can be interrupted. Baldwin and his colleagues have shown that it is possible to change these automatic reactions and attentional biases that characterize people with low self-esteem. Dandeneau and Baldwin (2004) developed a computer game that trains people with low self-esteem to ignore information about rejection. The game, EyeSpy, displays a set of 16 faces, one of which is smiling and the others with negative, rejecting expressions. The player is instructed to find and select the smiling face as quickly as possible. Dandeneau and Baldwin (2004) found that playing this game made those with low self-esteem less sensitive to rejection.

Environmental selection and environmental manipulation

The idea that individuals select environments consistent with their individual characteristics has a long history in psychology (e.g., Buss, 1987; Scarr & McCartney, 1983). An individual high in self-esteem may seek out intellectually challenging courses and opportunities, whereas an individual low in self-esteem may opt for more traditional educational fare. In this case, differences in traits motivate individuals to select certain situations over others. These processes will also facilitate continuity by the corresponsive principle – levels of self-esteem that influence individuals to select one context over another will likely be reinforced and accentuated in these new situations. Scarr and McCartney (1983) argued that these active person-environment transactions increase in frequency over the life span as the individual gains agency. This phenomenon may explain why the rank-order stability of self-esteem increases from early adolescence to late adolescence. Adolescents are granted more freedom and autonomy than children but their ability to select and manipulate environments is more constrained by social factors than adults. As individuals grow and gain more autonomy throughout adolescence and adulthood, they can select into environments that are more consistent with their self-esteem.

The idea that self-esteem is related to the kinds of environments individuals select for themselves is also consistent with Swann's self-verification theory, which proposes that individuals are motivated to confirm their pre-existing self-views (Kwang & Swann, 2010; Swann, 1983). That is, individuals with low self-esteem seek contexts that confirm and maintain their low self-regard whereas individuals with high self-esteem seek contexts that promote their high self-regard. This process might explain why individuals with low self-esteem prefer certain kinds of relationships that can involve negative feedback (see Kwang & Swann, 2010). An important caveat is that individuals with low self-esteem will prefer negative feedback in relationship contexts with a low risk of rejection. The gist is that a romantic partner can be negative but not rejecting. Nonetheless, the upshot of self-verification motives is that they tend to promote the consistency of self-views.

Self-esteem intervention efforts

A discussion of the mechanisms responsible for continuity and change in self-esteem naturally leads to questions about the impact of interventions aimed at modifying self-esteem levels. There are two critical questions – can interventions actually increase self-esteem and do they improve psychosocial outcomes for children and adults? Evidence about the effectiveness of interventions is critical for resolving debates about the potential dark side of self-esteem (Trzesniewski et al., 2008). Indeed, some commentators have gone as far as suggesting that the self-esteem movement has produced a generation of narcissists. Despite these concerns, meta-analytic research suggests that interventions can increase self-esteem and improve positive outcomes for children and adults. That is, there is evidence that it is possible to "significantly improve" levels of self-esteem and produce "concomitant positive changes in other areas of adjustment" (Haney & Durlak, 1998, p. 429).

More recently, O'Mara, Marsh, Craven, & Debus (2006) found that programs designed to enhance global and domain-specific self-esteem produced positive benefits for children and adolescents. Interestingly, programs targeting domain-specific self-evaluation tended to have larger effect sizes for relevant outcomes than programs targeting global self-esteem. For example, programs designed to increase academic self-worth led to larger improvements in grades than programs that increased global self-esteem. Thus, although O'Mara et al. found that global intervention efforts produced positive effects across a wide range of outcomes, they concluded that an ideal intervention should focus on "enhancing self-concept in specific areas relevant to the goals of the intervention" (O'Mara et al., 2006, p. 198). On the other hand, it might be most effective to attempt to do both – enhance domain-specific and global self-worth – given that global interventions are likely to have more pervasive effects on youth development, leading to cumulative, cascading benefits. O'Mara et al. also recommend combining self-esteem enhancement with interventions that directly target the outcome of interest. For example, if the goal is to improve academic achievement, then a combined intervention program might attempt to improve students' beliefs about their academic ability and promote skills and strategies that contribute to good grades. A combined intervention would provide the individual with the resources needed to maintain both high self-esteem and performance over longer periods of time.

In addition to testing the efficacy of various interventions, O'Mara et al. (2006) also identified the characteristics of the most successful interventions. This information is helpful for designing new programs and improving existing ones. They found that the most common type of intervention was one that focused on practice or training for a specific task. This strategy yielded a positive result, but was not nearly as powerful for increasing self-esteem as interventions that used praise and/or feedback. Specifically, interventions that used attributional feedback (e.g., helping individuals attribute outcomes to effort), goal feedback (e.g., promoting realistic and attainable goals), and contingent praise (e.g., praising individuals for positive performance) had the most powerful effect. The use of non-contingent praise was not effective. That is, it is not effective to tell people they are great in the absence of real accomplishments and/or mastery experiences.

We must emphasize that the term "self-esteem intervention" covers a range of programs and intervention strategies. Some programs are likely to be effective whereas others are likely to be ineffective. It is also possible that certain self-esteem programs may have negative consequences, as is true of any psychological intervention (see Lilienfeld, 2007). This is why careful and rigorous program evaluation is critical. In general, though, we believe there is sufficient evidence to conclude that intervention programs can increase self-esteem (at least in the short-term) and improve psychosocial adjustment and functioning.

Conclusions and future directions

Research on the development of self-esteem has progressed considerably over the past decade or two. There is now compelling evidence that the rank-order stability of self-esteem parallels the stability of basic personality traits, both in terms of the degree of stability and the way stability fluctuates across the life span. There is also replicable evidence that mean levels of self-esteem show normative changes across the life span: self-esteem increases during the transition to adulthood, peaks in midlife, and may decline in later life. However, many questions about the development of self-esteem remain. For example, self-esteem during childhood is not well understood. Why is self-esteem high in childhood? Is it due to measurement issues (e.g., young children do not understand the questions) or substantive issues (e.g., young children base their self-esteem on different things than adolescents and adults)? How are transactions between biological and social factors implicated in the development of self-esteem? What are the best strategies to enhance and maintain levels of self-esteem? We expect that the field will soon provide answers to these intriguing questions given the rapidly expanding body of research in this area.

Note

1 Individuals may also develop contingent self-esteem, linking their feelings of self-worth to specific successes and failures in academic and social domains. For example, an individual with contingent self-esteem would feel good about himself or herself after being asked to a dance, but that feeling would not last long and would be easily replaced by negative self-feelings after failing a test. When self-esteem becomes overly contingent on external factors, it can fluctuate dramatically and lead to a host of maladaptive psychological consequences (Crocker & Wolfe, 2001).

References

Ackerman, R. A., & Donnellan, M. B. (2011). Assessing narcissistic entitlement: Further evidence for the utility of the entitlement/exploitativeness subscale from the Narcissistic Personality Inventory. Manuscript submitted for publication.

Alsaker, F. D., & Olweus, D. (1992). Stability of global self-evaluations in early adolescence: A cohort longitudinal study. *Journal of Research on Adolescence, 2*, 123–145.

Arnett, J. J. (1999). Adolescent storm and stress, reconsidered. *American Psychologist, 54*, 317–326.

Asendorpf, J. B. (1992). Beyond stability: Predicting inter-individual differences in intra-individual change. *European Journal of Personality, 6*, 103–117.

Baird, B. M., Le, K., & Lucas, R. E. (2006). On the nature of intraindividual personality variability: Reliability, validity, and associations with well-being. *Journal of Personality and Social Psychology, 90*, 512–527.

Baumeister, R. F., Boden, J. M., & Smart, L. (1996). Relation of threatened egotism to violence and aggression: The dark side of high self-esteem. *Psychological Review, 103*, 5–33.

Baumeister, R. F., Campbell, F. A., Krueger, J. I., & Vohs, K. D. (2003). Does high self-esteem cause better performance, interpersonal success, happiness, or healthier lifestyles? *Psychological Science in Public Interest, 4*, 1–44.

Baumeister, R. F., Smart, L., & Boden, J. M. (1996). Relation of threatened egotism to violence and aggression: The dark side of high self-esteem. *Psychological Review, 103*, 5–33.

Brown, J. D. (2010). High self-esteem buffers negative feedback: Once more with feeling. *Cognition and Emotion, 24*, 1389–1404.

Buss, D. M. (1987). Selection, evocation, and manipulation. *Journal of Personality and Social Psychology, 53*, 1214–1221.

Caspi, A., & Roberts, B. W. (2001). Personality development across the life course: The argument for change and continuity. *Psychology Inquiry, 12*, 49–66.

Caspi, A., Roberts, B. W., & Shiner, R. L. (2005). Personality development: Stability and change. *Annual Review of Psychology, 56*, 453–484.

Chen, F. F. (2008). What happens if we compare chopsticks with forks? The impact of making innappropriate comparisons in cross-cultural research. *Journal of Personality and Social Psychology, 95*, 1005–1018.

Cole, D. A., Maxwell, S. E., Martin, J. M., Peeke, L. G., Serocyznski, A. D., & Tram, J. M. (2001). The development of multiple domains of child and adolescent self-concept: A cohort sequential longitudinal design. *Child Development, 72*, 1723–1746.

Conley, J. J. (1984). The hierarchy of consistency: A review and model of longitudinal findings on adult individual differences in intelligence, personality and self-opinion. *Personality and Individual Differences, 5*, 11–25.

Cooley, C. H. (1902). *Human nature and the social order*. New York: Charles Scribner's Sons.

Crocker, J., & Wolfe, C. T. (2001). Contingencies of self-worth. *Psychological Review, 108*, 593–623.

Dandeneau, S. D., & Baldwin, M. W. (2004). The inhibition of socially rejecting information among people with high versus low self-esteem; The role of attentional bias and the effects of bias reduction training. *Journal of Social and Clinical Psychology, 23*, 584–602.

Dannefer, D. (1984). Adult development and social theory: A paradigmatic reappraisal. *American Sociological Review, 49*, 100–116.

Davis-Kean, P. E., & Sandler, H. M. (2001). A meta-analysis for preschool self-concept measures: A framework for future measures. *Child Development, 72*, 887–906.

Demo, D. H. (1992). The self-concept over time: Research issues and directions. *Annual Review of Sociology, 18*, 303–326.

Donnellan, M. B., Kenny, D. A., Trzesniewski, K. H., Lucas, R. E., & Conger, R. D. (2011). Using trait-state models to examine the longitudinal consistency of global self-esteem from adolescence to adulthood. Manuscript submitted for review.

Donnellan, M. B., Trzesniewski, K. H., & Robins, R. W. (2006). Personality and self-esteem development in adolescence. In D. K. M. T. Little (ed.), *Handbook of personality development* (pp. 285–309). Hillsdale, NJ: Erlbaum.

Donnellan, M. B., Trzesniewski, K. H., & Robins, R. W. (2011). Self-esteem: Enduring issues and controversies. In A. F. T. Chamorro-Premuzic & S. von Stumm (eds.), *Handbook of Individual Differences* (pp. 718–746). New York: Wiley-Blackwell.

Donnellan, M. B., Trzesniewski, K. H., Robins, R. W., Moffitt, T. E., & Caspi, A. (2005). Low self-esteem is related to aggression, antisocial behavior, and delinquency. *Psychological Science, 16*, 328–335.

Egan, S. K., & Perry, D. G. (1998). Does low self-regard invite victimization? *Developmental Psychology, 34*, 299–309.

Erikson, E. H. (1968). *Identity, youth, and crisis*. New York, NY: W. Norton.

Erol, R. Y., & Orth, U. (2011). Self-esteem development from 14 to 30 years: A longitudinal study. *Journal of Personality and Social Psychology, 101*, 607–619.

Fenzel, L. M. (2000). Prospective study of changes in global self-worth and strain during the transition to middle school. *Journal of Early Adolescence, 20*, 93–116.

Ford, M. B., & Collins, N. L. (2010). Self-esteem moderates neuroendocrine and psychological responses to interpersonal rejection. *Journal of Personality and Social Psychology, 98*, 405–419.

Galambos, N. L., Barker, E. T., & Krahn, H. J. (2006). Depression, self-esteem, and anger in emerging adulthood: Seven-year trajectories. *Development Psychology, 42*, 350–365.

Gove, W. R., Ortega, S. T., & Style, C. B. (1989). The maturational and role perspectives on aging and self through the adult years: An empirical evaluation. *American Journal of Sociology, 94*, 1117–1145.

Hall, G. S. (1904). *Adolescence: Its psychology and its relations to physiology, anthropology, sociology, sex, crime, religion, and education*. Englewood Cliffs, NJ: Prentice Hall.

Haney, P., & Durlak, J. A. (1998). Changing self-esteem in children and adolescents: A meta-analytic review. *Journal of Clinical Child Psychology, 27*, 423–433.

Harter, S. (1999). *The construction of the self: A developmental perspective*. New York, NY: Guilford.

Harter, S. (2006). The self. In W. Damon, R. M. Lerner, & N. D. Eisenberg (eds.), *Handbook of Child Psychology: Vol. 3, Social, Emotional, and Personality Development* (6th edn, pp. 505–570). Hoboken, NJ: John Wiley & Sons.

Heimpel, S. A., Elliot, A. J., & Wood, J. V. (2006). Basic personality dimensions, self-esteem, and personal goals: An approach-avoidance analysis. *Journal of Personality, 74*, 1293–1320.

Helson, R., Mitchell, V., & Moane, G. (1984). Personality and patterns of adherence and nonadherence to the social clock. *Journal of Personality and Social Psychology, 46*, 1079–1096.

Hill, P. L., & Roberts, B. W. (in press). Narcissism, well-being, and observer-related personality across the lifespan. *Social Psychological & Personality Science*.

Hirsch, B. J., & Rapkin, B. D. (1987). The transition to junior high school: A longitudinal study of self-esteem psychological symptomology, school life, and social support. *Child Development, 58*, 1235–1243.

Hogan, R., & Roberts, B. W. (2004). A socioanalytic model of maturity. *Journal of Career Assessment, 12*, 207–217.

Holmes, J. G., & Wood, J. V. (2009). Interpersonal situations as affordances: The example of self-esteem. *Journal of Research in Personality, 43*, 250.

House, J. S. (1986). *Americans' Changing lives, Waves I, and II*. Ann Arbor, MI: Inter-University Consortium for Political and Social Research.

Huang, C. (2010). Mean-level change in self-esteem from childhood through adulthood: Meta-analysis of longitudinal studies. *Review of General Psychology, 14*, 251–260.

James, W. (1890/1983). *The principles of psychology*. Cambridge, MA: Harvard University Press.

Judge, T. A., & Bono, J. E. (2001). Relationship of core self-evaluation traits – self-esteem, generalized self-efficacy, locus of control, and emotional stability – with job satisfaction and job performance: A meta-analysis. *Journal of Applied Psychology, 86*, 80–92.

Jung, C. G. (1958). *The undiscovered self*. Boston, MA: Little, Brown.

Kenny, D. A., & Zautra, A. (2001). The trait-state models for longitudinal data. In L. M. C. A. G. Sayer (ed.), *New Methods for the Analysis of Change* (pp. 243–263). Washington, DC: American Psychological Association.

Kernis, M. H., Grannemann, B. D., & Barclay, L. C. (1989). Stability and level of self-esteem as predictors of anger arousal and hostility. *Journal of Personality and Social Psychology, 56*, 1013–1022.

Kwang, T., & Swann, W. B. (2010). Do people embrace praise even when they feel unworthy? A review of critical tests of self-enhancement versus self-verification. *Personality and Social Psychology Review, 14*, 263–280.

Lerner, R. M., & Busch-Rossnagel, N. (1981). *Individuals as producers of their development: A life-span perspective*. New York, NY: Academic Press.

Levinson, D. J. (1978). *The seasons of a man's life*. New York, NY: Knopf.

Lilienfeld, S. O. (2007). Psychological treatments that cause harm. *Perspectives on Psychological Science, 2*, 53–70.

Lucas, R. E., & Donnellan, M. B. (2011). Personality development across the life span: Longitudinal analyses with a national sample from Germany. *Journal of Personality and Social Psychology, 101*, 847–861.

Marsh, H. W., Craven, R. G., & Debus, R. L. (1991). Self-concepts of young children 5 to 8 years of age: Measurement of multidimensional structure. *Journal of Educational Psychology, 83*, 377–392.

Marsh, H. W., Ellis, L. A., & Craven, R. G. (2002). How do preschool children feel about themselves? Unraveling measurement and multidimensional self-concept structure. *Developmental Psychology, 38,* 376–393.

Maxwell, K., Donnellan, M. B., Hopwood, C. J., & Ackerman, R. A. (2011). The two faces of Narcissus? An empirical comparison of the Narcissistic Personality Inventory and the Pathological Narcissism Inventory. *Personality and Individual Differences, 50,* 577–582.

McCarthy, J. D., & Hoge, D. R. (1982). Analysis of age effects in longitudinal studies of adolescent self-esteem. *Developmental Psychology, 18,* 372–379.

Mitchell, V., & Helson, R. (1990). Women's prime of life: Is it the 50s? *Psychology of Women Quarterly, 14,* 451–470.

Moffitt, T. E. (1993). Adolescence-limited and life course-persistent antisocial behavior: A developmental taxonomy. *Psychological Review, 100,* 674–701.

Murray, S. L., Holmes, J. G., & Griffin, D. W. (2000). Self-esteem and the quest for felt security: How perceived regard regulates attachment processes. *Journal of Personality and Social Psychology, 78,* 478–498.

Neiss, M. B., Stevenson, J., & Sedikides, C. (2002). Self-esteem: A behavioral genetics perspective. *European Journal of Personality, 16,* 1–17.

Neugarten, B. L. (1967). The awareness of middle age. In R. Owen (ed.), *Middle Age* (pp. 93–98). London: BBC.

Nottlemann, E. D. (1987). Competence and self-esteem during transition from childhood to adolescence. *Developmental Psychology, 23,* 441–450.

O'Malley, P. M., & Bachman, J. G. (1983). Self-esteem: Change and stability between ages 13 and 23. *Developmental Psychology, 19,* 257–268.

O'Mara, A. J., Marsh, H. W., Craven, R. G., & Debus, R. L. (2006). Do self-concept interventions make a difference? A synergistic blend of construct validation and meta-analysis. *Educational Psychologist, 41,* 181–206.

Orth, U., Robins, R. W., & Widaman, K. F. (2012). Life-span development of self-esteem and its effect on important life outcomes. *Journal of Personality and Social Psychology, 102* (6), pp. 1271–1288.

Orth, U., Trzesniewski, K. H., & Robins, R. W. (2010). Self-esteem development from young adulthood to old age: A cohort-sequential longitudinal study. *Journal of Personality and Social Psychology, 98,* 645–658.

Pullmann, H., Allik, J., & Realo, A. (2009). Global self-esteem across the life span: A cross-sectional comparison between representative and self-selected internet samples. *Experimental Aging Research, 35,* 20–44.

Roberts, B. W., & DelVecchio, W. F. (2000). The rank-order consistency of personality traits from childhood to old age: A quantitative review of longitudinal studies. *Psychological Bulletin, 126,* 3–25.

Roberts, B. W., Donnellan, M. B., & Hill, P. L. (in press). Personality trait development in adulthood: Findings and implications. In H. Tennen (Ed.), *Handbook of Psychology. Volume 5: Personality and Social Psychology.* New York: Wiley.

Robins, R. W., & John, O. P. (1997). Effects of visual perspective and narcissism on self-perception: Is seeing believing? *Psychological Science, 8,* 37–42.

Robins, R. W., Trzesniewski, K. H., Tracy, J. L., Gosling, S. D., & Potter, J. (2002). Global self-esteem across the life span. *Psychology and Aging, 17,* 423–434.

Rosenberg, M. (1965). *Society and the adolescent self-image.* Princeton, NJ: Princeton University Press.

Rosenberg, R., Schooler, C., & Schoenbach, C. (1989). Self-esteem and adolescent problems: Modeling reciprocal effects. *American Sociological Review, 54,* 1004–1018.

Saphire-Bernstein, S., Way, B. M., Kim, H. S., Sherman, D. K., & Taylor, S. E. (2011). Oxytocin receptor gene (OXTR) is related to psychological resources. *Proceedings of the National Academy of Sciences, 108*, 15118–15122.

Sarbin, T. R. (1964). Role theoretical interpretation of psychological change. In P. W. D. Byrne (ed.), *Personality change* (pp. 176–219). New York, NY: John Wiley.

Scarr, S., & McCartney, K. (1983). How people make their own environments: A theory of genotype greater than environment effects. *Child Development, 54*, 424–435.

Shaw, B. A., Liang, J., & Krause, N. (2010). Age and race differences in the trajectories of self-esteem. *Psychology and Aging, 25*, 84–94.

Shiner, R. L., & Caspi, A. (2003). Personality differences in childhood and adolescence: measurement, development, and consequences. *Journal of Child Psychology and Psychiatry, 44*, 2–32.

Shrauger, S., & Schoeneman, T. J. (1979). Symbolic interactionist view of self-concept: Through the looking glass darkly. *Psychological Bulletin, 86*, 549–573.

Swann, W. B. (1983). Self-verification: Bringing social reality into harmony with the self. In J. Suls & A. G. Greenwald (eds.), *Social psychological perspectives on the self* (Vol. 2, pp. 33–66). Hillsdale, NJ: Erlbaum.

Swann, W. B., Chang-Scheider, C., & McClarty, K. L. (2007). Do people's self-views matter? Self-concept and self-esteem in everyday life. *American Psychologist, 62*, 84–94.

Tangney, J. P., & Leary, M. R. (2003). *The next generation of self-research*. In M. R. Leary & J. Tangney (eds.), *Handbook of self and identity* (pp. 667–674). New York, NY: Wiley.

Trzesniewski, K. H., & Donnellan, M. B. (2010). Rethinking "Generation Me": A study of cohort effects from 1976–2006. *Perspectives in Psychological Science, 5*, 58–75.

Trzesniewski, K. H., Donnellan, M. B., Moffitt, T. E., Robins, R. W., Poulton, R., & Caspi, A. (2006). Low self-esteem during adolescence predicts poor health, criminal behavior, and limited economic prospects during adulthood. *Developmental Psychology, 42*, 381–390.

Trzesniewski, K. H., Donnellan, M. B., & Robins, R. W. (2003). Stability of self-esteem across the life span. *Journal of Personality and Social Psychology, 84*, 205–220.

Trzesniewski, K. H., Donnellan, M. B., & Robins, R. W. (2008). Is "Generation Me" really more narcissistic than previous generations? *Journal of Personality, 76*, 4, 903–918.

Trzesniewski, K. H., Kinal, P. A., & Donnellan, M. B. (2010). Self-enhancement and self-protection in developmental context. In C. S. M. Alicke (ed.), *The handbook of self-enhancement and self-protection* (pp. 341–357). New York, NY: Guilford Press.

Twenge, J. M., & Campbell, W. K. (2001). Age and birth cohort differences in self-esteem: A cross-temporal meta-analysis. *Personality and Social Psychology Review, 5*, 321–344.

Wade, T. J., Thompson, V. D., Tashakkori, A., & Valente, F. (1989). A longitudinal analysis of sex by race differences in predictors of adolescent self-esteem. *Personality and Individual Differences, 10*, 717–729.

Wigfield, A., Eccles, J. S., Mac Iver, D., Reuman, D. A., & Midgley, C. (1991). Transitions during early adolescence: Changes in children's domain specific self-perceptions and general self-esteem across the transition to junior high school. *Developmental Psychology, 27*, 552–565.

Wortman, J., Lucas, R. E., & Donnellan, M. B. (in press). Stability and change in the Big Five personality domains: Evidence from a longitudinal study of Australians. *Psychology and Aging*.

Zeigler-Hill, V., & Myers, E. M. (2009). Is high self-esteem a path to the White House? The implicit theory of self-esteem and the willingness to vote for presidential candidates. *Personality and Individual Differences, 46*, 14–19.

Zeigler-Hill, V., & Myers, E. M. (2011). An implicit theory of self-esteem: The consequences of perceived self-esteem for romantic desirability. *Evolutionary Psychology, 9*, 147–180.

5   Fragile self-esteem

The perils and pitfalls of (some) high self-esteem

Christian H. Jordan and Virgil Zeigler-Hill

It is easy to understand why modern parents and educators are often uncertain about what constitutes healthy self-esteem. Low self-esteem is not optimal; it has been found to contribute to a number of maladaptive outcomes, including lower life satisfaction, depressive symptoms, and suicidal impulses (Harter, 1993; Myers & Diener, 1995; Orth, Robins, & Roberts, 2008). Yet high self-esteem has also come under increased scrutiny: there has been considerable recent debate about whether high self-esteem causes many of the positive outcomes it was once believed to produce, including academic achievement, occupational success, and popularity (Baumeister, Campbell, Krueger, & Vohs, 2003; Swann, Chang-Schneider, & Larsen McClarty, 2007; Trzesniewski, Donnellan, Moffitt, Robins, Poulton, & Caspi, 2006). Even more troubling for advocates of the virtues of high self-esteem is the fact that positive attitudes about the self have been associated with aggression and violence (Baumeister, Smart, & Boden, 1996), discrimination (Aberson, Healy, & Romero, 2000; Crocker, Thompson, McGraw & Ingerman, 1987), and pervasive self-serving biases (Blaine & Crocker, 1993). In addition, there is recent evidence that the rate of narcissism is on the rise – particularly among young people – and this may contribute to inflated self-views and a troubling sense of entitlement (Twenge, Konrath, Foster, & Campbell, 2008). In light of these considerations, just what is "healthy" self-esteem?

High self-esteem contributes to greater psychological well-being than low self-esteem overall, but the extent of its benefits depends on its psychological character. There is accumulating evidence that the label "high self-esteem" reflects a heterogeneous mix of individuals (Baumeister et al., 2003; Jordan, Logel, Spencer, Zanna, & Whitfield, 2009; Kernis, 2003). An influential distinction is the difference between *secure* and *fragile* high self-esteem (see Kernis, 2003; Kernis & Paradise, 2002). Secure high self-esteem is conceptualized as a well-anchored sense of self-worth that is based on realistic self-views that are not easily challenged. This view of high self-esteem has its roots in humanistic psychology (Rogers, 1959, 1961). Individuals with secure self-esteem recognize their weaknesses and they are disappointed by their failures but they do not view these experiences as impugning their overall sense of self-worth. In contrast, fragile high self-esteem is conceptualized as feelings of self-worth that are unrealistic, vulnerable to threat, and require constant validation. Individuals with fragile high self-esteem are preoccupied with protecting and enhancing their self-esteem, which is often accomplished at the expense of other people.

The conceptual distinction between secure and fragile high self-esteem is compelling but is it possible to distinguish these forms of high self-esteem empirically from each other? Separating those with secure high self-esteem from those with fragile high self-esteem requires going beyond standard measures of self-esteem that directly ask respondents to report their feelings of self-worth. For example, the Rosenberg Self-Esteem Scale (Rosenberg, 1965) is the most widely used measure of self-esteem, and simply asks respondents how much they agree with statements such as "On the whole I am satisfied with myself" and "I am able to do things as well as most other people." Direct measures of self-esteem do a good job of assessing one's overall level of self-esteem (i.e., global self-evaluation) but individuals with both secure and fragile forms of high self-esteem will report feeling good about themselves and they should score equally high on these measures of self-esteem. Consequently, researchers have begun considering factors beyond self-esteem level in order to identify individuals with the fragile form of high self-esteem. The three main approaches have been to consider whether high self-esteem is contingent, unstable, or accompanied by low implicit self-esteem (Kernis, 2003). We begin by reviewing each of these indicators of fragile self-esteem and the evidence that links each indicator to defensiveness and self-enhancement. We then consider how fragile high self-esteem differs from narcissism and how both fragile self-esteem and narcissism relate to psychological well-being and interpersonal functioning.

Indicators of fragile self-esteem

Contingent self-esteem

Contingent self-esteem refers to self-evaluations that depend on meeting standards of performance, approval, or acceptance in order to be maintained. This is a fragile form of high self-esteem because individuals only feel good about themselves when they are able to meet these standards. The idea that contingent self-esteem is fragile has a long pedigree. Carl Rogers (1959, 1961) theorized that basing self-worth on "conditional" criteria can cause self-esteem to become vulnerable. More recently, Deci and Ryan (1995; see also Ryan & Brown, 2003) argued in their self-determination theory that some people regulate their behavior and goals based on *introjected* standards – most typically they internalize significant others' conditional standards of approval – which causes them to develop contingent self-esteem. These individuals become preoccupied with meeting externally derived standards or expectations in order to maintain their feelings of self-worth. As a result, their self-esteem is continually "on the line." If these individuals fail to meet their self-imposed standards, they may experience intense feelings of shame, incompetence, or worthlessness.

Contingent self-esteem has been conceptualized globally such that the self-esteem of some individuals is contingent whereas it is relatively non-contingent for other individuals (Deci & Ryan, 1995; Kernis & Goldman, 2006a). Contingent self-esteem has also been conceptualized as a domain-specific construct such that individuals differ in the area of life that serves as the basis for their self-esteem. According to this view, few people have truly non-contingent self-esteem (Crocker & Wolfe, 2001; Pyszczynski, Greenberg, & Goldenberg, 2003). Rather, people differ with regard to the life domains upon which they stake their feelings of self-worth. Some people report basing their self-esteem on academic competence, whereas others report basing it on physical appearance, competition, God's love, family support, virtue, or others' approval (Crocker, Luhtanen, Cooper, & Bouvrette, 2003; Crocker & Wolfe, 2001). Other researchers have examined the extent to which people base their self-worth on friendships (Cambron, Acitelli, & Steinberg, 2010) or romantic relationships (Knee, Canevello, Bush, & Cook, 2008).

The areas of life that people identify as the basis of their self-worth have been found to predict changes in their state self-esteem and well-being. Students who base their self-worth on academic competence experience boosts to self-esteem when they receive good grades or an acceptance letter from a graduate program as well as significant drops in their self-esteem when they receive poor grades or a rejection letter from a graduate program (Crocker, Karpinski, Quinn & Chase, 2003; Crocker, Sommers, & Luhtanen, 2002). Individuals who base their self-worth on others' approval experience more negative affect and lower self-esteem when someone they interact with dislikes them (Park & Crocker, 2008) and those who base their self-esteem on friendships (Cambron et al., 2010) or romantic relationships (Knee et al., 2008) have self-esteem that is tied more closely to positive and negative events in those relationships. Tellingly, drops in self-esteem that result from failures in contingent domains are often greater in magnitude than boosts that result from successes (Crocker, Karpinski, et al., 2003; Crocker et al., 2002). This asymmetry may contribute to the overall fragility of contingent self-esteem.

As a result of their positive self-views being continuously on the line, individuals with contingent high self-esteem may go to great lengths to guard against threatening information by engaging in practices such as blaming others for their failures, derogating people who criticize them, or distorting or denying information that reflects poorly on them (Deci & Ryan, 1995; Kernis, 2003). Indeed, some evidence links contingent self-esteem to defensiveness. In one study, individuals with low self-esteem who based their self-worth on academic performance experienced significant drops in state self-esteem after performing poorly on a test of academic ability. In contrast, individuals with high self-esteem who based their self-worth on academic performance did not; if anything, they experienced somewhat higher self-esteem after a failure (Park, Crocker, & Kiefer, 2007). They also appeared to be more determined to demonstrate their competence to others. These results might indicate that individuals with contingent high self-esteem are actually relatively secure in their positive self-views.

However, they might indicate that their self-esteem was buffered by defensive reactions that they had to the threat prior to the state self-esteem measure. In Park and colleagues' terms, the results might suggest that individuals with contingent high self-esteem mobilize "their efforts to refute the negative feedback and affirm themselves" (Park et al., 2007, p. 1514) following failure experiences. We believe this latter interpretation is likely in light of additional evidence that contingent high self-esteem is related to defensiveness.

A defensive response to poor performance, for example, may help to explain why individuals with high self-esteem who base their feelings of self-worth on academic competence are viewed by interaction partners as more preoccupied, less supportive, and less likable following failure (Park & Crocker, 2005). In a similar vein, Kernis and Paradise (2003, reported in Kernis, 2003) found that individuals with globally contingent self-esteem became especially angry and hostile after an insulting evaluation, relative to individuals with non-contingent self-esteem or those evaluated positively. Anger and hostility often suggest defensiveness and attempts to restore threatened feelings of self-worth (Kernis, 2003). When their self-esteem is threatened, individuals with contingent high self-esteem may become preoccupied with defending their self-worth, which may make them insensitive and hostile toward others. However, these reactions may depend on the domains of contingency that are threatened, because other evidence suggests that some individuals with contingent self-esteem become more affiliative when their self-esteem is threatened (Park & Crocker, 2008; Park & Maner, 2011). This is a point that we will return to later in the chapter.

More direct evidence that contingent high self-esteem is related to defensiveness comes from an ambitious study of verbal defensiveness (Kernis, Lakey, & Heppner, 2008). One way that people defend against threatening information is by changing the way it is represented in their consciousness by limiting awareness of it or distorting its meaning (Feldman Barrett, Cleveland, Conner, & Williams, 2002). Kernis and colleagues (2008) used a structured interview technique (Feldman Barrett et al., 2002) to assess verbal defensiveness. Participants responded to stressful questions (e.g., "Tell me about a time when you felt your parents were really disappointed in you," "Tell me about a time when you have felt less sexually desirable than a friend") and their responses were coded for defensiveness. More defensive responses expressed less negative emotion, more positive emotion, rationalized negative behaviors, assigned fault to external sources or social norms, and distanced respondents from the threatening events. Individuals with contingent high self-esteem (assessed globally) expressed significantly more verbal defensiveness than individuals with non-contingent high self-esteem. Taken together, this evidence suggests that contingent high self-esteem is fragile and related to defensiveness.

Unstable self-esteem

Another indicator of fragile self-esteem is self-esteem instability (Kernis & Waschull, 1995). Although one's level of self-esteem is reasonably consistent over time (Rosenberg, 1965; Trzesniewski, Donnellan, & Robins, 2003), more imme-diate, context-specific feelings of self-worth fluctuate considerably. However, the state self-esteem of some individuals fluctuates more than it does for other individuals. Self-esteem stability is conceptualized as a dispositional tendency to experience variability in context-specific feelings of self-worth (Kernis, 2005; Kernis, Grannemann, & Barclay, 1989). Whereas self-esteem level is measured by asking respondents, on a single occasion, how much they value themselves "in general," self-esteem instability is measured by administering measures on multiple occasions (e.g., twice a day for five days). Respondents report how they feel about themselves "right now" or "at this moment." Self-esteem instability is captured by the within-person variability in state self-esteem over time as reflected by the standard deviation of each individual's momentary self-esteem scores. Larger standard deviations (i.e., more variability) reflect greater self-esteem instability. Unstable high self-esteem is considered to be a form of fragile high self-esteem because these fluctuations in feelings of self-worth suggest that the positive attitudes these individuals hold about themselves are vulnerable to challenges or threats.

Contingent self-esteem can contribute to self-esteem instability. As described earlier, performances in contingent domains are related to increases and decreases in state self-esteem (e.g., Crocker, Karpinski, et al., 2003; Crocker et al., 2002). More generally, individuals who demonstrate unstable self-esteem tend to report having contingent self-esteem (Gunn & Jordan, 2008; Kernis et al., 2008). Correlations between the two, however, are not so high that they are redundant (*r*s range from .29 to .44 for globally contingent self-esteem). Some self-esteem contingencies are more likely to induce self-esteem instability than others. For example, those contingencies of self-worth that have been identified by Crocker and her colleagues (e.g., Crocker, Luhtanen, et al., 2003) as *external* (e.g., academic competence, competition) appear to be more closely associated with self-esteem instability than those contingencies that are *internal* (e.g., virtue, family support). In addition, self-esteem instability is related to factors other than self-esteem contingency such as neuroticism and low self-concept clarity (Kernis, Cornell, Sun, Berry & Harlow, 1993; Kernis, Paradise, Whitaker, Wheatman, & Goldman, 2000; Roberts, Kassel, & Gotlib, 1995). Nevertheless, the overlap between contingent and unstable self-esteem suggests that they both reflect fragile self-esteem.

Unstable high self-esteem has been found to predict defensiveness and self-enhancement. As with contingent self-esteem, self-esteem instability is related to anger and hostility (Kernis et al., 1989). Considering both level and stability of self-esteem, individuals with unstable high self-esteem scored highest on a number of well-validated anger and hostility inventories. In contrast, individuals with stable high self-esteem scored the lowest. In addition, individuals with unstable high self-esteem are more self-aggrandizing and indicate they are more likely to boast to their friends about their successes than individuals with stable high self-esteem (Kernis, Greenier, Herlocker, Whisenhunt, & Abend, 1997). When they actually do perform well (e.g., on an exam), individuals with unstable high self-esteem are more likely to claim that they did so in spite of performance-inhibiting factors (e.g., a personal crisis or sleepless night), which makes their performance seem even more remarkable (Kernis, Grannemann, & Barclay, 1992). In the study of verbal defensiveness described earlier (Kernis et al., 2008), individuals with unstable high self-esteem also exhibited higher levels of verbal defensiveness than individuals with stable high self-esteem.

Low implicit self-esteem

The final major indicator of fragile self-esteem is high self-esteem that is accompanied by low levels of implicit self-esteem (Epstein & Morling, 1995; Kernis, 2003). A number of longstanding theories suggest that some individuals with high self-esteem are defensive, aggressive, and boastful because they harbor negative self-feelings at less conscious levels (Coopersmith, 1959; Harder, 1984; Horney, 1937). This possibility, however, remained largely untested until the advent of measures of implicit self-esteem. Implicit self-esteem is generally defined as efficient self-evaluations that exist largely outside of conscious awareness (e.g., Epstein & Morling, 1995; Farnham, Greenwald, & Banaji, 1999; Greenwald & Banaji, 1995; Koole & Pelham, 2003). The extent to which implicit self-esteem is nonconscious, however, is debatable (e.g., Bosson, 2006; Jordan, Logel, Spencer, & Zanna, 2006; Olson, Fazio, & Hermann, 2007), with some evidence indicating that people are aware of their implicit self-esteem but experience it as gut feelings or intuitive self-evaluations (Jordan, Whitfield, & Zeigler-Hill, 2007; cf. Olson et al., 2007). An alternative conceptualization of implicit self-esteem is to view it as the degree of cognitive association between one's self-concept and positive or negative affect (see Zeigler-Hill & Jordan, 2010; cf. Gawronski & Bodenhausen, 2006). Whereas implicit self-esteem is associative in this view, traditional or *explicit* self-esteem is propositional in nature and reflects deliberative evaluative judgments of the self.

Consistent with this distinction, explicit self-esteem is typically measured by self-report instruments that directly ask people how they feel about themselves, allowing them to deliberate and reflect on their self-evaluations. The Rosenberg Self-Esteem Scale (described earlier) is an example of an instrument that captures explicit self-esteem. Implicit self-esteem, in contrast, is measured with nonreactive measures that do not obviously assess self-esteem, with the most common of these instruments being the self-esteem version of the Implicit Association Test (IAT; see Greenwald & Farnham, 2000; Greenwald, McGhee, & Schwarz, 1998) and the Name-Letter Task (Nuttin, 1985, 1987). Despite the potential utility of implicit self-esteem, it is important to note that there are a number of psychometric problems with nonreactive measures of self-esteem (Bosson, Swann, & Pennebaker, 2000; Buhrmester, Blanton, & Swann, 2011) and some of these measures – such as the IAT – assess the underlying associative basis of implicit self-esteem better than others (Karpinski & Steinberg, 2006). Nevertheless, these nonreactive measures have been useful for studying defensiveness and fragile self-esteem. Notably, measures of implicit and explicit self-esteem typically do not correlate with each other (Bosson et al., 2000; Farnham et al., 1999). Thus, knowing a person's level of explicit self-esteem reveals virtually nothing about his or her level of implicit self-esteem, which could be either high or low. Individuals with high explicit self-esteem but low implicit self-esteem may have fragile self-esteem (Epstein & Morling, 1995; Jordan, Spencer, & Zanna, 2003; Kernis, 2003). This combination has also been referred to as *discrepant* high self-esteem (Zeigler-Hill & Jordan, 2010).

Supporting the view that discrepant high self-esteem is a form of fragile self-esteem, implicit self-esteem is associated with contingent and unstable self-esteem. Individuals with low implicit self-esteem (as measured by the IAT) report basing their self-worth on external contingencies, such as academic performance, appearance, others' approval, and competition (Jordan, Spencer, & Zanna, 2003). Consistent with this finding, those with discrepant high self-esteem also demonstrated greater drops in state self-esteem after receiving negative feedback on an apparent intelligence test. Other research demonstrates that individuals with low implicit self-esteem have more unstable self-esteem (Zeigler-Hill, 2006a). Two recent studies that included all three indicators of fragility found that low implicit self-esteem is related to unstable and contingent self-esteem, measured globally (Kernis et al., 2008) or in specific domains (Gunn & Jordan, 2008). In the latter case, low implicit self-esteem was again related more strongly to external contingencies.

Discrepant high self-esteem is also associated with defensiveness and self-enhancement. Among individuals with high explicit self-esteem, those with low implicit self-esteem show more unrealistic optimism, report that their actual selves more closely approximate their ideal selves, and endorse a highly flattering personality profile as more self-descriptive (Bosson, Brown, Zeigler-Hill, & Swann, 2003). They also engage in more rationalization of decisions (Jordan, Spencer, Zanna, Hoshino-Brown, & Correll, 2003, Study 3) and use discrimination as a means to protect and enhance their self-esteem by showing more ingroup bias in the minimal group paradigm (Jordan, Spencer, Zanna et al., 2003, Study 2) and more ethnic discrimination when their positive self-views are threatened (Jordan, Spencer & Zanna, 2005). Children with discrepant high self-esteem are described by teachers as more aggressive (Sandstrom & Jordan, 2008). Following self-threat, individuals with discrepant high self-esteem become more convinced of their opinions and perceive greater social support for them (McGregor & Marigold, 2003; McGregor, Nail, Marigold, & Kang, 2005). Lastly, in the study of verbal defensiveness described earlier, high self-esteem individuals with low implicit self-esteem were more defensive than those with high implicit self-esteem (Kernis et al., 2008).

Is narcissism a form of fragile self-esteem?

Self-esteem that is contingent, unstable, or accompanied by low implicit self-esteem reflects fragile self-esteem. Narcissism shares many conceptual similarities with fragile self-esteem. Narcissists have unrealistic and inflated positive self-views and frequently strive to validate and enhance their self-esteem (e.g., Campbell & Foster, 2007; Morf, Torchetti, & Schürch, 2011). They are egoistic, aggressive, and self-serving. A number of theoretical models of narcissism, moreover, posit that the grandiosity of narcissists conceals a more fragile underlying sense of self (Akhtar & Thomson, 1982; Kernberg, 1966, 1975; Kohut & Wolf, 1986; Morf & Rhodewalt, 2001; Morf et al., 2011; see Bosson et al., 2008, or Zeigler-Hill & Jordan, 2011, for reviews). Nevertheless, narcissism is considered to be a distinct syndrome from fragile self-esteem (Kernis, 2003; Kernis et al., 2008). Throughout the rest of this chapter, we explore similarities and differences between narcissism and fragile self-esteem. We focus on narcissism as a "normal" personality variable – that is most often measured by the Narcissistic Personality Inventory (NPI; see Raskin & Hall, 1979) – rather than narcissistic personality disorder or more pathological forms of narcissism (Pincus & Lukowitsky, 2010; Rhodewalt & Peterson, 2009).

Despite shared concerns with protecting and enhancing self-esteem, empirical relations between narcissism and fragile self-esteem are weak and inconsistent. Some studies have observed relations between narcissism and indicators of fragile self-esteem, including unstable self-esteem (Rhodewalt, Madrian, & Cheney, 1998) and low implicit self-esteem (Gregg & Sedikides, 2010; Jordan, Spencer, Zanna, et al., 2003; Zeigler-Hill, 2006a; see Bosson et al., 2008 for a review). Two studies found that amongst individuals with high self-esteem, those with low implicit self-esteem were most narcissistic (Jordan, Spencer, Zanna, et al., 2003; Zeigler-Hill, 2006a). Other studies, however, have failed to replicate this pattern consistently. A recent series of meta-analyses failed to find any consistent associations between narcissism and unstable self-esteem, global contingent self-esteem, or low implicit self-esteem (Bosson et al., 2008). The lack of overall convergence between narcissism and fragile self-esteem may reflect the fact that narcissists stake their self-worth in only certain domains. Narcissists tend to be concerned with enhancing and maintaining *agentic* self-views (in terms of surgency, extraversion, action, competence, and skill) but not *communal* self-views (in terms of agreeableness, warmth, nurturance, kindness, and affection; see Campbell & Foster, 2007; Campbell, Rudich, & Sedikides, 2002). Consistent with this idea, narcissism is positively related to self-esteem contingencies based on competition but negatively associated with contingencies based on affiliation (Crocker, Luhtanen, et al., 2003; Zeigler-Hill, Clark, & Pickard, 2008). Narcissists' self-esteem also appears to be affected by mundane achievement-related events but more so by failures (e.g., falling behind on tasks) than successes (e.g., getting ahead on tasks; Zeigler-Hill, Myers, & Clark, 2010; see also, Rhodewalt & Morf, 1998). To the extent that narcissists have fragile self-esteem, it may thus be limited to agentic rather than communal domains, at least with respect to unstable and contingent self-esteem. With respect to implicit self-esteem, narcissists actually demonstrate relatively high levels of implicit self-esteem on agentic traits, which suggests that any feelings of low implicit self-esteem for narcissistic individuals may only emerge for communal traits (Campbell, Bosson, Goheen, Lakey, & Kernis, 2007).

Is fragile self-esteem or narcissism beneficial?

Psychological well-being

There is ongoing debate in social psychology over whether unrealistically posi-tive self-views are detrimental or beneficial to psychological well-being (e.g., Taylor & Brown, 1988; Colvin, Block, & Funder, 1995). Consistent with the possibility that it promotes well-being, narcissism is negatively related to depres-sion, loneliness, and daily sadness, as well as being positively related to daily happiness, subjective well-being, and life satisfaction (e.g., Hill & Roberts, in press; Sedikides, Rudich, Gregg, Kumashiro, & Rusbult, 2004). There are limits to these associations, however (Campbell & Campbell, 2009). More extreme levels of narcissism are linked to depression (Miller, Campbell, & Pilkonis, 2007) and only younger respondents show a link between narcissism and life satisfaction (Hill & Roberts, in press). To the extent that narcissism is associated at all with greater psychological well-being, however, this is another way that narcissism diverges from fragile self-esteem.

Contingent self-esteem has been linked to a variety of negative mental health outcomes. Adolescent females who base their self-esteem on appearance tend to be preoccupied with their appearance, have lower levels of self-esteem, and report more depressive symptoms (Harter, 1997; Harter, Stocker, & Robinson, 1996; see also Crocker, 2002). Contingent self-esteem is also related to problem drinking (Neighbors, Larimer, Geisner, & Knee, 2004). People with unstable self-esteem experience more depression in response to daily hassles (Greenier et al., 1999; Kernis et al., 1998; Roberts & Monroe, 1992). They tend to see broad implications for their self-worth in circumscribed failures (Kernis et al., 1998) and focus more on the threatening and aversive aspects of interpersonal events (Waschull & Kernis, 1996). Compared to individuals with stable high self-esteem, those with unstable high self-esteem demonstrate lower levels of auton-omy, environmental mastery, sense of purpose in life, self-acceptance, and positive relations with others (Kernis, 2003). Discrepancies between implicit and explicit self-esteem are also related to negative outcomes, such as anger suppres-sion, nervousness, and poorer physical health (Schröder-Abé, Rudolph, & Schütz, 2007).

The defensive tendencies of individuals with fragile self-esteem do not appear to be very effective at enhancing their well-being because each indicator of fragile self-esteem has been linked to maladaptive outcomes. In contrast, overall narcissism scores have been found to be related to greater psychological well-being. This divergence between narcissism and fragile self-esteem may be more apparent than real, however. The psychological benefits of narcissism are attributable entirely to high self-esteem (Sedikides et al., 2004). This suggests that narcissists may only demonstrate enhanced well-being in comparison to individuals with low self-esteem. It is not clear that narcissists have greater well-being than non-narcissists who have high self-esteem. In fact, narcissists may demonstrate lower levels of well-being than these individuals in the same way that individuals with fragile high self-esteem demonstrate lower levels of well-being than those with secure high self-esteem (Kernis, 2003; Schröder-Abé et al., 2007). This is a possibility that is worth exploring in future research.

Interpersonal relationships

In contrast to intrapersonal well-being, narcissism is more clearly related to negative interpersonal outcomes. Narcissists tend to value other people only to the extent that they enhance their status or validate their positive self-views (Campbell & Foster, 2007; Campbell & Campbell, 2009). Although narcissists are often well liked initially in group settings, they are among the least well liked over the longer term (Paulhus, 1998). Although narcissists report greater relationship satisfaction than non-narcissists (Sedikides et al., 2004), narcissism is associated with a host of relationship problems (see Campbell & Campbell, 2009, for a review) including a lack of emotional closeness (Foster, Shrira, & Campbell, 2006) and an increased likelihood of infidelity (Buss & Shackelford, 1997). Narcissists, moreover, react with aggression toward those who criticize them (Bushman & Baumeister, 1998). As we have seen, narcissists do not typically value communal traits such as warmth, kindness, or affection. They value traits that distinguish them from other people (Campbell & Foster, 2007; Campbell et al., 2002).

Fragile high self-esteem similarly predicts negative interpersonal outcomes. Individuals with fragile self-esteem are frequently angry, hostile, and aggressive, especially when their positive self-views have been challenged. As we have seen, this is specifically true of individuals with contingent self-esteem (Kernis & Paradise, 2002; Park & Crocker, 2005), unstable self-esteem (Kernis et al., 1989) and low implicit self-esteem (Melwani & Barsade, 2011; Sandstrom & Jordan, 2008). Similarly, individuals with high explicit but low implicit self-esteem are less forgiving and report greater intentions to retaliate against a transgressor especially when the transgressor apologizes, because they view the apology as an admission of guilt (Eaton, Struthers, Shomrony, & Santelli, 2007). Men with fragile high self-esteem, moreover, demonstrate interpersonal styles that are more hostile (less communal) than those with secure high self-esteem across all three indicators of fragility (Zeigler-Hill, Clark, & Beckman, 2011).

Yet, in contrast to narcissism, fragile self-esteem is sometimes associated with more affiliative and warmer interpersonal behaviors. Women with fragile high self-esteem demonstrate interpersonal styles that are just as communal as those with secure high self-esteem (Zeigler-Hill, Clark, & Beckman, 2011). High self-esteem individuals who base their self-worth on others' approval become more motivated to appear warm, caring, and kind after receiving negative social feedback (Park & Crocker, 2008). High self-esteem individuals who base their self-esteem on physical appearance respond to appearance-related threats with greater motivation to affiliate with close others (e.g., friends and family; see Park & Maner, 2011). Men with unstable high self-esteem, despite their generally more hostile interpersonal styles, view their close relationships more positively in terms of closeness, satisfaction, and commitment than men with stable high self-esteem (Zeigler-Hill, Fulton, & McLemore, 2011).

Whether fragile self-esteem is associated with more positive or negative interpersonal outcomes may depend, in part, on one's domains of self-esteem contingency. Basing self-worth on others' approval (Park & Crocker, 2008) or attractiveness (Park & Maner, 2011) is related to more affiliative responses to threat than basing self-worth on academic competence. Recall that individuals with academic contingencies were rated as more preoccupied, less supportive, and less likable following an academic threat (Park & Crocker, 2005). Individuals who base their feelings of self-worth on God's love or family support demonstrate more communal interpersonal styles, whereas those who base their self-worth on competition demonstrate more hostile interpersonal styles (Zeigler-Hill, 2006b). Considering the fact that narcissism predicts predominantly negative interpersonal outcomes, this latter finding is consistent with the fact that narcissists base self-worth on competition and not domains that require others' validation (Crocker, Luhtanen, et al., 2003; Zeigler-Hill et al., 2008). Thus, some contingencies of self-worth may promote affiliation more than others.

Nevertheless, even the more positive interpersonal motives associated with fragile self-esteem are likely to reflect concerns with protecting and enhancing self-worth (Park & Crocker, 2008; Zeigler-Hill, Clark, & Beckman, 2011). Individuals with fragile high self-esteem, especially those with contingencies that require others' validation, may pursue positive relationships primarily because they want others to support and affirm their positive self-views. They may thus pursue relationships primarily as a means of self-image maintenance rather than an expression of support or caring for others. Longitudinal studies demonstrate that having predominant self-image goals in relationships predicts decreased well-being for oneself and one's relationships, particularly compared to having compassionate goals (Crocker & Canevello, 2008; Crocker, Canevello, Breines, & Flynn, 2010). Thus, even the more prosocial responses of fragile self-esteem individuals may be relatively detrimental over time.

Conclusions

We can now offer a provisional answer to the question of what constitutes "healthy" self-esteem: it is high self-esteem that is relatively non-contingent, stable, and accompanied by high implicit self-esteem. Although narcissism is distinct from fragile self-esteem and may be positively related to intrapersonal well-being overall, we suggest that healthy self-esteem is also non-narcissistic. The common thread connecting fragile self-esteem and narcissism appears to be a preoccupation with self-image. Narcissists and individuals with fragile high self-esteem focus a great deal of energy on avoiding losses to self-esteem or feelings of shame at the same time that they try to bolster their self-esteem and feelings of pride (Baumeister & Vohs, 2001; Park & Crocker, 2008; Tracy, Cheng, Robins, & Trzesniewski, 2009). They may pursue their self-esteem goals to the detriment of basic psychological needs such as those concerning competence, relatedness, and autonomy (Park & Crocker, 2005; Deci & Ryan, 1995; Ryan & Brown, 2003). It may indeed be the case that "when self-esteeming processes are salient there is something awry with self-regulation, and with well-being" (Ryan & Brown, 2003, p. 71).

The key to healthy self-esteem may thus be to take one's focus away from self-esteem. Self-determination theory posits that secure (or "true") high self-esteem arises from acting in accordance with one's authentic values and interests rather than regulating behavior around self-esteem concerns (Deci & Ryan, 1995; see also, Kernis & Goldman, 2006b; Rogers, 1961). Indeed, behaving more authentically is associated with greater self-esteem stability, satisfaction of psychological needs, and less defensiveness (Heppner, Kernia, Nezlek, Foster, Lakey, & Goldman, 2008; Lakey, Kernis, Heppner, & Lance, 2008). Other recent perspectives also emphasize a more "self-less" orientation as a route to healthy self-esteem and well-being through strategies such as mindful attention to present experiences or a greater focus on other people and one's shared humanity (Ryan and Brown, 2003; Park & Crocker, 2005; Fredrickson, Cohen, Coffey, Pek, & Finkel, 2008; Leary & Guadagno, 2011; Neff, 2003). Somewhat ironically, the most effective way to cultivate healthy self-esteem may be to worry less about having high self-esteem.

References

Aberson, C. L., Healy, M., & Romero, V. (2000). Ingroup bias and self-esteem: A meta-analysis. *Personality and Social Psychology Review, 4,* 157–173.

Akhtar, S., & Thomson, J. A. (1982). Overview: Narcissistic personality disorder. *American Journal of Psychiatry, 139,* 12–20.

Baumeister, R. F., Campbell, J. D., Krueger, J. I., & Vohs, K. D. (2003). Does high self-esteem cause better performance, interpersonal success, happiness, or healthier lifestyles? *Psychological Science in the Public Interest, 4,* 1–44.

Baumeister, R. F., Smart, L., & Boden, J. M. (1996). Relation of threatened egotism to violence and aggression: The dark side of high self-esteem. *Psychological Review, 103,* 5–33.

Baumeister, R. F., & Vohs, K. D. (2001). Narcissism as addiction to esteem. *Psychological Inquiry, 12,* 206–210.

Blaine, B., & Crocker, J. (1993). Self-esteem and self-serving biases in reactions to positive and negative events: An integrative review. In R. F. Baumeister (ed.), *Self-esteem: The puzzle of low self-regard* (pp. 55–85). Hillsdale, NJ: Erlbaum.

Bosson, J. K. (2006). Assessing self-esteem via self-reports and nonreactive instruments: Issues and recommendations. In M. Kernis (ed.), *Self-esteem issues and answers: A sourcebook of current perspectives* (pp. 88–95). New York, NY: Psychology Press.

Bosson, J. K., Brown, R. P., Zeigler-Hill, V., & Swann, W. B. (2003). Self-enhancement tendencies among people with high explicit self-esteem: The moderating role of implicit self-esteem. *Self and Identity, 2,* 169–187.

Bosson, J. K., Lakey, C. E., Campbell, W. K., Zeigler-Hill, V., Jordan, C. H., & Kernis, M. H. (2008). Untangling the links between narcissism and self-esteem: A theoretical and empirical review. *Social and Personality Psychology Compass, 2,* 1415–1439.

Bosson, J. K., Swann, W. B., & Pennebaker, J. W. (2000). Stalking the perfect measure of implicit self-esteem: The blind men and the elephant revisited? *Journal of Personality and Social Psychology, 79*, 631–643.

Bushman, B. J., & Baumeister, R. (1998). Threatened egotism, narcissism, self-esteem, and direct and displaced aggression: Does self-love or self-hate lead to violence? *Journal of Personality and Social Psychology, 75*, 219–229.

Buss, D. M., & Shackelford, T. K. (1997). Susceptibility to infidelity in the first year of marriage. *Journal of Research in Personality, 31*, 193–221.

Cambron, M. J., Acitelli, L. K., & Steinberg, L. (2010). When friends make you blue: The role of friendship contingent self-esteem in predicting self-esteem and depressive symptoms. *Personality and Social Psychology Bulletin, 36*, 384–397.

Campbell, W. K., & Campbell, S. (2009). On the self-regulatory dynamics created by the peculiar benefits and costs of narcissism: A contextual reinforcement model and examination of leadership. *Self and Identity, 8*, 214–232.

Campbell, W. K., & Foster, J. D. (2007). The narcissistic self: Background, an extended agency model, and ongoing controversies. In C. Sedikides, & S. J. Spencer (eds.), *The self* (pp. 115–138). New York, NY: Psychology Press.

Campbell, W. K., Rudich, E., & Sedikides, C. (2002). Narcissism, self-esteem, and the positivity of self-views: Two portraits of self-love. *Personality and Social Psychology Bulletin, 28*, 358–368.

Campbell, W. K., Bosson, J. K., Goheen, T. W., Lakey, C. E., & Kernis, M. H. (2007). Do narcissists like themselves "deep down inside"? *Psychological Science, 18*, 227–229.

Colvin, C. R., Block, J., & Funder, D. C. (1995). Overly positive self-evaluations and personality: Negative implications for mental health. *Journal of Personality and Social Psychology, 68*, 1152–1162.

Coopersmith, S. (1959). A method for determining types of self-esteem. *Journal of Abnormal and Social Psychology, 59*, 87–94.

Crocker, J. (2002). Contingencies of self-worth: Implications for self-regulation and psychological vulnerability. *Self and Identity, 1*, 143–150.

Crocker, J. (2008). From egosystem to ecosystem: Implications for relationships, learning and well-being. In H. A. Wayment & J. Bauer (eds.), *Transcending self-interest: Psychological explorations of the quiet ego* (pp. 63–72). Washington, DC: American Psychological Association.

Crocker, J., & Canevello, A. (2008). Creating and undermining social support in communal relationships: The role of compassionate and self-image goals. *Journal of Personality and Social Psychology, 95*, 555–575.

Crocker, J., & Park, L. E. (2004). The costly pursuit of self-esteem. *Psychological Bulletin, 130*, 392–414.

Crocker, J., & Wolfe, C. T. (2001). Contingencies of self-worth. *Psychological Review, 108*, 593–623.

Crocker, J., Canevello, A., Breines, J. G., & Flynn, H. (2010). Interpersonal goals and change in anxiety and dysphoria in first-semester college students. *Journal of Personality and Social Psychology, 98*, 1009–1024.

Crocker, J., Karpinski, A., Quinn, D. M., & Chase, S. (2003). When grades determine self-worth: Consequences of contingent self-worth for male and female engineering and psychology majors. *Journal of Personality and Social Psychology, 85*, 507–516.

Crocker, J., Luhtanen, R. K., Cooper, M. L., & Bouvrette, A. (2003). Contingencies of self-worth in college students: Theory and measurement. *Journal of Personality and Social Psychology, 85*, 894–908.

Crocker, J., Sommers, S. R., & Luhtanen, R. K. (2002). Hopes dashed and dreams fulfilled: Contingencies of self-worth and admissions to graduate school. *Personality and Social Psychology Bulletin, 28*, 1275–1286.

Crocker, J., Thompson, L., McGraw, K., & Ingerman, C. (1987). Downward comparison, prejudice, and evaluations of others: Effects of self-esteem and threat. *Journal of Personality and Social Psychology*, *52*, 907–916.

Deci, E. L., & Ryan, R. M. (1995). Human autonomy: The basis for true self-esteem. In M. H. Kernis (ed.), *Efficacy, agency, and self-esteem* (pp. 31–49). New York, NY: Plenum Press.

Eaton, J., Struters, C. W., Shomrony, A., & Santinelli, A. G. (2007). When apologies fail: The moderating effects of explicity and implicity self-esteem on apology and forgiveness. *Self and Identity, 6*, 209–222.

Emler, N. (2001). *Self-esteem: The costs and causes of low self-worth*. York: York Publishing Services for the Joseph Rowntree Foundation.

Epstein, S., & Morling, B. (1995). Is the self motivated to do more than enhance and/or verify itself? In M. H. Kernis (ed.), *Efficacy, agency, and self-esteem* (pp. 9–29). New York, NY: Plenum.

Farnham, S. D., Greenwald, A. G., & Banaji, M. R. (1999). Implicit self-esteem. In D. Abrams & M. A. Hogg (eds.), *Social identity and social cognition* (pp. 230–248). Oxford: Blackwell.

Feldman Barrett, L., Cleveland, J., Conner, T., & Williams, N. L. (2002). Defensive verbal behavior assessment. *Personality and Social Psychology Bulletin, 28*, 776–788.

Foster, J. D., Shrira, I., & Campbell, W. K. (2006). Theoretical models of narcissism, sexuality, and relationship commitment. *Journal of Social and Personal Relationships, 23*, 367–386.

Fredrickson, B. L., Cohen, M. A., Coffey, K. A., Pek, J., & Finkel, S. M. (2008). Open hearts build lives: Positive emotions, induced through loving-kindness meditation, build consequential personal resources. *Journal of Personality and Social Psychology, 95*, 1045–1062.

Gawronski, B., & Bodenhausen, G. V. (2006). Associative and propositional processes in evaluation: An integrative review of implicit and explicit attitude change. *Psychological Bulletin, 132*, 692–731.

Greenier, K. G., Kernis, M. H., Whisenhunt, C. R., Waschull, S. B., Berry, A. J., Herlocker, C. E., & Abend, T. (1999). Individual differences in reactivity to daily events: Examining the roles of stability and level of self-esteem. *Journal of Personality, 67*, 185–208.

Greenwald, A. G., & Banaji, M. R. (1995). Implicit social cognition: Attitudes, self-esteem, and stereotypes. *Psychological Review, 102*, 4–27.

Greenwald, A. G., & Farnham, S. D. (2000). Using the implicit association test to measure self-esteem and self-concept. *Journal of Personality and Social Psychology, 79*, 1022–1038.

Greenwald, A. G., McGhee, D. E., & Schwartz, J. L. K. (1998). Measuring individual differences in implicit cognition: The Implicit Association Test. *Journal of Personality and Social Psychology, 74*, 1464–1480.

Gregg, A. P., & Sedikides, C. (2010). Implicit self-esteem and narcissism: Rethinking the link. *Self and Identity, 9*, 142–161.

Gunn, G. R., & Jordan, C. H. (2008). Convergence between implicit, unstable, and contingent self-esteem. Unpublished data, Wilfrid Laurier University.

Harder, D. W. (1984). Character style of the defensively high self-esteem man. *Journal of Clinical Psychology, 40*, 26–35.

Harter, S. (1993). Causes and consequences of low self-esteem in children and adolescents. In R. F. Baumeister (ed.), *Self-esteem: The puzzle of low self-regard* (pp. 87–116). New York, NY: Plenum.

Harter, S. (1997). The personal self in social context: Barriers to authenticity. In R. D. Ashmore & L. Jussim (eds.), *Self and identity* (Vol. 1, pp. 81–105). Oxford: Oxford University Press.

Harter, S., Stocker, C., & Robinson, N. S. (1996). The perceived directionality of the link between approval and self-worth: The liabilities of a looking glass self-orientation among young adolescents. *Journal of Research on Adolescence, 6*, 285–308.

Heppner, W., L., Kernia, M. H., Nezlek, J. B., Foster, J., Lakey, C. E., & Goldman, B. M. (2008). Within-person relationships among daily self-esteem, need satisfaction, and authenticity. *Psychological Science, 19*, 1140–1145.

Hill, P. L., & Roberts, B. W. (in press). Narcissism, well-being, and observer-rated personality across the lifespan. *Social Psychological and Personality Science*.

Horney, K. (1937). *The neurotic personality of our time*. New York, NY: Norton.

Jordan, C. H., Logel, C., Spencer, S. J., & Zanna, M. P. (2006). Nonconscious self-esteem: Is there something you're not telling yourself? In M. Kernis (ed.), *Self-esteem issues and answers: A sourcebook of current perspectives* (pp. 60–68). New York, NY: Psychology Press.

Jordan, C. H., Logel, C., Spencer, S. J., Zanna, M. P., & Whitfield, M. L. (2009). The heterogeneity of self-esteem: Exploring the interplay between implicit and explicit self-esteem (pp. 251–284). In R. E. Petty, R. H. Fazio, & P. Brinol (eds.), *Attitudes: Insights from the new implicit measures*. New York, NY: Psychology Press.

Jordan, C. H., Spencer, S. J., & Zanna, M. P. (2003). "I love me … I love me not": Implicit self-esteem, explicit self-esteem, and defensiveness. In S. J. Spencer, S. Fein, M. P. Zanna, & J. M. Olson (eds.), *Motivated social cognition: The Ontario symposium* (Vol. 9, pp. 117–145). Mahwah, NJ: Erlbaum.

Jordan, C. H., Spencer, S. J., & Zanna, M. P. (2005). Types of high self-esteem and prejudice: How implicit self-esteem relates to ethnic discrimination among high explicit self-esteem individuals. *Personality and Social Psychology Bulletin, 31*, 693–702.

Jordan, C. H., Spencer, S. J., Zanna, M. P., Hoshino-Browne, E., & Correll, J. (2003). Secure and defensive high self-esteem. *Journal of Personality and Social Psychology, 85*, 969–978.

Jordan, C. H., Whitfield, M., & Zeigler-Hill, V. (2007). Intuition and the correspondence between implicit and explicit self-esteem. *Journal of Personality and Social Psychology, 93*, 1067–1079.

Karpinski, A., & Steinberg, J. A. (2006). Implicit and explitic self-esteem: Theoretical and methodological refinements. In M. H. Kernis (ed.), *Self-esteem issues and answers: A source book of current perspectives* (pp. 102–109). New York, NY: Psychological Press.

Kernberg, O. F. (1966). Structural derivatives of object relationships. *International Journal of Psychoanalysis, 47*, 236–252.

Kernberg, O. F. (1975). *Borderline conditions and pathological narcissism*. New York, NY: Jason Aronson.

Kernis, M. H. (2003). Toward a conceptualization of optimal self-esteem. *Psychological Inquiry, 14*, 1–26.

Kernis, M. H. (2005). Measuring self-esteem in context: The importance of stability of self-esteem in psychological functioning. *Journal of Personality, 73*, 1569–1605.

Kernis, M. H., Cornell, D. P., Sun, C. R., Berry, A., & Harlow, T. (1993). There's more to self-esteem than whether it is high or low: The importance of stability of self-esteem. *Journal of Personality, 65* (6): 1190–1204.

Kernis, M. H., & Goldman, B. M. (2006a). Assessing stability of self-esteem and contingent self-esteem. In M. H. Kernis (ed.), *Self-esteem: Issues and answers* (pp. 77–85). New York, NY: Psychology Press.

Kernis, M. H., & Goldman, B. M. (2006b). A multicomponent conceptualization of authenticity: Theory and research. In M. P. Zanna (ed.), *Advances in Experimental Social Psychology* (Vol. 38, pp. 283–357). San Diego, CA: Academic Press.

Kernis, M. H., Grannemann, B. D., & Barclay, L. C. (1989). Stability and level of self-esteem as predictors of anger arousal and hostility. *Journal of Personality and Social Psychology, 56*, 1013–1023.

Kernis, M. H., Grannemann, B. D., & Barclay, L. C. (1992). Stability of self-esteem: Assessment, correlates, and excuse making. *Journal of Personality, 60*, 621–644.

Kernis, M. H., Greenier, K. D., Herlocker, C. E., Whisenhunt, C. R., & Abend, T. A. (1997). Self-perceptions of reactions to doing well or poorly: The roles of stability and level of self-esteem. *Personality and Individual Differences, 22*, 845–854.

Kernis, M. H., Lakey, C. E., & Heppner, W. L. (2008). Secure versus fragile high self-esteem as a predictor of verbal defensiveness: Converging findings across three different markers. *Journal of Personality, 76*, 477–512.

Kernis, M. H., & Paradise, A. W. (2002). Distinguishing between secure and fragile forms of high self-esteem. In E. L. Deci & R. M. Ryan (eds.), *Handbook of self-determination research* (pp. 339–360). Rochester, NY: University of Rochester Press.

Kernis, M. H., Paradise, A. W., Whitaker, D. J., Wheatman, S. R., & Goldman, B. N. (2000). Master of one's psychological domain? Not likely if one's self-esteem is unstable. *Personality and Social Psychology Bulletin, 26*, 1297–1305.

Kernis, M. H., & Waschull, S. B. (1995). The interactive roles of stability and level of self-esteem: Research and theory. In M. P. Zanna (ed.), *Advances in Experimental Social Psychology* (Vol. 27, pp. 93–141). San Diego, CA: Academic Press.

Kernis, M. H., Whisenhunt, C. R., Washull, S. B., Greenier, K. D., Berry, A. J., Herlocker, C. E., & Anderson, C. A. (1998). Multiple facets of self-esteem and their relation to depressive symptoms. *Personality and Social Psychology Bulletin, 24*, 657–668.

Knee, C. R., Canevello, A., Bush, A. L., & Cook, A. (2008). Relationship-contingent self-esteem and the ups and downs of romantic relationships. *Journal of Personality and Social Psychology, 95*, 608–627.

Kohut, H., & Wolf, E. S. (1986). The disorders of self and their treatment: An outline. In A. P. Morrison (ed.), *Essential papers on narcissism* (pp. 175–196). New York and London: New York University Press.

Koole, S. L., & Pelham, B. W. (2003). On the nature of implicity self-esteem. The case of the name letter effect. In S. J. Spencer, S. Fein, M. P. Zanna, & J. M. Olson (eds.), *Motivated social perception: The Ontario symposium* (Vol. 9, pp. 93–116). Mahwah, NJ: Lawrence Erlbaum Associates.

Lakey, C. E., Kernis, M. H., Heppner, W. L., & Lance, C. E. (2008). Individual differences in authenticity and mindfulness as predictors of verbal defensiveness. *Journal of Research in Personality, 42*, 230–238.

Leary, M. R., & Guadango, J. (2011). The role of hypo-egoic self-processes in optimal functioning and subjective well-being. In K. M. Sheldon, T. B. Kashdan, & M. F. Steiger (eds.), *Designing positive psychology: Taking stock and moving forward* (pp. 135–146). New York, NY: Oxford University Press.

McGregor, I., & Marigold, D. C. (2003). Defensive zeal and the uncertain self: What makes you so sure? *Journal of Personality and Social Psychology, 85*, 838–852.

McGregor, I., Nail, P. R., Marigold, D. C., & Kang, S-J. (2005). Defensive pride and consensus: Strength in imaginary numbers. *Journal of Personality and Social Psychology, 89*, 978–996.

Melwani, S., & Barsade, S. G. (2011). Held in contempt: The psychological, interpersonal, and performance consequences of contempt in a work context. *Journal of Personality and Social Psychology, 101*, 503–520.

Miller, J. D., Campbell, W. K., & Pilkonis, P. A. (2007). Narcissistic personality disorder: Relations with distress and functional impairment. *Comprehensive Psychiatry, 48*, 170–177.

Morf, C. C., & Rhodewalt, F. (2001). Unraveling the paradoxes of narcissism: A dynamic self-regulatory processing model. *Psychological Inquiry, 12*, 177–196.

Morf, C. C., Torchetti, T., & Schürch, E. (2011). Narcissism from the perspective of the dynamic self-regulatory processing model. In W. K. Campbell & J. D. Miller (eds.), *The handbook of narcissism and narcissistic personality disorder: Theoretical approaches, empirical findings, and treatments* (pp. 56–70). Hoboken, NJ: Wiley.

Myers, D. G., & Diener, E. (1995). Who is happy? *Psychological Science, 6*, 10–19.

Neff, K. (2003). Self-compassion: An alternative conceptualization of a healthy attitude toward oneself. *Self and Identity, 2*, 85–102.

Neighbors, C., Larimer, M. E., Geisner, I. M., & Knee, C. R. (2004). Feeling controlled and drinking motives among college students: Contingent self-esteem as a mediator. *Self and Identity, 3*, 207–224.

Nuttin, J. M. (1985). Narcissism beyond Gestalt and awareness: The name-letter effect. *European Journal of Social Psychology, 15* (3), pp. 353–361.

Nuttin, J. M. (1987). Affective consequences of mere ownership: The name letter effect in twelve European languages. *European Journal of Social Psychology, 17*, 381–402.

Olson, M. A., Fazio, R. H., & Hermann, A. D. (2007). Reporting tendencies underlie discrepancies between implicit and explicit measures of self-esteem. *Psychological Science, 18*, 287–291.

Orth, U., Robins, R. W., & Roberts, B. W. (2008). Low self-esteem prospectively predicts depression in adolescence and young adulthood. *Journal of Personality and Social Psychology, 95*, 695–708.

Park, L. E., & Crocker, J. (2005). Interpersonal consequences of seeking self-esteem. *Personality and Social Psychology Bulletin, 11*, 1587–1598.

Park, L. E., & Crocker, J. (2008). Contingencies of self-worth and responses to negative interpersonal feedback. *Self & Identity, 7*, 184–203.

Park, L. E., & Maner, J. K. (2011). Does self-threat promote social connection? The role of self-esteem and contingences of self-worth. *Journal of Personality and Social Psychology, 96*, 203–271.

Park, L. E., Crocker, J., & Kiefer, A. K. (2007). Contingencies of self-worth, academic failure, and goal pursuit. *Personality and Social Psychology Bulletin, 33*, 1503–1517.

Paulhus, D. H. (1998). Interpersonal adaptiveness of trait self-enhancement: A mixed blessing? *Journal of Personality and Social Psychology, 74*, 1197–1208.

Pincus, A. L., & Lukowitsky, M. R. (2010). Pathological narcissism and narcissistic personality disorder. *Annual Review of Clinical Psychology, 6*, 421–446.

Pyszcynski, T., Greenberg, J., & Goldenberg, J. L. (2003). Freedom versus fear: On the defense, growth, and expansion of the self. In M. R. Leary & J. P. Tangney (eds.), *Handbook of self and identity* (pp. 314–343). New York, NY: Guilford Press.

Rhodewalt, F. (2005). Social motivation and object relations: Narcissism and interpersonal self-esteem regulation. In J. P. Forgas, K. D. Williams, & S. M. Laham (eds.), *Social motivation: Conscious and unconscious processes* (pp. 332–350). Cambridge: Cambridge University Press.

Rhodewalt, F., & Morf, C. C. (1998). On self-aggrandizement and anger: A temporal analysis of narcissism and affective reactions to success and failure. *Journal of Personality and Social Psychology, 74*, 672–685.

Rhodewalt, F., & Peterson, B. (2009). Narcissism. In M. R. Leary & R. H. Hoyle (eds.), *Handbook of individual differences* (pp. 547–560). New York, NY: Guilford Press.

Rhodewalt, F., Madrian, J. C., & Cheney, S. (1998). Narcissism, self-knowledge organization, and emotional reactivity: The effect of daily experiences on self-esteem and affect. *Personality and Social Psychology Bulletin, 24*, 75–87.

Roberts, J. E., Kassel, J. D., & Gotlib, I. H. (1995). Level and stability of self-esteem as predictors of depressive symptoms. *Personality and Individual Differences, 19*, 217–224.

Roberts, J. E., & Monroe, S. M. (1992). Vulnerable self-esteem and depressive symptoms: Prospective findings comparing three alternative conceptualizations. *Journal of Personality and Social Psychology, 62*, 804–812.

Rogers, C. R. (1959). A theory of therapy, personality, and interpersonal relationships, as developed in the client-centered framework. In S. Koch (ed.), *Psychology: A study of science* (Vol. 3, pp. 184–256). New York, NY: McGraw-Hill.

Rogers, C. R. (1961). *On becoming a person: A therapist's view of psychotherapy*. Boston, MA: Houghton Mifflin.

Rosenberg, M. (1965). *Society and the adolescent self-image*. Princeton, NJ: Princeton University Press.

Ryan, R. M., & Brown, K. W. (2003). Why we don't need self-esteem: On fundamental needs, contingent love, and mindfulness. *Psychological Inquiry, 14*, 71–76.

Sandstrom, M. J., & Jordan, R. (2008). Defensive self-esteem and aggression in childhood. *Journal of Research in Personality, 42*, 506–514.

Schröder-Abé, M., Rudolph, A., & Schütz, A. (2007). High implicit self-esteem is not necessarily advantageous: Discrepancies between implicit and explicit self-esteem and their relationship with anger suppression and psychological health. *European Journal of Personality, 21*, 319–339.

Sedikides, C., Rudich, E. A., Gregg, A. P., Kumashiro, M., & Rusbult, C. (2004). Are normal narcissists psychologically healthy?: Self-esteem matters. *Journal of Personality and Social Psychology, 87*, 400–416.

Swann, W. B., Jr., Chang-Schneider, C. & Larsen McClarty, K. (2007). Do people's self-views matter? Self-concept and self-esteem in everyday life. *American Psychologist, 62*, 84–94.

Taylor, S. E., & Brown, J. D. (1988). Positive illusions and well-being revisited: Separating fact from fiction. *Psychological Bulletin, 116*, 21–27.

Tracy, J. L., Cheng, J. T., Robins, R. W., & Trzesniewski, K. H. (2009). Authentic and hubristic pride: The affective core of self-esteem and narcissism. *Self and Identity, 8*, 196–213.

Trzesniewski, K. H., Donnellan, M. B., Moffitt, T. E., Robins, R. W., Poulton, R., & Caspi, A. (2006). Low self-esteem during adolescence predicts poor health, criminal behavior, and limited economic prospects during adulthood. *Developmental Psychology, 42*, 381–390.

Trzesniewski, K. H., Donnellan, M. B., & Robins, R. W. (2003). Stability of self-esteem across the life span. *Journal of Personality and Social Psychology, 84*, 205–220.

Twenge, J. M., Konrath, S., Foster, J. D., & Campbell, W. K. (2008). Egos inflating over time: A cross-temporal meta-analysis of the Narcissistic Personality Inventory. *Journal of Personality, 76*, 875–902.

Waschull, S. B., & Kernis, M. H. (1996). Level and stability of self-esteem as predictors of children's intrinsic motivation and reasons for anger. *Personality and Social Psychology Bulletin, 22*, 4–13.

Zeigler-Hill, V. (2006a). Discrepancies between implicit and explicit self-esteem: Implications for narcissism and self-esteem instability? *Journal of Personality, 74*, 119–143.

Zeigler-Hill, V. (2006b). Contingent self-esteem and the interpersonal circumplex: The interpersonal pursuit of self-esteem. *Personality and Individual Differences, 40*, 713–723.

Zeigler-Hill, V., Clark, C. B., & Beckman, T. E. (2011). Fragile self-esteem and the interpersonal circumplex: Are feelings of self-worth associated with interpersonal style? *Self and Identity, 10*, 509–536.

Zeigler-Hill, V., Clark, C. B., & Pickard, J. D. (2008). Narcissistic subtypes and contingent self-esteem: Do all narcissists base their self-esteem on the same domains? *Journal of Personality, 76*, 753–774.

Zeigler-Hill, V., Fulton, J. J., & McLemore, C. (2011). The role of unstable self-esteem in the appraisal of romantic relationships. *Personality and Individual Differences, 51*, 51–56.

Zeigler-Hill, V, & Jordan, C. H. (2010). Two faces of self-esteem: Implicit and explicit forms of self-esteem. In B. Gawronski & B. K. Payne (eds.), *Handbook of implicit social cognition: Measurement, theory, and applications* (pp. 392–407). New York, NY: Guilford Press.

Zeigler-Hill, V., & Jordan, C. H. (2011). Behind the mask: Narcissism and implicit self-esteem. *The handbook of narcissism and narcissistic personality disorder: Theoretical approaches, empirical findings, and treatments* (pp. 101–115). Hoboken, NJ: Wiley.

Zeigler-Hill, V., Myers, E. M., & Clark, C. B. (2010). Narcissism and self-esteem reactivity: The role of negative achievement events. *Journal of Research in Personality, 44*, 285–292.

6 The development of explicit and implicit self-esteem and their role in psychological adjustment

Tracy DeHart, Reyna Peña, and Howard Tennen

Self-esteem plays a key role in most formulations of psychopathological pro-cesses (Cooper, 1986) and in many models of therapeutic techniques (Bednar, Wells, & Peterson, 1989). For several highly prevalent emotional disorders, such as depression and borderline personality, vulnerable self-esteem is a defining characteristic. For other disorders, such as narcissistic personality disorder and eating disorders, fluctuations in self-esteem triggered by stressful interpersonal encounters prompt self-destructive behavior and maladaptive responses to others. Recently, researchers have begun to focus on people's *implicit* (i.e., unconscious, relatively uncontrolled, and overlearned) self-evaluations (for reviews, see Greenwald & Banaji, 1995; Koole & DeHart, 2007). Research has demonstrated that implicit self-esteem predicts important psychological and physical outcomes independent of explicit self-esteem (i.e., feelings of self-worth that are consciously considered and relatively controlled). In this chapter we review and integrate theory and research from social psychology and clinical psychology to elucidate the role of implicit and explicit self-esteem in emotional disorders.

We begin with an overview of the development of explicit and implicit self-esteem. Then, we examine the role of both explicit and implicit self-esteem in psychological adjustment. Specifically, we illustrate how the dynamics of self-esteem are manifested in psychopathology through the lens of three emotional disorders: depression, narcissistic personality disorder, and eating disorders. Next, because research on implicit self-esteem and emotional disorders is rela-tively new, we offer several avenues for future research. Finally, we offer sug-gestions regarding daily process methodology as a promising way to examine self-esteem disturbances in emotional disorders and the therapeutic processes designed for their alleviation.

Implicit versus explicit self-esteem

In the history of research on the self-concept, no topic has been more heavily studied than self-esteem. Presumably this is the case because low self-esteem is a vulnerability that has been linked to susceptibility to mental illness (Bardone, Vohs, Abramson, Heatherton, & Joiner, 2000; Roberts & Monroe, 1994) and even physical illness (Brown & McGill, 1989). However, most of this research has focused on people's explicit self-evaluations. The Rosenberg Self-Esteem Scale is the measure used most widely to assess people's explicit beliefs about the self (Rosenberg, 1965). People are asked to reflect upon and self-report on their self-worth and feelings about themselves. However, one major limitation of explicit measures of self-esteem is that many people are unable to articulate self-concept vulnerabilities as a part of their conscious belief systems (DeHart & Tennen, 2006). Both cognitive and psychoanalytic perspectives underscore the importance of implicit (automatic, unconscious) beliefs and cognition in psychological disorders (Friedman & Whisman, 2004; Phillips, Hine, & Thorsteinsson, 2010). Investigators have recently begun to use indirect methods to assess the role of people's implicit beliefs about the self in psychological disorders (Cockerham, Stopa, Bell, & Gregg, 2009; de Jong, 2002; Phillips et al., 2010). Below we will discuss two measures developed to assess implicit self-esteem.

Measures of implicit self-esteem

One of the most widely used, reliable, and valid measures of implicit self-esteem is based on research concerning the name-letter effect (Kitayama & Karasawa, 1997; Nuttin, 1987). Individuals' evaluation of their first and last initials is assessed by asking them to rate their preferences for each letter of the alphabet. A letter-liking score is computed, which is the difference between a person's rating of his or her first and last name initials and the mean liking for these two letters provided by people whose names did not include that letter (thus, more positive values would indicate higher name-letter preferences). Name-letter preference is computed by taking the average liking scores for an individual's first and last-name initials (for detailed information on scoring name-letter measures see DeHart, Pelham, & Tennen, 2006). The name-letter test has been used to assess implicit self-esteem as both a stable trait (DeHart et al., 2006) and a temporary state (DeHart & Pelham, 2007).

Another widely used measure of implicit self-esteem is the Self-Esteem Implicit Association Test (IAT; see Greenwald & Farnham, 2000). Participants are asked to categorize different combinations of self-related words and positive and negative words. Implicit self-esteem is determined by comparing how quickly participants are able to categorize self-related and negative words and how quickly they are able to categorize self-related and positive words together. Like the name-letter test, the self-esteem IAT has been used to assess implicit self-esteem at the trait level (Greenwald & Farnam, 2000; Jordan, Spencer, Zanna, Hoshino-Browne, & Correll, 2003) and also as a temporary state (Dijksterhuis, 2004).

Although both the name-letter effect and the IAT are believed to assess people's implicit self-esteem, these measures are often weakly correlated with one another (Bosson, Swann, & Pennebaker, 2000; Rudolph, Schröder-Abé, Schütz, Gregg, & Sedikides, 2008). However, recent research has observed similar effects associated with different measures of implicit self-esteem that are typically uncorrelated with one another (Baccus, Baldwin, & Packer, 2004; Dijksterhuis, 2004; Pelham et al., 2005). For instance, research using the IAT (Jordan et al., 2003) and the name-letter measure (Bosson, Brown, Zeigler-Hill, & Swann, 2003; Gregg & Sedikides, 2010) has linked high explicit and low implicit self-esteem with greater defensiveness and higher levels of narcissism.

Measures of implicit self-esteem are also weakly correlated with measures of explicit self-esteem (Bosson et al., 2000; DeHart et al., 2006; Gregg & Sedikides, 2010; Hetts, Sakuma, & Pelham, 1999). Presumably, this has to do with differences in the nature of people's implicit and explicit beliefs (DeHart et al., 2006; Epstein, 1994; Strack & Deutsch, 2004). For example, dual-process models suggest that people's implicit and explicit beliefs about the self are represented by two distinct attitudes (Strack & Deutsch, 2004). In addition, people's implicit beliefs about the self likely develop earlier than their explicit beliefs (DeHart et al., 2006; Rudman, Phelan, & Heppen, 2007), and implicit self-esteem appears to change much more slowly compared with explicit self-esteem (Gregg, Seibt, & Banaji, 2006; Hetts et al., 1999), and self-enhancement motives may cause people to reinterpret negative social experiences on an explicit level (Crocker & Major, 1989), although leaving a clear mark on the implicit level.

However, other investigators have argued that implicit and explicit attitudes toward the self are not independent of one another (Gawronski & Bodenhausen, 2007; Olson & Fazio, 2009). Therefore, another potential explanation for the dissociation between people's implicit and explicit self-esteem is that self-enhancement motives influence some people to inflate their self-esteem on explicit measures only (Olson, Fazio, & Hermann, 2007). There is no easy answer to the question of whether implicit and explicit self-esteem measures tap distinct attitudes. However, the accumulating evidence for the validity of implicit self-esteem clearly suggests that implicit measures of self-esteem provide important information not provided by measures of explicit self-esteem (DeHart et al., 2006; Koole, Dijksterhuis, & van Knippenberg, 2001; Shimizu & Pelham, 2004).

Origins of explicit and implicit self-esteem

People's explicit and implicit self-evaluations are presumably formed through interactions with significant others (Bartholomew, 1990; Bowlby, 1982; Cooley, 1902; Leary, Tambor, Terdal, & Downs, 1995; Mead, 1934). Theories in the tradition of symbolic interactionism suggest that people develop a sense of self on the basis of how other people treat them (Cooley, 1902; Mead, 1934). Over time, people internalize their perceptions of others' view of them. In addition, the sociometer theory of self-esteem suggests that self-esteem is a consequence of people's perceived social standing through their interactions with others (Leary et al., 1995). Specifically, individuals with low self-esteem have repeatedly experienced perceived interpersonal rejection. Conversely, most people with high self-esteem have experienced many subjectively successful or non-rejecting interpersonal relationships. In fact, the interpersonal monitoring system is believed continuously to monitor acceptance by functioning preconsciously (Leary et al., 1995). Therefore, both explicit and implicit self-esteem should be indicators of people's perceived acceptance.

Most parents have a major influence on the psychological development of their children (Baumrind, 1971; Bowlby, 1982; Harter, 1993; Parker, Tupling, & Brown, 1979; Pomerantz & Newman, 2000). For example, attachment theorists argue that people develop beliefs about the self on the basis of the responsiveness and sensitivity of their primary caregivers in childhood (Bartholomew, 1990; Bowlby, 1982). Repeated interpersonal experiences within the family thus form the basis for mental representations of the self in relation to others. Over time, how caretakers respond to infants presumably becomes internalized into working mental models, which are a set of conscious and unconscious beliefs for organizing information about the self in relation to other people.

In keeping with these theoretical perspectives, parenting style should be related to both implicit and explicit self-esteem (Baumrind, 1971; Parker et al., 1979). DeHart and colleagues (2006) examined the influence of recalled early childhood experiences on explicit and implicit self-esteem. DeHart and colleagues found that adults who reported that their parents were more nurturing during childhood reported high implicit and explicit self-esteem compared with those whose parents were less nurturing. Individuals who reported that their parents were more overprotective reported lower implicit self-esteem as adults. Moreover, permissive parenting was related to explicit, but not implicit self-esteem. Finally, mother's independent reports of their parenting were also related to their child's level of implicit and explicit self-esteem.

DeHart and colleagues (2006) also found that different aspects of parenting were differentially related to implicit and explicit self-esteem. For example, people's perceptions of parental overprotectiveness were reliably related to implicit self-esteem but were not reliably related to explicit self-esteem. This may reflect changes in children's ability to make self-protective attributions as they grow older (Wilson, Smith, Ross, & Ross, 2004). Given that very young children are not as adept as older children at self-protection, the quality of very early parenting, such as being overprotective, might have a stronger influence on implicit than on explicit self-esteem. In other words, overprotectiveness may undermine very young children's (mostly implicit) sense of autonomy or competence (Gilbert & Silvera, 1996) but may be less problematic once children are old enough to engage in high levels of attributional correction. When older children make such corrections for parental overprotectiveness they may protect their explicit self-esteem, but fail to repair their implicit self-esteem (Hetts et al., 1999).

DeHart and colleagues' (2006) findings are consistent with attachment theory, which suggests that people's conscious and unconscious working models are based upon the same types of experiences with primary caretakers. It is also plausible that *different* aspects of the same parenting style may have differential effects on implicit and explicit self-esteem. For example, parents who are nurturing may influence their children's implicit self-esteem through non-verbal channels, and their explicit self-esteem through verbal channels. It is also possible that people's current level of implicit self-esteem may influence their recollections of childhood interactions with their parents. The convergence of children's and mothers' descriptions of mothers' parenting style provides additional support for these retrospective reports. Nonetheless, determining the precise causal relation between parenting and implicit self-esteem will require prospective longitudinal research examining the relations among these variables.

Although both implicit and explicit self-esteem are formed based on interactions with significant others, the relation between people's explicit and implicit self-esteem is weak at best (Bosson, Swann, & Pennebaker, 2000; DeHart et al., 2006; Hetts et al., 1999). Presumably, this has to do with differences in the nature of people's implicit and explicit beliefs (for a more detailed explanation, see DeHart et al., 2006; Epstein, 1994). For example, implicit beliefs that presumably have their origins in early childhood experiences may become automatic over time. Because the quality of people's relationships may change over time and be reflected in their explicit belief system, their previously formed implicit beliefs may not be available for conscious articulation, but may still be elicited automatically (DeHart et al., 2006; Rudman et al., 2007).

Origins of insecure high self-esteem

The consistently weak association found between implicit and explicit self-esteem indicates that there are discrepancies between many people's implicit and explicit self-esteem. Researchers have recently been examining some important outcomes related to secure (high explicit and high implicit) versus insecure (high explicit and low implicit) high self-esteem (Bosson et al., 2003; Jordan et al., 2003). Individuals with high explicit but low implicit self-esteem (insecure high self-esteem) report higher levels of self-protective defensiveness (Jordan et al., 2003).

To our knowledge no research has directly examined the origins of secure versus insecure high self-esteem. However, there is theory and some research on early experiences related to other types of defensiveness, such as narcissism and unstable high self-esteem (for a review see Kernis, 2005). For example, Kernis and colleagues have argued that people possess a certain trait level of explicit self-esteem – around which their state self-esteem fluctuates. Unstable (or labile) high self-esteem has been linked to anger (Waschull & Kernis, 1996), emotional reactivity (Rhodewalt, Madrian, & Cheney, 1998), and depression (Butler, Hokanson, & Flynn, 1994; Kernis, Grannemann, & Mathis, 1991). Presumably, negative events activate negative self-evaluations among people with reactive self-esteem.

Kernis and colleagues have examined the role of parent-child communication in the development of stable versus unstable self-esteem (Kernis, Brown, & Brody, 2000). Eleven- and twelve-year-old children were asked to report on their parents' communication patterns (e.g., critical and controlling) and to complete the Rosenberg's (1965) self-esteem scale (to assess trait self-esteem). Then, the children were asked to complete reworded versions of the Rosenberg measure that asked them to report how they felt "right at this moment" every morning and evening for five days. Children with unstable self-esteem (i.e., a higher standard deviation in their daily self-esteem ratings) reported that their parents were more critical and that their fathers were more controlling compared with children with more stable self-esteem. Presumably, children with unstable self-esteem are able to make self-protective attributions for their parents' critical and controlling behavior (Wilson et al., 2004). Engaging in self-protective attributions may result in having explicit self-esteem that is high, but negative daily events may activate negative self-evaluations, resulting in labile self-esteem.

Origins of narcissism

Clinical conceptions depict narcissistic individuals as having excessively positive self-views that are believed to be defensive and mask underlying insecurities (Kernberg, 1975). Most psychodynamic perspectives on narcissism point to the important role of early object relations in the development of the disorder (Kernberg, 1975; Nemiah, 1973). That is, early relationships with parents who are rejecting, neglectful, disapproving, and do not meet the child's needs are internalized into negative feelings about others as well as feelings of inferiority and insecurity (Nemiah, 1973). Therefore, a vulnerable self-structure develops, and narcissistic individuals try constantly to compensate for their insecurities by exaggerating their accomplishments, preoccupying themselves with thoughts of success, and seeking excessive admiration from others.

Previous research has examined some early experiences related to sub-clinical levels of narcissism (Otway & Vignoles, 2006; Ramsey, Watson, Biderman, & Reeves, 1996; Watson, Little, & Biderman, 1992). For example, research has examined the relations among parenting styles and narcissism among college students (Ramsey et al., 1996; Watson et al., 1992). Children who reported that their parents were more authoritarian reported higher levels of narcissism. In addition, children who reported that their parents were more permissive reported higher levels of narcissism. Presumably, parents who do not provide emotional warmth or parents who do not provide structure are contributing to higher levels of narcissism in their children. Although these findings are consistent with the idea that early parent-child relations are related to the development of narcissism, the retrospective reports of parenting are open to alternative causal interpretations. Nevertheless, this is some of the first empirical evidence linking early childhood experiences to narcissism.

Researchers examined the association of parental coldness and parental overvaluation (of their child) to narcissism (Otway & Vignoles, 2006). A non-clinical sample of adults completed measures of childhood experiences and narcissism. Those who reported more parental coldness also reported higher narcissism. In addition, those who reported that their parents engaged in more overvaluation of them also reported higher narcissism. These findings may help explain why narcissists have both a grandiose sense of self and underlying insecurities. The researchers suggest that people high in narcissism received constant praise and overvaluation from their parents, while at the same time their parents were cold and distant. Presumably, having cold and distant parents left a mark on the child's implicit self-esteem, but over time these individuals were able to explain away and rationalize their parent's behavior and form positive explicit beliefs about the self.

In sum, the existing research suggests that people's implicit and explicit beliefs about the self develop based on their interactions with significant others. Both explicit and implicit self-esteem are believed to be indicators of people's perceived relational value (DeHart, Pelham, Fiedorowicz, Carvallo, & Gabriel, 2011; Leary, 2005). In the next section, we will examine the role of explicit and implicit self-esteem in clinical psychological disorders.

Self-esteem and psychological disorders

Although people's overall feelings of worth and acceptance play an important role in their psychological functioning, the dynamics of self-esteem vary among emotional disorders. We have selected two disorders from DSM IV's (American Psychiatric Association, 2000) Axis I, major depressive disorder and eating disorders, and one from Axis II, narcissistic personality disorder, in which self-esteem plays an especially important role. We discuss how implicit and explicit self-esteem motives are related to each disorder, and we highlight potential difficulties that certain manifestations of implicit self-esteem pose for the therapeutic process.

Major depressive disorder

Major depressive disorder is characterized by a depressed mood, loss of interest or pleasure in activities, and disturbances in thought processes (American Psychiatric Association, 2000). Depression is one of the most serious and widespread mental health disorders (World Health Organization, 2001). Sub-clinical levels of depression are even more common and also have negative implications for people's mental and physical health and well-being (Kim, Thibodeau, & Jorgensen, 2011). Therefore, it is important to understand predictors and outcomes of depression. Clinicians have recently been examining the important role of implicit cognition in depression (Friedman & Whisman, 2004; for a review, see Phillips, Hine, & Thorsteinsson, 2010).

Early psychodynamic perspectives assumed that depression is anger that is directed toward the self, which is the result of unconscious anger felt toward the loss of an inconsistent attachment relationship (Arieti & Bemporad, 1978; Basch, 1975). In contrast, cognitive perspectives on depression contend that early experiences with close others create explicit and implicit beliefs about the self that serve as vulnerability factors, which in turn interact with negative daily experiences to initiate and maintain depression (Bandura, 1997; Beck, Rush, Shaw, & Emery, 1979; Brown & Harris, 1978; 1989; Maddux, 1995; Phillips et al., 2010;

Weich, Patterson, Shaw, & Stewart-Brown, 2009). Daily negative experiences may activate self-conscious emotions (shame and guilt), which are believed to be evolutionarily adaptive because of their social and interpersonal functions. Recently, a meta-analysis confirmed that shame and guilt are reliably associated with depression (Kim et al., 2011).

These theoretical perspectives suggest that negative of self-esteem and poor self-esteem regulation in the face of adverse events may play a key role in depression. Joiner's (2000) distinction between erosive and self-propagating processes in depression suggests two distinct mechanisms through which low self-esteem might influence depression chronicity and vulnerability to recurrence. One possibility is that a depressive episode erodes an individual's personal (and potentially protective) resources, including self-esteem, which leaves him or her at greater risk for an extended depressive episode or a recurrence. In other words, depression erodes self-esteem. A variant of this view is that individuals vulnerable to a first depressive episode have pre-existing low or vulnerable self-esteem. Joiner offers another possibility, however: rather than representing an eroded resource, the low self-esteem noted frequently among depressed and formerly depressed individuals may propel them to engage in active interpersonal strategies that interfere with effective interpersonal functioning and potentially undermine social support. Excessively seeking reassurance and seeking negative feedback consistent with one's low self-esteem are two such active, self-propagating processes delineated by Joiner (2000).

One common theme of both psychodynamic and cognitive perspectives is that self-esteem is a vulnerability factor for depression, with low explicit self-esteem being associated with increased depression (Brown & Harris, 1978, 1989). Social and clinical psychologists have argued that it is not low explicit self-esteem per se that is related to depression, but rather labile (Kernis et al., 1991) or reactive explicit self-esteem (Butler et al., 1994; Roberts & Monroe, 1992, 1994). Presumably, negative events activate negative explicit self-evaluations among individuals with labile or reactive self-esteem, which in turn compromise their ability to regulate depressed moods. More recent dual-process models of depression (Beevers, 2005; Phillips et al., 2010) have suggested that both controlled and automatic beliefs about the self are likely to influence people's ability to regulate depressed moods in response to negative events.

As mentioned above, the sociometer theory of self-esteem suggests that both implicit and explicit self-esteem are indicators of low relational value (DeHart et al., 2011; Leary, 2005). Therefore, it is no surprise that depressed individuals also experience relationship difficulties (Brown & Harris, 1978; Davila, Bradbury, Cohan, & Tochluk, 1997; Fincham, Beach, Harold, & Osborne, 1997). For example, wives who are depressed act in ways that elicit rejection from their partners, which results in their feeling more distressed (Davila et al., 1997). This is an example of a self-propagating process. A client's depression can also influence the therapeutic relationship. Because people's explicit beliefs about the self can influence the imagined appraisals of others (Kenny, 1994; Shrauger & Schoeneman, 1979), the negative self-appraisals of depressed individuals make them inclined to anticipate, and perhaps even evoke signs of rejection from the therapist that interfere with the therapeutic alliance.

Although psychodynamic and cognitive perspectives on depression both suggest that overlearned and automatic negative beliefs play a role in depression (Friedman & Whisman, 2004), most of the empirical research on self-esteem and depression has focused on people's explicit (conscious) self-esteem. However, recently researchers have been examining conscious versus unconscious perspectives on depression in the context of dual-process models of depression (see Phililips et al., 2010, for a review). In addition, researchers have started to examine the role of implicit (independent of explicit) self-esteem in depression.

Implicit self-esteem and depression

Despite the widespread use of dual-process models in social psychology, it was not until recently that dual-process models were applied to understanding cognitive vulnerabilities to depression (Beevers, 2005; Haeffel et al., 2007). Dual-process models of depression suggest that when people encounter a negative event, there are two different types of processes that both play a role in determining how they will respond to that negative event. First, people have an automatic (i.e., unconscious) cognitive response to the negative event. In response to the stressful event, implicit schemas about the self are activated quickly and unintentionally. If these automatic beliefs are negative, this can lead the person to experience negative affect (shame or guilt) in response to the event (Kim et al., 2011). However, people can also respond to the negative event in a more deliberate and controlled (conscious) fashion, which may override or even increase the automatic negative response (Beevers, 2005; Haeffel et al., 2007). Beevers (2005) has suggested that negative automatic schemas are the primary source of cognitive vulnerability to depression. In contrast, Haeffel and colleagues (2007) assert that both automatic and controlled beliefs play a role in cognitive vulnerability to depression. Haeffel and colleagues argue that it is people's final conscious interpretation of an event that makes them most at risk for depression – even if positive automatic schemas are activated in response to negative events.

Several studies have examined the relation between implicit self-esteem and depression. One study (Segal, Truchon, Gemar, Guirguis, & Horowitz, 1995) found that negative self-relevant information is more readily accessible for depressed compared to non-depressed individuals. Consistent with these findings, currently depressed participants reported lower implicit self-esteem (IAT) compared with a group of healthy controls (Risch et al., 2010). Another study examined implicit self-esteem (IAT) in a group of currently depressed participants, with and without suicidal ideation, and a group of non-depressed controls (Franck, De Raedt, Dereu, & Van den Abbeele, 2007; Haeffel et al., 2007). This study revealed that low implicit self-esteem was associated with depression, but only for participants without suicidal ideation. Depressed participants with suicidal ideation did not differ from non-depressed controls in their level of implicit self-esteem.

Other studies, however, have found that *high* implicit self-esteem is associated with depression (Franck, De Raedt, & De Houwer, 2007; 2008; De Raedt, Schacht, Franck, & De Houwer, 2006). Across three different studies (and three different measures of implicit self-esteem), De Raedt and colleagues (2006) demonstrated that the implicit self-esteem of currently depressed patients did not differ from the implicit self-esteem of a non-depressed control group. That is, currently depressed people had implicit self-esteem that was just as high as non-depressed people. However, participants' suicidal ideation was not assessed in these studies. Because previous research has demonstrated that depression is related to higher implicit self-esteem only among depressed participants who are also high on suicidal ideation (Franck, De Raedt, et al., 2007), one potentially fruitful direction for future research would be to determine whether these effects are due to depressed patients being relatively high in suicidal ideation.

However, Franck et al. (2008) found that *formerly* depressed individuals reported higher implicit self-esteem (IAT) compared with their currently depressed and never depressed counterparts (which did not differ from one another) in an initial assessment (see Gemar, Segal, Sagrati, & Kennedy, 2001, for similar findings). On the other hand, formerly depressed people with three or more depressive episodes reported lower implicit self-esteem compared with formerly depressed people with less than three depressive episodes (Risch et al., 2010). In addition, Franck et al. (2008) found that the formerly depressed participants showed a stronger decrease in implicit self-esteem in response to a negative mood induction compared with participants who had never been depressed. These findings may reflect more reactive implicit beliefs among formerly depressed participants. That is, consistent with cognitive theories (Beevers, 2005; Haeffel et al., 2007; Roberts & Monroe, 1992), vulnerable implicit beliefs about the self are a latent diathesis that may become activated in response to negative events or moods. Previous research has also found that people's implicit self-evaluations appear to become activated when assessed under conditions of threat (DeHart & Pelham, 2007; Jones, Pelham, Mirenberg, & Hetts, 2002).

In one of the few tests of the dual-process model of depression, Haeffel and colleagues (2007) employed an experimental design in one study and a five-week prospective longitudinal design in a second study. In the experimental study, Haeffel and colleagues assessed college students' implicit feelings of self-worth with the self-worth IAT and then randomly assigned them to either a difficult anagram condition, after which they were told that they had done poorly, or to a control condition. They were then assessed for feelings of distress. Participants who scored low on the implicit measure of self-worth and had received negative feedback reported more distress than those who scored higher in implicit self-worth. These effects were not evident in the control condition. These experimental findings suggest that people's initial affective response to a threatening event is influenced by their negative automatic beliefs about the self. The results of the five-week prospective study revealed that both implicit (self-worth IAT) and explicit (cognitive-style questionnaire) vulnerabilities interacted with stressful negative life events to predict depression at Time 2 (controlling for depression at Time 1). However, when entered into the same regression model, only explicit vulnerabilities interacted with stressful life events to predict subsequent depression. Haeffel and colleagues assert that people's implicit self-esteem vulnerabilities influence their immediate affective response to stressful events, whereas their explicit self-esteem vulnerabilities influence their long-term depressive responsive to events.

Another study of young adults examined the influence of explicit and implicit self-esteem, cognitive vulnerability (cognitive-style questionnaire), and stressful negative events in predicting depression over four months (Steinberg, Karpinski, & Alloy, 2007). This study revealed that low implicit self-esteem (IAT) predicted increased depression in response to high levels of stressful negative events over four months, but only for participants who were at risk for depression based on their attributional style. Neither explicit self-esteem nor the name-letter measure of implicit self-esteem interacted with cognitive vulnerability and stressful negative events to predict subsequent depression.

Other research has examined the influence of implicit self-esteem on depression relapse (Franck, De Raedt, & De Houwer, 2007). Currently depressed, formerly depressed, and never depressed individuals completed the Beck Depression Inventory II (BDI-II; see Beck, Steer, & Brown, 1996), and measures of explicit and implicit self-esteem (name-letter measure). Six months later, participants completed the BDI-II again. At the initial session, implicit self-esteem did not differ across the currently depressed, formerly depressed and never depressed participants. However, currently depressed participants reported lower explicit self-esteem compared with their formerly depressed and never depressed counterparts (who did not differ from one another). Interestingly, when both Time 1 implicit and explicit self-esteem predicted Time 2 depression (controlling for Time 1 depression), only implicit self-esteem predicted depression six months later.

Some of the initial evidence linking implicit self-esteem to depression suggests that implicit self-esteem is related to depression among individuals who do not have suicidal ideation (Franck, De Raedt, et al., 2007), predicts depression over six months (Franck, De Raedt, & De Houwer, 2007), and interacts with negative life events to predict depression over time (Steinberg et al., 2007). In addition, formerly depressed participants showed a stronger decrease in implicit self-esteem in response to a negative mood induction (Franck et al., 2008) and formerly depressed people with three or more depressive episodes reported lower implicit self-esteem (Risch et al., 2010). Therefore, the implicit self-esteem among people who are formerly depressed appears to be vulnerable.

Eating disorders

Eating disorders are marked by extreme disturbances in eating behavior. Anorexia nervosa and bulimia nervosa are the two main diagnoses classified in the *Diagnostic and Statistical Manual of Mental Disorders* (DSM; see American Psychiatric Association, 2000). DSM criteria for anorexia nervosa include refusal to maintain a normal body weight in proportion to height and age, exaggerated fear of gaining weight even if underweight, disturbances in how body shape and weight are evaluated, and amenorrhea. Diagnostic criteria for bulimia nervosa include recurrent episodes of binge eating, recurrent inappropriate compensatory behavior to prevent weight gain (e.g., vomiting; misuse of laxatives, diuretics, enemas, or other medications; fasting; or excessive exercise), and disturbances in how body shape and weight are evaluated. About nine out of ten individuals diagnosed with either bulimia or anorexia are women.

Anorexia and bulimia diagnoses have increased in the last few decades. A wide number of risk factors and correlates have been explored in the literature, including negative body shape self-concepts, appearance dissatisfaction, negative self-evaluation, and low self-esteem (Ackard, Fulkerson & Neumark-Sztainer, 2011; Jacobi, Hayward, de Zwaan, Kraemer, & Agras, 2004; Polivy & Herman, 2002; Stice, 2002). Notably, low self-esteem has been implicated in the development and maintenance of disordered eating, and is also a feature of associated risk factors and correlates such as perfectionism, poor self-regulation, and appearance dissatisfaction (Baumeister & Heatherton, 1996; Bos, Huijding, Muris, Vogel & Biesheuvel, 2010; Cockerham, Stopa, Bell, & Gregg, 2009; Tylka & Sabik, 2010).

Earlier work on eating disorders from a psychodynamic perspective focused on disturbances in maternal relationships and failure to separate from the mother in hindering development of healthy self-representations, and the use of disordered dietary restriction in defensive displacement of aggression toward the self onto the body (Johnson, 1991). Negative self-evaluations and overly critical body evaluations are features of anorexia and bulimia that have received considerable attention from psychodynamic perspectives. The role of perceived personal ineffectiveness has been associated with both anorexic and bulimic eating patterns (Jacobi, Paul, de Zwaan, Nutzinger, & Dahme, 2004; Wagner, Halmi & Maguire, 1987). Consistent with this idea, an adult clinical population with anorexia or bulimia did report lower levels of explicit self-esteem and ineffectiveness compared to healthy controls (Jacob et al., 2004). Additionally, a similar pattern has been observed in a school-aged sample: explicit self-esteem levels declined linearly along a continuum in relation to severity of common disordered eating behaviors – those with no symptoms having higher self-esteem than those at sub-threshold, while threshold symptomatic had the lowest self-esteem (Ackard et al., 2011).

Cognitive behavioral theories contend that negative self-cognitions and unrealistic self-evaluations play a role in the development and maintenance of eating disorders (Fairburn, Cooper, & Shafran, 2003; Polivy & Herman, 2002). For those with anorexia, extreme restrictions represent a primary method used to exert control over negative or irrational (i.e., perfectionist) self-evaluations. For bulimics, low self-esteem becomes linked with concerns about weight, which becomes linked with self-worth. Binges are often triggered by an inability to deal with negative moods or other aversive cognitive and affective states (Fairburn et al., 2003). In fact, Heatherton and Baumeister (1991) suggest that binge eaters are motivated by the need to escape aversive self-awareness. Low self-esteem may be indicative of a type of false belief about the self that affects the ability to regulate stress and eating behaviors effectively.

Lower self-esteem is thought to be a predisposing factor to eating disorders, as women with low self-esteem are particularly likely to turn to societal norms and unrealistic thinness ideals in evaluating their bodies (Fairburn et al., 2003; Tylka & Sabik, 2010). Extreme caloric restriction and other behaviors found among anorexia sufferers with low explicit self-esteem represent attempts to attain internalized ideals they hold regarding body type. However, some recent longitudinal research by Barker and Bornstein (2010) within an adolescent population showed that although appearance dissatisfaction predicted later lowered self-esteem, self-esteem did not predict later reports of body dissatisfaction. However, the evidence linking explicit self-esteem to eating disorders is inconsistent (Cockerham et al., 2009), which has led researchers to start examining the role of implicit self-esteem in eating disorders.

Implicit self-esteem and eating disorders

While most research in this area has examined explicit self-esteem, there is some emerging research examining the association of implicit self-esteem in the development, prediction, and treatment of anorexia and bulimia. Dual-process models of attitudes have been used to examine the role of both explicit and implicit self-esteem in eating disorders (Cockerham et al., 2009). Cockerham and colleagues (2009) examined the relations between implicit (IAT) and explicit self-esteem and bulimia nervosa (controlling for depression scores). They found that individuals in their clinical sample with disordered eating displayed lower explicit self-esteem compared with the control group. However, participants with disordered eating reported higher implicit self-esteem compared with a control group. These findings are consistent with findings demonstrating that high implicit self-esteem is associated with depression (Franck, De Raedt, & De Houwer, 2007; 2008; De Raedt et al., 2006). However, the findings suggesting that depression is related to higher implicit self-esteem may only hold for depressed participants who are also high on suicidal ideation (Franck, De Raedt, Dereu, & Van den Abbeele, 2007).

Findings by Bos and colleagues (2010) indicated that there was no significant relation between implicit self-esteem and psychopathology in a sample of healthy adolescents. In their assessment of the relation between various types of self-esteem (contingent, explicit, and implicit) and pathological symptoms like those associated with anorexia and bulimia, implicit self-esteem was found to not be associated with psychopathology. The authors suggest that implicit self-esteem, since it is automatic and developmentally predates adolescence, may be less susceptible to stresses related to adolescence in comparison to explicit self-esteem. That is, the relation between declines in explicit self-esteem and increases in psychopathological symptoms may be more telling in understanding inclinations toward developing pathologies like disordered eating in healthy adolescents, since implicit esteem and possibly attitudes toward body concept are more enduring.

Within a sample of adult women presenting with an eating disorder (anorexia or bulimia), however, implicit self-esteem figures more prominently and definitively. Research by Vanderlinden et al. (2009) showed that, in response to positive and negative feedback on an intellectual test, both implicit and explicit self-esteem levels of control group members without an eating disorder remained the same. But, in response to positive feedback, women with an eating disorder reported higher implicit and explicit self-esteem scores. In response to negative feedback, women with an eating disorder reported lower explicit but not implicit scores. Their results suggest women with an eating disorder exhibited more labile self-esteem (especially explicit) in response to feedback.

Research by Hoffmeister and colleagues (Hoffmeister, Teige-Mocigemba, Blechert, Klauer, & Tuschen-Caffier, 2010) investigated body concerns alongside implicit self-esteem (IAT) and explicit self-esteem, utilizing a non-clinical sample of restrained and unrestrained eaters. After exposure to a mirror-task condition designed to increase body awareness, unrestrained eaters reported an increase in implicit self-esteem but restrained eaters demonstrated a decrease in implicit self-esteem. Other research on gender differences in implicit weight identity suggest that implicit attitudes regarding being overweight predicted implicit self-esteem among women, but not men (Grover, Keel & Mitchell, 2003). This suggests that women may indeed internalize thinness ideals, predisposing some women to be overly preoccupied with eating behavior and weight (Tylka & Sabik, 2010). In addition, O'Conner and colleagues (2011) reported higher implicit self-esteem among women having undergone a written disclosure intervention related to their body concept compared to a control intervention.

In the absence of clearer evidence on the nature of the relationship between implicit self-esteem and eating disorders, the above findings indicate that understanding the role of implicit self-esteem – and implicit body concepts – in eating disorder development has implications for prediction, prevention, and treatment efforts. While some research exists that examines the relation between low implicit self-esteem and eating disorders, more research is needed to understand the role of implicit self-esteem in the development of eating disorders. Indeed, such an understanding would aid the treatment of anorexia and bulimia in individuals with low implicit self-esteem – but it may also aid in the treatment of body image and appearance satisfaction.

Narcissistic personality disorder

Narcissistic personality disorder is characterized by a grandiose sense of self-importance, constant need for admiration from others, lack of empathy, and interpersonal exploitativeness that begins by early adulthood (American Psychiatric Association, 2000). Most psychodynamic perspectives on narcissism point to the important role of early relations with attachment figures in the development of the disorder (Cooper, 1986; Kernberg, 1975; Nemiah, 1973; cf. Lasch,

1979). That is, early relationships with parents who are rejecting, neglectful, disapproving, and do not meet the child's needs are internalized into negative feelings about others as well as feelings of inferiority and insecurity (DeHart et al., 2006; Nemiah, 1973). Therefore, a vulnerable self-structure develops, and narcissistic individuals try constantly to compensate for their insecurities by exaggerating their accomplishments, preoccupying themselves with thoughts of success, and seeking excessive admiration from others.

Considerable evidence indicates that narcissism is associated with high explicit self-esteem (e.g., Bosson et al., 2008; Campbell, Rudich, & Sedikides, 2002; Emmons, 1987). However, narcissism is not just extremely high self-esteem. Compared to people with high explicit self-esteem, narcissists self-enhance in less socially acceptable ways (Horvath & Morf, 2010), and they are motivated to display superiority. However, recent research suggests that narcissists are aware that they see themselves more positively than others see them (Carlson, Vazire, & Oltmanns, 2011). Compared to self-ratings, their meta-perceptions (i.e., reflected appraisals, perceptions of how others perceive them) are lower on positive traits. Narcissists also appear to recognize that they possess narcissistic traits.

Clinical conceptions depict narcissistic individuals as demonstrating emotional instability, despite their grandiose sense of self (Kernberg, 1975; Kohut, 1986; Nemiah, 1973). Narcissists' excessively positive self-views are believed to be defensive and mask underlying insecurities (Kernberg, 1975), which is consistent with research and theory on sub-clinical levels of narcissism among young adults who have high explicit and low implicit self-esteem (Brown & Bosson, 2001; Jordan et al., 2003; Kernis, 2003).

Another reason why narcissistic individuals experience emotional instability is that they set excessively high goals for themselves, which they fail to meet (Kernberg, 1975; Kohut, 1986; Lasch, 1979; Nemiah, 1973). In fact, it has been argued that narcissistic individuals may be especially well suited for bureaucratic institutions because of the ambition and confidence they exude (Lasch, 1979). However, their vulnerable self-esteem makes them particularly sensitive to criticism or setbacks, and their awareness of this sensitivity makes it difficult for narcissists to take risks. Excessively high personal goals, an impoverished sense of self, and extreme sensitivity to criticism converge in individuals with pathological narcissism to engender unstable self-esteem and affect (Rhodewalt et al., 1998).

Narcissistic individuals also have impaired interpersonal relationships. They are caught in an approach-avoidance dilemma. On the one hand, they must rely on the admiration of others to combat the negative appraisals they maintain about themselves – appraisals they are unable to regulate (Stolorow, 1986). At the same time, however, they are terrified of becoming emotionally dependent on others, because others are viewed "as without exception undependable" (Lasch, 1979, p. 84). Problems in relying on others make it difficult for the narcissist to form a productive client-therapist relationship (Bromberg, 1986; Cooper, 1986; Lasch, 1979). A major goal in the psychodynamic treatment of narcissistic individuals is to make their unconscious insecurities more introspectively available, so they can be more fully integrated into their conscious beliefs (Kernberg, 1975; Kohut & Wolf, 1986; White, 1986).

Implicit self-esteem and narcissism

As mentioned previously, people with high levels of narcissism have developed fragile self-structures (Bosson et al., 2003; Gregg & Sedikides, 2010; Jordan et al., 2003). Insecure high self-esteem refers to a combination of high explicit self-esteem and low implicit self-esteem. People with insecure high self-esteem scored higher on measures of narcissism and engage in more defensive behaviors than people with secure high (high explicit and high implicit) self-esteem (Campbell, Bosson, Goheen, Lakey, & Kernis, 2007; Jordan et al., 2003). Individuals with insecure high self-esteem also report higher levels of self-esteem instability than those with secure high self-esteem (Zeigler-Hill, 2006). Presumably, negative events activate negative self-evaluations among people with labile self-esteem, although negative events were not examined in this research.

Self-esteem instability (and insecure high self-esteem) is related to increased levels of verbal defensiveness (Kernis, Lakey, & Heppner, 2008), and people with insecure high self-esteem report higher levels of anger suppression behaviors than do those with secure high self-esteem (Schröder-Abé, Rudolf, & Schütz, 2007). People with insecure high self-esteem (compared to secure high) also report more days of impaired health (Schröder-Abé et al., 2007). Overall, insecure high self-esteem is associated with more negative outcomes compared to secure high self-esteem.

Although other studies have found that both explicit and implicit self-esteem have only main-effect relations with narcissism (Gregg & Sedikides, 2010), a recent meta-analysis revealed that implicit self-esteem was positively related to narcissism (Bosson et al., 2008). In addition, narcissists' implicit (e.g., Campbell et al., 2007) and explicit self-evaluations (e.g., Campbell, Brunell, & Finkel, 2006; Campbell, Rudich, & Sedikides, 2002) vary depending on whether they are reporting on agentic (e.g., intelligence, attractiveness) or communal (e.g., warmth, caring) traits (Campbell et al., 2007). Based on these findings, Bosson and colleagues (2008) posited that narcissists may possess deep-seated insecurities about communal traits. Although it appears that both explicit and implicit self-esteem are related to narcissism, the exact nature of that relation is unclear.

Directions for future research

Examining the role of implicit self-esteem in emotional disorders is a relatively new and exciting area of research (see Phillips et al., 2010, for a recent review). The research reviewed above suggests that both explicit and implicit self-esteem may play a role (as both a predictor and a consequence) in psychological disorders. Although the existing research is provocative, there are still many unanswered questions regarding the relation between implicit and explicit self-esteem and emotional disorders.

Many of the cognitive perspectives on psychological disorders we reviewed suggest that early experiences influence explicit and implicit beliefs about the self that serve as vulnerability factors, which in turn interact with negative daily experiences to predict depression (Beck et al., 1979; Phillips et al., 2010; Weich et al., 2009) and eating disorders (Fairburn et al., 2003; Polivy & Herman, 2002). However, most of the research reviewed was cross-sectional and only examined the association between implicit and explicit self-concept vulnerabilities and emotional disorders. A few prospective studies did assess these relations over several months (Haeffel et al., 2007; Steinberg et al., 2007). Previous research has occasionally looked at how explicit cognitive vulnerabilities influence how people respond to daily negative events (Tennen, Affleck, Armeli, & Carney, 2000; Tolpin, Gunthert, Cohen, & O'Neill, 2004). To our knowledge no research has examined how implicit cognitive vulnerabilities interact with daily negative events to predict daily depression or eating disorder symptoms.

Previous research has found that people's implicit self-evaluations appear to be most informative when assessed under conditions of threat or cognitive load (DeHart, Tennen, Armeli, Todd, & Mohr, 2009; Jones et al., 2002; Koole et al., 2001). For example, self-concept threat seems to activate beliefs that are typically not available to conscious reflection (DeHart & Pelham, 2007; Jones et al., 2002). Therefore, we encourage researchers to examine how people's implicit self-esteem is influenced by daily negative events and impacts psychological disorders. Researchers have been using daily diary recording (Stone, Lennox, & Neale, 1985), ecological momentary assessment (Stone & Shiffman, 1994), or experience sampling (Csikszentmihalyi & Larson, 1984) – to capture hypothesized psychological processes in situ. We believe that the inherently idiographic nature of these implicit and explicit if-then contingencies is exceptionally well suited to study through daily process designs.

Cognitive therapy for depression and eating disorders teaches patients to use more adaptive cognitive and behavioral strategies to deal with stressful situations (Beck et al., 1979). For example, cognitive therapy for depression teaches patients to change negative beliefs about the self, changing negative thoughts that are elicited more or less automatically, and engage in more healthy activities (Parrish et al., 2009). Cognitive therapy for eating disorders focuses on bolstering the self-esteem and confidence of patients (Vanderlinden et al., 2009). However, very little research has looked at the influence of these therapeutic techniques on people's overlearned and automatic beliefs about the self.

Finally, daily process methods can provide unique self-esteem-related outcome indicators in studies of psychotherapy's effectiveness. Rather than comparing pre-treatment and post-treatment *levels* of self-esteem as indicators of effective treatment, daily process methods would allow clinical researchers to examine changes in how low self-esteem clients respond to self-threatening information, whether after treatment they are better able to evoke positive memories when they experience negative moods, and if treatment made them more resilient to setbacks in their daily lives (Cohen et al., 2008; Parrish et al., 2009). These are the very processes described by traditional clinical theory and current social psychological models of self-esteem.

References

Ackard, D. M., Fulkerson, J. A., & Neumark-Sztainer, D. (2011). Psychological and behavioral risk profiles as they relate to eating disorder diagnoses as symptomatology among a school-based sample of youth. *International Journal of Eating Disorders, 44,* 440–446.

American Psychiatric Association. (2000). *Diagnostic and statistical manual of mental disorders* (4th edn, Text Revision). Washington, DC: American Psychiatric Association.

Arieti, S., & Bemporad, J. (1978). *Severe and mild depression: The psychotherapeutic approach.* New York, NY: Basic Books.

Baccus, J. R., Baldwin, M. W., & Packer, D. J. (2004). Increasing implicit self-esteem through classical conditioning. *Psychological Science, 15,* 498–502.

Bandura, A. (1997). Self-efficacy: The exercise of control. New York, NY: W. H. Freeman and Company.

Bardone, A. M., Vohs, K. D., Abramson, L. Y., Heatherton, T. F., & Joiner, T. E., Jr. (2000). The confluence of perfectionism, body dissatisfaction, and low self-esteem predicts bulimic symptoms: Clinical implications. *Behavior Therapy, 31,* 265–280.

Barker, E. T., & Bornstein, M. H. (2010). Global self-esteem, appearance satisfaction, and self-reported dieting in early adolescence. *Journal of Early Adolescence, 30,* 205–224.

Bartholomew, K. (1990). Avoidance of intimacy: An attachment perspective. *Journal of Social and Personal Relationships, 7,* 147–178.

Basch, M. F. (1975). Toward a theory that encompasses depression: A revision of existing causal hypotheses in psychoanalysis. In E. J. Anthony & T. Benedek (eds.), *Depression and human existence* (pp. 485–515). Boston, MA: Little, Brown and Company.

Baumeister, R. F., & Heatherton, T. F. (1996). Self-regulation failure: An overview. *Psychological Inquiry, 7,* 1–15.

Baumrind, D. (1971). Current patterns of parental authority. *Developmental Psychology Monographs, 4,* 1–103.

Beck, A. T., Rush, A. J., Shaw, B. F., & Emery, G. (1979). *Cognitive therapy of depression.* New York, NY: Guilford Press.

Beck, A. T., Steer, R. A., & Brown, G. K. (1996). *Manual for the Beck Depression Inventory II.* San Antonio, TX: Psychological Corporation.

Bednar, R. L., Wells, M. G., & Peterson, S. R. (1989*). Self-esteem: Paradoxes and innovations in clinical theory and practice.* Washington, DC: American Psychological Association.

Beevers, C. G. (2005). Cognitive vulnerability to depression: A dual process model. *Clinical Psychology Review, 25,* 975–1002.

Bos, A. E. R., Huijding, J., Muris, P., Vogel, L. R. R., & Biesheuvel, J. (2010). Global, contingent and implicit self-esteem and psychopathological symptoms in adolescents. *Personality and Individual Differences, 48,* 311–316.

Bosson, J. K., Brown, R. P., Zeigler-Hill, V., & Swann, W. B. (2003). Self-enhancement tendencies among people with high explicit self-esteem: The moderating role of implicit self-esteem. *Self and Identity, 2*, 169–187.

Bosson, J. K., Lakey, C. E., Campbell, K. W., Zeigler-Hill, V., Jordan, C. H., & Kernis, M. H. (2008). Untangling the links between narcissism and self-esteem: A theoretical and empirical review. *Social and Personality Psychology Compass, 2/3*, 1415–1439.

Bosson, J. K., Swann, W. B., Jr, & Pennebaker, J. W. (2000). Stalking the perfect measure of implicit self-esteem: The blind men and the elephant revisited*. Journal of Personality and Social Psychology, 79*, 631–643.

Bowlby, J. (1982). *Attachment and loss. Vol. 1: Attachment.* London: Hogarth Press.

Bromberg, P. M. (1986). The mirror and the mask: On narcissism and psychoanalytic growth. In A. P. Morrison (ed.), *Essential papers on narcissism* (pp. 420–463). New York, NY: New York University Press.

Brown, G. W., & Harris, T. (1978). *Social origins of depression: A study of psychiatric disorder in women.* New York, NY: Free Press.

Brown, G. W., & Harris, T. (1989). Depression. In G. W. Brown & T. O Harris (eds.), *Life events and illness* (pp. 49–89). New York, NY: Guilford Press.

Brown, J. D., & McGill, K. L. (1989). The cost of good fortune: When positive life events produce negative health consequences. *Journal of Personality and Social Psychology, 57*, 1103–1110.

Brown, R. P., & Bosson, J. K. (2001). Narcissus meets Sisyphus: Self-love, self-loathing, and the never-ending pursuit of self-worth. *Psychological Inquiry, 12*, 210–213.

Butler, A. C., Hokanson, J. E., & Flynn, H. A. (1994). A comparison of self-esteem lability and low trait self-esteem as vulnerability factors for depression. *Journal of Personality and Social Psychology, 66*, 166–177.

Campbell, W. K., Bosson, J. K., Goheen, T. W., Lakey, C. E., & Kernis, M. H. (2007). Do narcissists dislike themselves "Deep down inside"? *Psychological Science, 18*, 227–229.

Campbell, W. K., Brunell, A. B., & Finkel, E. J. (2006). Narcissism, interpersonal self-regulation, and romantic relationships: An agency model approach. In K. D. Vohs & E. J. Finkel (eds.), *Self and relationships: Connecting intrapersonal and interpersonal processes* (pp. 57–83). New York, NY: Guilford Press.

Campbell, W. K., Rudich, E. A., & Sedikides, C. (2002). Narcissism, self-esteem, and the positivity of self-views: Two portraits of self-love. *Personality and Social Psychological Bulletin, 28*, 358–368.

Carlson, E. N., Vazire, S., & Oltmanns, T. F. (2011). You probably think this paper's about you: Narcissists' perceptions of their personality and reputation. *Journal of Personality and Social Psychology, 101*, 185–201.

Cockerham, E., Stopa, L., Bell, L., & Gregg, A. (2009). Implicit self-esteem in bulimia nervosa. *Journal of Behavior Therapy and Experimental Psychiatry, 40*, 265–273.

Cohen, L., Gunthert, K., Butler, A., Parrish, P., Wenze, S., & Beck, J. (2008). Negative affective spillover from daily events predicts early response to cognitive therapy for depression. *Journal of Consulting and Clinical Psychology, 76*, 955–965.

Cooley, C. H. (1902). *Human nature and the social order.* New York, NY: Schocken.

Cooper, A. M. (1986). Narcissism. In A. P. Morrison (ed.), *Essential papers on narcissism* (pp. 111–141). New York, NY: New York University Press.

Crocker, J., & Major, B. (1989). Social stigma and self-esteem: The self-protective properties of stigma. *Psychological Review, 96*, 608–630.

Csikszentmihalyi, M., & Larson, R. (1984). *Being adolescent: Conflict and growth in the teenage years.* New York, NY: Basic Books.

Davila, J., Bradbury, T. N., Cohan, C. L., & Tochluk, S. (1997). Marital functioning and depressive symptoms: Evidence for a stress generation model. *Journal of Personality and Social Psychology, 73*, 849–861.

DeHart, T., & Pelham, B. W. (2007). Fluctuations in state implicit self-esteem in response to daily negative events. *Journal of Experimental Social Psychology, 43*, 157–165.

DeHart, T., & Tennen, H. (2006). Self-esteem in therapeutic settings and emotional disorders. In Michael Kernis (ed.), *Self-esteem: Issues and answers* (pp. 316–325). New York, NY: Psychology Press.

DeHart, T., Pelham, B. W., Fiedorowicz, L., Carvallo, M., & Gabriel, S. (2011). Including others in the implicit self: Implicit evaluation of significant others. *Self and Identity, 10*, 127–135.

DeHart, T., Pelham, B. W., & Tennen, H. (2006). What lies beneath: Parenting style and implicit self-esteem. *Journal of Experimental Social Psychology, 42*, 1–17.

DeHart, T., Tennen, H., Armeli, S., Todd, M., & Mohr, C. (2009). A diary study of implicit self-esteem, interpersonal interactions, and alcohol consumption in college students. *Journal of Experimental Social Psychology, 45*, 720–730.

de Jong, P. J. (2002). Implicit self-esteem and social anxiety: Differential self-favouring effects in high and low anxious individuals. *Behaviour Research and Therapy, 40*, 501–508.

De Raedt, R., Schacht, R., Franck, E., & De Houwer, J. (2006). Self-esteem and depression revisited: Implicit positive self-esteem in depressed patients? *Behaviour Research and Therapy, 44*, 1017–1028.

Dijksterhuis, A. (2004). I like myself but I don't know why: Enhancing implicit self-esteem by subliminal evaluative conditioning. *Journal of Personality and Social Psychology, 86*, 345–355.

Emmons, R. A. (1987). Narcissism: Theory and measurement. *Journal of Personality and Social Psychology, 52*, 11–17.

Epstein, S. (1994). Integration of the cognitive and the psychodynamic unconscious. *American Psychologist, 49*, 709–724.

Fairburn, C. G., Cooper, Z. & Shafran, R. (2003). Cognitive behaviour therapy for eating disorders: A "transdiagnostic" theory and treatment. *Behavior Research and Therapy, 41*, 509–528.

Fincham, F. D., Beach, S. R., Harold, G. T., & Osborne, L. N. (1997). Marital satisfaction and depression: Different causal relationships for men and women? *Psychological Science, 8*, 351–357.

Franck. E., De Raedt, R., & De Houwer, J. (2007). Implicit but not explicit self-esteem predicts future depressive symptomatology. *Behaviour Research and Therapy, 45*, 2448–2455.

Franck. E., De Raedt, R., & De Houwer, J. (2008). Activation of latent negative self-schemas as a cognitive vulnerability factor in depression: The potential role of implicit self-esteem. *Cognition and Emotion, 22*, 1588–1599.

Franck, E., De Raedt, R., Dereu, M., & Van den Abbeele, D. (2007). Implicit and explicit self-esteem in currently depressed individuals with and without suicidal ideation. *Journal of Behavior Therapy and Experimental Psychiatry, 38*, 75–85.

Friedman, M. A., & Whisman, M. A. (2004). Implicit cognition and the maintenance and treatment of major depression. *Cognitive and Behavioral Practice, 11*, 168–177.

Gawronski, B., & Bodenhausen, G. V. (2007). Unraveling the processes underlying evaluation: Attitudes from the perspective of the APE model. *Social Cognition, 5*, 687–717.

Gemar, M. C., Segal, Z. V., Sagrati, S., & Kennedy, S. J. (2001). Mood-inducted changes in the Implicit Association Test in recovered depressed patients. *Journal of Abnormal Psychology, 110*, 282–289.

Gilbert, D. T., & Silvera, D. H. (1996). Overhelping. *Journal of Personality and Social Psychology, 70*, 678–690.

Gilboa, E., Roberts, J. E., & Gotlib, I. H. (1997). The effects of induced and naturally occurring dysphoric mood on biases in self-evaluation and memory. *Cognition and Emotion, 11*, 65–82.

Greenwald, A. G., & Banaji, M. R. (1995). Implicit social cognition: Attitudes, self-esteem, and stereotypes. *Psychological Review, 102*, 4–27.

Greenwald, A. G., & Farnham, S. D. (2000). Using the implicit association test to measure self-esteem and self-concept. *Journal of Personality and Social Psychology, 79*, 1022–1038.

Gregg, A. P., & Sedikides, C. (2010). Narcissistic fragility: Rethinking its links to explicit and implicit self-esteem. *Self and Identity, 9*, 142–161.

Gregg, A. P., Seibt, B., & Banaji, M. R. (2006). Easier said than undone: Asymmetry in the malleability of implicit preferences. *Journal of Personality and Social Psychology, 90*, 1–20.

Grover, V. P., Keel, P. K., & Mitchell, J. P. (2003). Gender differences in implicit weight identity. *International Journal of Eating Disorders, 34*, 125–135.

Haeffel, G. J., Abramson, L. Y., Brazy, P. C., Shah, J. Y., Teachman, B. A., & Nosek, B. A. (2007). Explicit and implicit cognition: A preliminary test of a dual-process theory of cognitive vulnerability to depression. *Behaviour Research and Therapy, 45*, 1155–1167.

Harter, S. (1993). Causes and consequences of low self-esteem in children and adolescents. In R. Baumeister (ed.), *Self-esteem: The puzzle of low self-regard* (pp. 87–111). New York, NY: Plenum Press.

Heatherton, T. F., & Baumeister, R. F. (1991). Binge eating as escape from self-awareness. *Psychological Bulletin, 110*, 86–108.

Hetts, J. J., Sakuma, M., & Pelham, B. W. (1999). Two roads to positive regard: Implicit and explicit self-evaluation and culture. *Journal of Experimental Social Psychology, 35*, 512–559.

Hoffmeister K., Teige-Mocigemba, S., Blechert, J., Klauer, K. C., & Tuschen-Caffier, B. (2010). Is implicit self-esteem linked to shape and weight concerns in restrained and unrestrained eaters? *Journal of Behavior Therapy and Experimental Psychiatry, 41*, 31–38.

Horton, R. S., Bleau, G., & Drwecki, B. (2006). Parenting narcissus: What are the links between parenting and narcissism? *Journal of Personality, 74*, 345–376.

Horvath, S., & Morf, C. C. (2010). To be grandiose or to not be worthless: Different routes to self-enhancement for narcissism and self-esteem. *Journal of Research and Personality, 44*, 585–592.

Jacobi, C., Hayward, C., de Zwaan, M., Kraemer, H. C., & Agras, W. S. (2004). Coming to terms with risk factors for eating disorders: Application of risk terminology and suggestions for a general taxonomy. *Psychological Bulletin, 130*, 19–65.

Jacobi, C., Paul, T., de Zwaan, M., Nutzinger, D. O., & Dahme, B. (2004). Specificity of self-concept disturbances in eating disorders. *International Journal of Eating Disorders, 35*, 204–210.

Johnson, C. (ed.) (1991). *Psychodynamic treatment of anorexia nervosa and bulimia* (pp. 3–33). New York, NY: Guilford Press.

Joiner, T. E. (2000). Depression's vicious scree: Self-propagating and erosive processes in depression. *Clinical Psychology: Science and Practice, 7*, 203–218.

Jones, J. T., Pelham, B. W., Mirenberg, M. C., & Hetts, J. J. (2002). Name letter preferences are not merely mere exposure: Implicit egotism as self-regulation. *Journal of Experimental Social Psychology, 38*, 170–177.

Jordan, C. H., Spencer, S. J., Zanna, M. P., Hoshino-Browne, E., & Correll, J. (2003). Secure and defensive high self-esteem. *Journal of Personality and Social Psychology, 85*, 969–978.

Karpinski, A., Steinberg, J. A., Bersek, B., & Alloy, L. B. (2007). The Breadth-Based Adjective Rating Task (BART) as an indirect measure of self-esteem. *Social Cognition, 25*, 778–818.

Kenny, D. A. (1994). *Interpersonal perception: A social relations analysis*. New York, NY: Guilford Press.

Kernberg, O. F. (1975). *Borderline conditions and pathological narcissism*. New York, NY: Jason Aronson, Inc.

Kernis, M. H. (2003). Toward a conceptualization of optimal self-esteem. *Psychological Inquiry, 14*, 1–26.

Kernis, M. H. (2005). Measuring self-esteem in context: The importance of stability of self-esteem in psychological functioning. *Journal of Personality, 73*, 1569–1606.

Kernis, M. H., Brown, A. C., & Brody, G. H. (2000). Fragile self-esteem in children and its associations with perceived patterns of parent-child communication. *Journal of Personality, 68*, 225–252.

Kernis, M. H., Grannemann, B. D., & Mathis, L. C. (1991). Stability of self-esteem as a moderator of the relation between level of self-esteem and depression. *Journal of Personality and Social Psychology, 61*, 80–84.

Kernis, M. H., Lakey, C. E., & Heppner, W. L. (2008). Secure versus fragile high self-esteem as a predictor of verbal defensiveness: Converging findings across three different markers. *Journal of Personality, 76*, 477–512.

Kim, S., Thibodeau, R., & Jorgensen, R. S. (2011). Shame, guilt, and depressive symptoms: A meta-analytic review. *Psychological Bulletin, 137*, 68–96.

Kinderman, P. (1994). Attentional bias, persecutory delusions and the self-concept. *British Journal of Medical Psychology, 67*, 53–66.

Kitayama, S., & Karasawa, M. (1997). Implicit self-esteem in Japan: Name letters and birthday numbers. *Personality and Social Psychology Bulletin, 23*, 736–742.

Kohut, H. (1986). Forms and transformations of narcissism. In A. P. Morrison (ed.), *Essential papers on narcissism* (pp. 60–68). New York, NY: New York University Press.

Kohut, H., & Wolf, E. S. (1986). The disorders of the self and their treatment: An outline. In A. P. Morrison (ed.), *Essential papers on narcissism* (pp. 175–197). New York, NY: New York University Press.

Koole, S. L., & DeHart, T. (2007). Self-affection without self-reflection: Origins, models, and consequences of implicit self-esteem. In C. Sedikides & S. Spencer (eds.), *The self in social psychology* (pp. 36–86). New York, NY: Psychology Press.

Koole, S. L., Dijksterhuis, A., & van Knippenberg, A. (2001). What's in a name: Implicit self-esteem and the automatic self. *Journal of Personality and Social Psychology, 80*, 669–685.

Lasch, C. (1979). *The culture of narcissism: American life in an age of diminishing expectations*. New York, NY: W. W. Norton & Company, Inc.

Leary. M. R. (2005). Sociometer theory and the pursuit of relational value: Getting to the root of self-esteem. *European Review of Social Psychology, 16*, 75–111.

Leary, M. R., Tambor, E. S., Terdal, S. K., & Downs, D. L. (1995). Self-esteem as an interpersonal monitor: The sociometer hypothesis. *Journal of Personality and Social Psychology, 68*, 518–530.

Maddux, J. E. (1995). Self-efficacy theory: An introduction. In J. E. Maddux (ed.), *Self-efficacy, adaptation, and adjustment* (pp. 3–27). New York, NY: Plenum Press.

Mead, G. H. (1934). *Mind, self, and society*. Chicago, IL: University of Chicago Press.

Nemiah, J. C. (1973). *Foundations of psychopathology*. New York, NY: Jason Aronson, Inc.

Nuttin, J. M. (1987). Affective consequences of mere ownership: The name letter effect in twelve European languages. *European Journal of Social Psychology, 17*, 381–402.

O'Conner, D. B., Hurling, R., Hendrickx, H., Osborne, G., Hall, J., Walklet, E., et al. (2011). Effects of written emotional disclosure on implicit self-esteem and body image. *British Journal of Health Psychology, 16*, 488–501.

Olson, M. A., & Fazio, R. H. (2009). Implicit and explicit measures of attitudes: The perspective of the MODE model. In R. E. Petty, R. H. Fazio, and P. Briñol (eds.), *Insights from the new implicit measures* (pp. 19–63). New York, NY: Psychology Press.

Olson, M. A., Fazio, R. H., & Hermann, A. D. (2007). Reporting tendencies underlie discrepancies between implicit and explicit measures of self-esteem. *Psychological Science, 18*, 287–291.

Otway, L. J., & Vignoles, V. L. (2006). Narcissism and childhood recollections: A quantitative test of psychoanalytic predictions. *Personality and Social Psychology Bulletin, 32*, 104–116.

Parker, G., Tupling, H., & Brown, L. B. (1979) A parental bonding instrument. *British Journal of Medical Psychology, 52*, 1–10.

Parrish, B., Cohen, L., Gunthert, K., Butler, A., Laurenceau, J.-P., & Beck, J. (2009). Effects of cognitive therapy for depression on daily stress-related variables. *Behaviour Research and Therapy, 47*, 444–448.

Pavlove, B., Uher, R., Dennington, L., Wright, K., & Donaldson, C. (2011). Reactivity of affect and self-esteem during remission in bipolar affective disorder: An experimental investigation. *Journal of Affective Disorders, 134*, 102–111.

Pelham, B. W., Koole, S. L., Hardin, C. D., Hetts, J. J., Seah, E., & DeHart, T. (2005). Gender moderates the relation between implicit and explicit self-esteem. *Journal of Experimental Social Psychology, 41*, 84–89.

Phillips, W. J., Hine, D. W., & Thorsteinsson, E. B. (2010). Implicit cognition and depression: A meta-analysis. *Clinical Psychology Review, 30*, 691–709.

Polivy, J., & Herman, C. P. (2002). Causes of eating disorders. *Annual Review of Psychology, 53*, 187–213.

Pomerantz, E. M., & Newman, L. S. (2000). Looking in on the children: Using developmental psychology as a tool for hypothesis testing and model building in social psychology. *Personality and Social Psychology Review, 4*, 300–316.

Ramsey, A., Watson, P. J., Biderman, M. D., & Reeves, A. L. (1996). Self-reported narcissism and perceived parental permissiveness and authoritarianism. *Journal of Genetic Psychology, 157*, 227–238.

Rhodewalt, F., Madrian, J. C., & Cheney, S. (1998). Narcissism, self-knowledge, organization, and emotional reactivity: The effect of daily experience on self-esteem and affect. *Journal of Personality & Social Psychology, 24*, 75–87.

Risch, A. K., Buba, A., Birk, U., Morina, N., Steffens, M. C., & Stangier, U. (2010). Implicit self-esteem in recurrently depressed patients. *Journal of Behavior Therapy and Experimental Psychiatry, 41*, 199–206.

Roberts, J. E., & Monroe, S. M. (1992). Vulnerable self-esteem and depressive symptoms: Prospective findings comparing three alternative conceptualizations. *Journal of Personality and Social Psychology, 62*, 804–812.

Roberts, J. E., & Monroe, S. M. (1994). A multidimensional model of self-esteem in depression. *Clinical Psychology Review, 14*, 161–181.

Rosenberg, M. (1965). *Society and the adolescent self-image.* Princeton, NJ: Princeton University Press.

Rudman, L. A., Phelan, J. E., & Heppen, J. B. (2007). Developmental sources of implicit attitudes. *Personality and Social Psychology Bulletin, 33*, 1700–1713.

Rudolph, A., Schröder-Abé, M., Schütz, A., Gregg, A. P., & Sedikides, C. (2008). Through a glass, less darkly? Reassessing convergent and discriminant validity in measures of implicit self-esteem. *European Journal of Psychological Assessment, 24*, 273–281.

Schröder-Abé, M., Rudolph, A., & Schütz, A. (2007). High implicit self-esteem is not necessarily advantageous: Discrepancies between explicit and implicit self-esteem and their relationship with anger expression and psychological health. *European Journal of Personality, 21*, 319–339.

Segal, Z. V., Truchon, C., Gemar, M., Guirguis, M., & Horowitz, L. M. (1995). A priming methodology for studying self-representation in major depressive disorder. *Journal of Abnormal Psychology, 104*, 205–213.

Sheppes, G., Meiran, N., Gilboa-Schechtman, E., & Shahar, G. (2008). Cognitive mechanisms underlying implicit negative self-concept in dysphoria. *Emotion, 8*, 386–394.

Shimizu, M., & Pelham, B. W. (2004). The unconscious cost of good fortune: Implicit and explicit self-esteem, positive life events, and health. *Health Psychology, 23*, 101–105.

Shrauger, S. J., & Schoeneman, T. J. (1979). Symbolic interactionist view of self-concept: Through the looking glass darkly. *Psychological Bulletin, 86*, 549–573.

Steinberg, J. A., Karpinski, A., & Alloy, L. B. (2007). The exploration of implicit aspects of self-esteem in vulnerability – stress models of depression. *Self and Identity, 6* (2–3), 101–117.

Stice, E. (2002). Risk and maintenance factors for eating pathology: A meta-analytic review. *Psychological Bulletin, 128*, 825–848.

Stolorow, R. D. (1986). Toward a functional definition of narcissism. In A. P. Morrison (ed.), *Essential papers on narcissism* (pp. 198–208). New York, NY: New York University Press.

Stone, A. A., Lennox, S., & Neale, J. M. (1985). Daily coping and alcohol use in a sample of community adults. In S. Shiffman & T. A. Wills (eds.), *Coping and substance abuse* (pp. 199–220). New York, NY: Academic Press.

Stone, A. A., & Shiffman, S. (1994). Ecological momentary assessment (EMA) in behavioral medicine. *Annals of Behavioral Medicine, 16*, 199–202.

Strack, F., & Deutsch, R. (2004). Reflective and impulsive determinants of social behavior. *Personality and Social Psychology Review, 8*, 220–247.

Sugarman, A. (1991). Bulimia: A displacement from psychological self to body self. In C. Johnson (ed.), *Psychodynamic treatment of anorexia nervosa and bulimia* (pp. 3–33). New York, NY: Guilford Press.

Tennen, H., Affleck, G., Armeli, S., & Carney, M. A. (2000). A daily process approach to coping: Linking theory, research, and practice. *American Psychologist, 55*, 626–636.

Tolpin, L. H., Gunthert, K. C., Cohen, L. H., & O'Neill, S. C. (2004). Borderline personality features and instability of daily negative affect and self-esteem. *Journal of Personality, 72*, 111–137.

Tylka, T. L., & Sabik, N. J. (2010). Integrating social comparison theory and self-esteem within objectification theory to predict women's disordered eating. *Sex Roles, 63,* 18–31.

Vanderlinden, J., Kamphuis, J. H., Slagmolen, D., Wigboldus, D., Pieters, G., & Probst, M. (2009). Be kind to your eating disorder patients: The impact of positive and negative feedback on the explicit and implicit self-esteem of female patients with eating disorders. *Eating and Weight Disorders, 14,* 237–242.

Wagner, S., Halmi, K. A., & Maguire, T. V. (1987). The sense of personal ineffectiveness in patients with eating disorders: One construct or several? *International Journal of Eating Disorders, 6,* 495–505.

Waschull, S. B., & Kernis, M. H. (1996). Level and stability of self-esteem as predictors of children's intrinsic motivation and reasons for anger. *Personality and Social Psychology Bulletin, 22,* 4–13.

Watson, P. J., Little, T., & Biderman, M. D. (1992). Narcissism and parenting styles. *Psychoanalytic Psychology, 9,* 231–244.

Weich, S., Patterson, J., Shaw, R., & Stewart-Brown, S. (2009). Family relationships in childhood and common psychiatric disorders in later life: Systematic review of prospective studies. *British Journal of Psychiatry, 194,* 392–398.

White, M. T. (1986). Self relations, object relations, and pathological narcissism. In A. P. Morrison (ed.), *Essential papers on narcissism* (pp. 143–174). New York, NY: New York University Press.

Wilson, A. E., Smith, M. D., Ross, H. S., & Ross, M. (2004). Young children's personal accounts of their sibling disputes. *Merrill-Palmer Quarterly, 50,* 39–60.

World Health Organization. (2001). *World health report 2001. Mental health: New understanding, new hope.* Geneva: World Health Organization.

Zeigler-Hill, V. (2006). Discrepancies between implicit and explicit self-esteem: Implications for narcissism and self-esteem instability. *Journal of Personality, 74,* 119–144.

7 An existential perspective on the need for self-esteem

Tom Pyszczynski and Pelin Kesebir

It is a universally acknowledged truth that people want to feel good about themselves. This desire plays a fundamental role in our lives, affecting virtually everything we do. Sometimes even the distortion of reality, leading to an inaccurate perception of ourselves and others, is not too steep a price to pay to maintain a positive view of ourselves. In this chapter, we adopt an existential perspective to address some basic questions about the self-esteem motive: What is self-esteem? Why do people need it? How do they get it, lose it, and maintain it? And what role does it play in adaptive goal-directed behavior, psychological dysfunction, and the maximization of one's capacities?

What is self-esteem?

The nature and function of self-esteem is one of psychology's oldest and most studied topics, yet it remains highly controversial. In the first ever reference to the topic, William James conceived of self-esteem as a "certain average tone of self-feeling which each one of us carries about with him" (James, 1890/1950, p. 306). Well over a century after James, the field has converged on defining self-esteem as an affectively laden global evaluation of the self (Gecas, 1982; Leary & McDonald, 2003; Rosenberg, Schooler, Schoenbach, & Rosenberg, 1995). Despite conflicting views of its function, antecedents, and consequences, there is broad consensus that self-esteem is an orientation toward the self, a feeling born from the *I*'s evaluation of the *me*, a general sense of satisfaction and happiness with what one is, does, and has. Psychologists also generally agree that self-esteem has two, albeit intertwined, dimensions – one based on a sense of competence, power, and efficacy, and one based on a sense of virtue and moral worth (Gecas, 1982; Mruk, 2006; Tafarodi & Swann, 1995). The first dimension (*self-competence*) involves evaluation of the self as globally strong or weak, whereas the second dimension (*self-liking*) involves evaluation of the self as globally acceptable or unacceptable (Tafarodi & Swann, 1995). Self-esteem results from the extent of concordance between one's ideal self and real self along both of these dimensions (James, 1890/1950).

Self-esteem is a critical facet of the self-system and has immense emotional impact and motivational power. Of all the judgments that people pass in life, few have consequences as broad as the ones they pass on themselves: "No significant aspect of our thinking, motivation, feelings, or behavior is unaffected by our self-evaluation," notes Nathaniel Branden (1985, p. xi). Epstein similarly argues that if one's level of self-esteem is altered it affects the entire self-system (Epstein, 1980, p. 106). How we evaluate ourselves has a powerful impact on our emotional well-being, how we relate to others and the world around us, what we approach and avoid, and what we make out of our lives. In support of this view, empirical research reveals that a wide range of desirable life outcomes, including mental health and happiness, quality of personal relationships, and success and achievement, are associated with high levels of self-esteem (Leary & MacDonald, 2003; Mruk, 2006; Trzesniewski et al., 2006). But why is self-esteem of such critical importance? What functions does it serve that make people seek it so desperately?

Why do we need self-esteem?

Unlike other animals, human beings are not only conscious but also self-conscious. Though other animals think, feel, and behave, they do not contemplate the fact that they are thinking, feeling, and behaving. The human capacity for self-awareness is central to the processes through which members of our species control and regulate their behavior. Life is weaved from an incessant thread of choices, decisions, and possible courses of action. Stepping back from our ongoing stream of behavior, turning attention inward, and comparing our current state with our goals and standards makes it possible for us to stay "on track" by adjusting our behavior, and even changing the goals we are pursuing, when circumstances call for it. The twin human capacities for self-consciousness and self-evaluation substantially facilitate goal attainment and probably evolved because they helped our ancestors navigate the material and social world more flexibly, and thus effectively, ultimately increasing their chances of surviving, reproducing, and passing on their genes (Becker, 1971; Greenberg, Pyszczynski, & Solomon, 1986).

Carver and Scheier (1981, 2002) posit that all self-regulating systems operate by comparing their current state with an ideal reference value, noting any discrepancies that exist, and then taking action to reduce these discrepancies (see Trope & Lieberman, 2010, or Vallacher & Wegner, 1987, for related conceptualizations). The standards against which one's current state is compared are organized hierarchically with goal-directed behavior (e.g., studying for an exam) at the intermediate levels, the specific actions through which these behaviors are enacted (e.g., reading over one's notes) at the lower or more concrete levels, and the goals that these behaviors seek to achieve (e.g., earning a good grade) at the higher or more abstract levels. The lower levels of the hierarchy consist of increasingly concrete actions and components of actions that explain *how* behavior is enacted (e.g., turning pages, moving one's hands, changing levels of muscle tension). The higher levels of the hierarchy consist of increasingly abstract goals and aspirations that explain *why* the behavior is performed (e.g., getting a college degree, pursuing a career, living a good life). Carver and Scheier argued that viewing oneself as a good person – in other words, having self-esteem – is the superordinate goal toward which most other goals in life are oriented. In other words, most of the more specific goals that people seek over the course of their lives are ultimately oriented toward being a valuable person: having self-esteem. Only animals with self-consciousness – the ability to direct attention inward and reflect on their thoughts, feelings, and behaviors – could turn themselves and their existence into objects of global evaluation and then orient themselves toward pursuing goals that continually document their value (Leary, 2004). But why is it so important to feel valuable?

Although self-consciousness is immensely advantageous, it comes with some major costs. Perhaps the most onerous one is that it leads us to realize that, like all other living things, we will die someday. This is the starting point of terror management theory (TMT; see Greenberg, Pyszczynski, & Solomon, 1986), a broad theory of diverse aspects of human social behavior that was initially developed to explain why people need self-esteem. Inspired by cultural anthropologist Ernest Becker's (e.g., 1971, 1973, 1975) attempts to integrate the various human science disciplines, TMT posits that awareness of the inevitability of death in an animal that has evolved to prioritize survival creates the potential for paralyzing terror. This terror would seriously undermine the effective pursuit of goal-directed behavior necessary for survival, unless effectively managed. Consequently, this potential for terror put a "press" on the explanations for life and the prescriptions for how to live it that early humans were inventing. Beliefs and values that were useful in managing terror were especially appealing and likely to be shared with others, and eventually became part of the meaning systems that people used to organize and direct their lives. People manage the potential for terror that results from their awareness of the inevitability of death by construing themselves as valuable participants in a meaningful and never-ending existence. This is accomplished by: (1) maintaining faith in one's own individualized version of the cultural worldview, which is abstracted from one's experiences interacting with diverse elements of the culture in which one lives; and (2) attaining self-esteem by living up to the standards of value that are part of one's cultural worldview.

From this perspective, self-esteem and culture are humanly created shields against existential anxiety, with self-esteem being heavily dependent on the cultural worldview from which it is derived. What provides self-esteem within one cultural context might be utterly irrelevant or even cause shame within another. For example, although most college students get enormous boosts to self-esteem when they get high scores on college tests, this might be a meaningless accomplishment for a Tibetan monk or a source of shame for a gang member who views such efforts as "selling out to the man." Regardless of how it is obtained, anxiety is minimized when self-esteem is strong; but when self-esteem is threatened, anxiety leaks through and instigates behavior to shore up the damaged shield, usually by striving to reassert one's value or find an excuse for one's shortcomings. Because it is a cultural creation, self-esteem requires that one not only live up to the values that are part of one's culture but also believe in the absolute validity of the worldview from which those standards come. If the worldview from which one's self-esteem is derived is incorrect, it is impossible to derive value from meeting that culture's standards.

Since its inception in the mid-1980s, a large body of research has provided empirical support for the central tenets of TMT regarding the anxiety-buffering functions of self-esteem and cultural worldviews (see Greenberg, Solomon, & Arndt, 2008; Kesebir & Pyszczynski, 2012, for recent reviews). For present purposes, we provide only a brief overview of some of the highlights of the research documenting the terror management function of self-esteem (see Pyszczynski, Greenberg, Solomon, Arndt, & Schimel, 2004, for a more thorough review of research on TMT and self-esteem). The earliest research on these issues established that, as the theory predicts, self-esteem provides a cushion against the fear of death. In the first test of this anxiety-buffer hypothesis, Greenberg and colleagues (1992) demonstrated that raising participants' self-esteem through bogus positive feedback decreased self-reported anxiety in response to vivid images of death and lowered the physiological arousal of participants awaiting painful electric shocks. Subsequent studies showed that both experimentally enhanced and dispositionally high self-esteem are associated with lower levels of worldview defense and death-thought accessibility in response to reminders of one's mortality (Harmon-Jones et al., 1997), as well as diminished defensive distortions aimed at denying vulnerability to death (Greenberg et al., 1993). More recently, Schmeichel and colleagues (2009) demonstrated that this anxiety-buffering capacity stems more from implicit than explicit self-esteem. Implicit self-esteem is a global evaluation of the self that is less filtered, less susceptible to self-presentational biases and impression management attempts, one "that people are unable or unwilling to report" (Buhrmester et al., 2011, p. 366). To the extent that implicit self-esteem is a more accurate reflection of people's affective response to self, it makes good sense that it would be a better predictor of how people will respond when mortality thoughts are salient.

A second wave of research on the existential functions of self-esteem tested the hypothesis that mortality reminders would increase people's striving for self-esteem. If self-esteem is a balm against death anxiety, as the theory posits, then death thoughts would intensify the craving for it. Ample evidence supports this hypothesis. For example, studies reveal that death reminders magnify self-serving biases in the form of internal, stable, and global attributions for positive outcomes and external, unstable, and specific attributions for negative outcomes (Mikulincer & Florian, 2002). Along similar lines, Cox and Arndt (in press) found that after mortality reminders, people were more likely to exaggerate how positively their romantic partners perceive them, as a way to enhance their own self-esteem. Consistent with the idea that self-esteem depends on faith in one's worldview, Landau, Greenberg, and Sullivan (2009) documented that the tendency to resort to self-enhancement as a way to manage death anxiety takes a backseat if the self-enhancement has negative connotations for significant elements of one's cultural worldview. For example, participants self-enhanced less after mortality salience if doing so suggested that they viewed themselves more positively than their admired cultural icons. This is consonant with the TMT proposition that people attain symbolic immortality by means of their association with worldviews and institutions larger than themselves – because people are cognizant that they will eventually perish, regardless of how great or unique they are personally, they must believe that the grander culture and its worldview will endure.

Mortality salience also amplifies people's striving to demonstrate their prowess in domains that are important to them. For instance, Taubman Ben-Ari, Florian, and Mikulincer (1999) found that Israeli soldiers whose self-esteem contingencies included their driving ability engaged in more reckless driving following mortality reminders. Similarly, heightened mortality awareness increased identification with one's body and one's interest in sex among people with high, but not low, body self-esteem (Goldenberg, McCoy, Pyszczynski, Greenberg, & Solomon, 2000); it improved strength performance among individuals who are invested, but not for those not invested, in strength training (Peters, Greenberg, & Williams, 2005); and led to greater environmental concern for those who acquire self-esteem from environmental activism but not for those who do not (Vess & Arndt, 2008).

Other research has shown that mortality salience induces people to distance themselves from identities with negative implications for their self-esteem. For example, participants reminded of mortality exhibit reduced identification with their college football team after the team's loss (Dechesne, Greenberg, Arndt, & Schimel, 2000); in a related vein, Mexican-American participants primed with death affiliated less with their ethnicity after being exposed to a negative depiction of an ingroup member (Arndt, Greenberg, Schimel, Pyszczynski, & Solomon, 2002). These findings are consistent with the social identity theory (Tajfel & Turner, 1979) view that group affiliations have powerful effects on self-esteem and suggest that, as TMT suggests, part of the motivation underlying group identification is the protection from existential anxiety that being part of a valued group provides. Little existential solace can be obtained from being affiliated with a group or ideology with undesirable, unwelcome implications for oneself.

If self-esteem acts as a barricade against anxiety-ridden thoughts about death, then weakening this barricade should make it easier for death-related thoughts to permeate consciousness. An array of studies have tested and lent support to this hypothesis: Hayes, Schimel, Faucher, and Williams (2008) showed that threatening participants' self-esteem by telling them that they scored below average on an intelligence test or that their personality is ill-suited for their career aspirations increased the accessibility of death-related thoughts but not other negative or aversive thoughts. Yet, when participants were allowed to reaffirm their self-esteem by writing about values that are most important to them, this eliminated the effect of the self-esteem threat on death-thought accessibility. Similarly, Ogilvie, Cohen, and Solomon (2008) reported that participants induced to think about their *undesired self* – themselves at their worst – evinced increased death-thought accessibility.

More recently, Cox and Arndt (in press) documented that when reminded of death, participants induced to think about a time when their romantic partners made them feel bad about themselves displayed higher death-thought accessibility. Conversely, recalling an instance in which their romantic partners made them feel good about themselves reduced death-related thoughts provoked by the mortality salience. This line of studies reveals the one-to-one relationship between self-esteem and death-thought accessibility, and offers what we view as particularly convincing evidence for the existentially charged nature of self-esteem.

Studies have also revealed the important role that self-esteem and terror management processes play in the maintenance of physical health. Goldenberg and Arndt (2008) proposed in their terror management health model (TMHM) that the conscious and nonconscious awareness of death differentially influence people's health decisions. Whereas people typically respond to conscious death thoughts with health-oriented responses (e.g., increased sun protection and exercise intentions), in the case of activated but nonconscious death thoughts, they forgo their health to protect and enhance their self-esteem. In other words, whether responses to nonconscious death thoughts are conducive to health depends to a large degree on the implications of the response for the individual's self-esteem rather than its relevance for health. This hypothesis has been tested and supported by studies examining smoking, dieting, tanning, and risk-taking in general. Hansen, Winzeler, and Topolinski (2010), for example, found that to the extent that smoking is a source of self-esteem, mortality-salient warning messages on cigarette packages cause more positive attitudes toward smoking. Similarly, Cox and colleagues (2009) reported that mortality salience led to higher tanning intentions when tanned skin was portrayed as physically attractive, but reduced intentions when the attractiveness of paler skin was highlighted. These and other similar studies testify to the crucial function of self-esteem in managing death anxiety in the important context of health decisions.

The research presented in this section converges on the conclusion that self-esteem plays a critical role in helping people manage existential anxiety. When mortality is made salient, high levels of self-esteem reduce anxiety and the defensive maneuvers aimed at dealing with this anxiety. Reminders of death increase the pursuit and defense of self-esteem. Threats to self-esteem bring death thoughts closer to consciousness, while reaffirming self-esteem lowers the accessibility of death thoughts. Across studies, being satisfied with oneself emerges as a bulwark against existential anxiety and a provider of power and serenity in the face of death and other threatening, unpleasant realities of life. This usefulness of self-esteem for making the pains of existence more bearable helps explain why self-esteem is important to people and sought with such vigor. We turn now to a consideration of where self-esteem comes from – how it is acquired, lost, and restored.

How is self-esteem acquired and maintained?

Granting that there is a heritable component to self-esteem (e.g., McGuire et al., 1999; Roy, Neale, & Kendler, 1995), psychologists generally agree that self-esteem is rooted in interpersonal experience, reflected appraisals from others, relationships, social comparisons, and group comparisons. It is also generally agreed that the foundations of self-esteem are laid in early life through interactions with one's family. Summarizing decades of theory and research on the issue, Hewitt writes that self-esteem depends on "unqualified acceptance of the child early in life, the provision of positive evaluations by significant others, favorable comparisons with others and with an ideal self, and the capacity for effective conduct" (Hewitt, 2009, p. 883). Children whose early experiences make them feel loved and accepted for who they are by their parents have a distinct advantage in developing a healthy sense of self-competence and self-liking (Branden, 1985). Basic human warmth, encouragement, respect, and support received from close others in these early years are essential to the development and maintenance of self-esteem throughout life (Harter, 1999; Mruk, 2006).

These early experiences have such great impact on the development of self-esteem because they shape the lenses through which the child comes to see her self and life – they constitute "Self 101" and "Existence 101" for the child. They not only inform the child as to his or her competence and lovability, but also provide a template for understanding the world and the people in it. These early experiences thus provide the beginnings of the self-esteem and worldview that TMT views as essential for emotional security and protection from anxiety throughout life. As discussed throughout this chapter, construing oneself as a person of value living in a meaningful, benevolent, and eternal world are the twin components of the cultural anxiety buffer that shields us from the anxiety that is an inherent consequence of the human condition. Uncertainty and unease regarding one's competence and worthiness or a sense of the world as chaotic, meaningless, or malevolent practically translates into an inability to encounter existence without anxiety and an over-reliance on less adaptive mechanisms to defuse anxiety.

Becker (1973) argued that a child who is cared for and loved is more likely to develop feelings of proven power and secure support, resulting in sturdier defenses against death anxiety. Recent research has demonstrated that secure parental attachment continues to buffer existential anxiety in adulthood. Cox and colleagues (2008), for instance, found that thinking about a secure, positive experience with one's mother increases self-esteem, and decreases both the accessibility of death thoughts and the need for worldview defense after mortality reminders. Similarly, secure parental attachment has been linked to higher levels of self-esteem (e.g., Arbona & Power, 2003; Armsden & Greenberg, 1987; Cassidy, 1988), lower levels of death fear (Mikulincer, Florian, & Tolmacz, 1990), and lower defensiveness in the face of mortality thoughts (Mikulincer & Florian, 2000). Attachment to romantic partners has been shown to fulfill a similar terror management function. For example, death reminders increase people's desire for intimacy and commitment in romantic relationships, and imagining separation from a romantic partner increases the accessibility of death-related thoughts and instigates worldview defense (Florian, Mikulincer, & Hirschberger, 2002). Studies have also shown that whereas securely attached persons are more likely to rely on their current romantic attachments to manage existential concerns, those with high levels of attachment insecurity continue to rely on the earlier bonds with their parents (Cox et al., 2008).

Early experiences within the family are clearly essential for the development of healthy self-esteem. Reliable and warm relationships with primary caretakers furnish the child with a sense of his or her own competence and worth, which, in turn, shield the child against the anxiety-inducing knowledge of life's fragile and finite nature. Whereas attachment figures constitute the initial source of self-esteem and protection against existential anxiety, as the child develops and matures, perceived success in meeting the standards of an increasingly individualized cultural worldview grow in importance as the basis for self-esteem and existential protection. Although cultural worldviews are initially learned by internalizing the parents' beliefs and values, children individuate as they develop, and they gradually construct their own worldviews by combining the beliefs and values of their close others, the groups they belong to, and the broader society that surrounds them. Cultural norms, moral values, and religious beliefs are among the most central ingredients of cultural worldviews. By explaining what life is and how it should be lived, cultural worldviews imbue existence with meaning, purpose, structure, and permanence, thereby helping to control anxiety. According to TMT, self-esteem is attained throughout life by living up to the standards of one's worldview or at least perceiving oneself as doing so.

The idea that self-esteem entails one's perception of oneself rather than objective reality helps to explain the diverse range of self-serving biases that have been found in people's self-relevant judgments. Self-serving attributional biases, downward social comparison, compensatory self-inflation, basking in reflected glory, cutting off reflected failure, self-handicapping, optimistic biases about one's future, and selective memory for ego-relevant events are just a few examples of the many forms of self-deceptive cognitive distortions that people use to defend their self-esteem against threats (for a review, see Greenberg et al., 1986; Greenberg, 2008).

If self-esteem fulfills this profoundly comforting function, it should also have wide-reaching implications for psychological well-being. Next, we examine the well-established association between self-esteem and psychological health from an existential perspective.

Psychological well-being and self-esteem

Decades of self-esteem research make one thing abundantly clear: self-esteem is linked to the good life and having high self-esteem is far preferable to having low self-esteem (Mruk, 2006). People with lower self-esteem experience virtually every aversive emotion more frequently than those with higher self-esteem and "virtually every clinically recognized variety of emotional and behavioral problem is more common among people with low than high self-esteem" (Leary & MacDonald, 2003, p. 412). Low self-esteem is correlated with, among other things, general negative affectivity, neuroticism, sadness, hostility, anger, social anxiety, shame, guilt, embarrassment proneness, and loneliness (Mruk, 2006). A host of psychological disorders, including major depression, anxiety disorder, eating disorders, sexual dysfunction, and pathological shame, have been found to be associated with low self-esteem in both children and adults (Leary & Mac-Donald, 2003). Indeed, as reported by O'Brien, Bartoletti, and Leitzel (2006), low self-esteem is listed as either a diagnostic criterion or associated feature of at least 24 mental disorders in the *Diagnostic and Statistical Manual of Mental Disorders* (DSM-IV-TR). Low self-esteem and an insufficient ability to experience self-relevant positive emotions such as pride is particularly strongly linked to depression, to such a degree that some even suggest conceptualizing self-esteem and depression as opposing end points of a bipolar continuum (Gruber, Oveis, Keltner, & Johnson, 2011; Watson, Suls, & Haig, 2002). It should come as no surprise, then, that low self-esteem predicts suicidal ideation, suicidal attempts, and completed suicides. Low self-esteem is a risk factor for suicide not only at the individual level, but also at the collective level – in nations with low overall levels of self-esteem, national suicide rates turn out to be higher (Chatard, Selimbegovic, & Konan, 2009).

In stark opposition to the gloomy prospects of low self-esteem, high self-esteem is robustly interrelated with happiness and mental health (Baumeister, Campbell, Krueger, & Vohs, 2003). Epstein concluded that high levels of self-esteem are accompanied by high levels of "happiness, security, affection, energy availability, alertness, calmness, clear-mindedness, singleness of purpose, lack of restraint, and spontaneity" (Epstein, 1979, p. 62). Over and above its benefits for psychological health, studies also suggest that high levels of self-esteem are beneficial to one's physical health (Higgins, Tykocinsky, & Vookles, 1990; Strauman, Lemieux, & Coe, 1993). Smaller discrepancies between one's actual self and desired self are associated with better immune system responses and decreased reports of a variety of physical complaints (e.g., diarrhea, migraine headaches, menstrual problems). O'Connor and Vallerand (1998) notably demonstrated that low self-esteem was associated with increased likelihood of mortality among nursing home residents over a four-year period, even after controlling for age, sex, and physical health.

Interestingly, Baumeister et al., (2003) have argued that although self-esteem makes people feel good, it has few tangible benefits beyond that. They concluded that high self-esteem does not cause socially important and desirable behaviors (e.g., high academic achievement, good job performance, leadership); nor does low self-esteem cause undesirable behaviors (e.g., violence, smoking, drinking, taking drugs). We contend, together with other scholars (e.g., Bosson & Swann, 2009; Swann, Chang-Schneider, & McClarty, 2007, 2008), that this criticism neglects to factor in the specificity matching principle, according to which global measures predict global outcomes and specific measures predict specific outcomes. Indeed, the capacity of global self-esteem to predict global or bundled behaviors has been demonstrated in impressive longitudinal studies (e.g., Donnellan, Trzesniewski, Robins, Moffitt, & Caspi, 2005; Trzesniewski et al., 2006; Werner & Smith, 1992). Trzesniewski and colleagues (2006), for example, showed that low self-esteem in adolescence was a significant predictor of major depressive disorder, anxiety disorder, tobacco dependence, criminal convictions, school dropout, and money and work problems 11 years later. Furthermore, the predictive power of self-esteem was bolstered when outcomes were aggregated. Results revealed that only 17% of low self-esteem adolescents were free from the above-mentioned problems as adults, whereas 56% of them had multiple problems. In contrast, 51% of high self-esteem adolescents were free from problems as adults, whereas only 17% had multiple problems. Additionally, meta-analyses show that interventions aimed at increasing self-esteem produce significant improvements in behavioral, personality, and academic functioning (Haney & Durlak, 1998).

Narcissism – a sense of self-superiority, entitlement, and over-confidence – has also been increasingly studied as the dark side of self-esteem (e.g., Twenge & Campbell, 2009). Although we acknowledge the individually and socially toxic consequences of narcissism, we view the distinction between self-esteem and narcissism as an extremely important one. As Swann and colleagues note, "conflating narcissism and true high self-esteem is profoundly problematic for the same reasons that it is problematic to mistake for a friend an enemy who is merely masquerading as a friend" (Swann et al., 2007, p. 87). The pursuit of self-esteem can doubtlessly take dangerous forms and be costly (Crocker & Park, 2004). That said, the literature makes it clear that positive self-esteem is an extraordinarily important resource in dealing with anxiety. Importantly, it is only a genuine, implicit, stable sense of self-esteem that effectively buffers existential anxiety and engenders positive life outcomes (see Schmeichel et al., 2009), and clearly *not* uncertain fragile high self-esteem or narcissism.

How to explain the remarkable psychological advantages associated with an authentically strong sense of self-worth? An existential analysis implies that these advantages arise from self-esteem's crucial role in buffering anxiety. TMT posits that without effective management the existential anxiety that results from awareness of the inevitability of death would interfere with effective action and lead to greater defensive distortions of one's perceptions to control it. Similarly, existentially oriented psychiatrists and scholars have frequently suggested that psychological disorders reflect extreme, graceless, or inefficient ways of dealing with existential anxiety (Becker, 1971, 1973; Lifton, 1979; Yalom, 1980). In this view, psychological dysfunction often results from mismanaged death anxiety. A small but growing number of TMT studies support this notion (Arndt, Routledge, Cox, & Goldenberg, 2005). For example, mortality reminders have been shown to exacerbate anxiety symptoms in those who suffer from anxiety disorders such as phobias and obsessive-compulsive disorder (Strachan et al., 2007). Other studies have demonstrated that the personality trait of neuroticism – a stable tendency to experience negative emotional states – makes it more difficult for individuals to manage death anxiety (e.g., Arndt & Solomon, 2003; Goldenberg, Pyszczynski, McCoy, Greenberg, & Solomon, 1999; Goldenberg, Routledge, & Arndt, 2009). Neuroticism is indeed robustly linked to low self-esteem (Judge, Erez, Bono, & Thoresen, 2002), death anxiety (Frazier & Foss-Goodman, 1988), and a broad array of psychological disorders (Malouff, Thorsteinsson, & Schutte, 2005).

More recently, TMT has been applied to understanding post-traumatic stress disorder (PTSD) in the form of anxiety-buffer disruption theory (ABDT; see Pyszczynski & Kesebir, 2011). According to ABDT, PTSD results from a disruption in people's anxiety-buffering systems, which normally provide protection from anxiety – both anxiety in general and death anxiety in particular. This type of breakdown occurs when people experience horrifying events that violate the core assumptions of their worldviews and self-esteem and therefore undermine the ability of these psychological structures to protect them effectively from anxiety. This makes the person chronically vulnerable to anxiety in response to both reminders of the event itself and other threatening events, which, in turn, produces the three symptom clusters that define the state of PTSD. Hyper-arousal is a simple and direct effect of the absence of the protection that a well-functioning anxiety buffer ordinarily provides. Intrusive thoughts occur as traumatized people struggle to cope with this overwhelming anxiety. Avoidance of things related to the trauma reflect the extreme fear that such stimuli produce in the absence of an effective anxiety buffer; and self-medication through alcohol and other drugs – another form of avoidance – are similar attempts to deal with the onslaught of anxiety that results from a malfunctioning anxiety buffer. A growing body of research (e.g., Abdollahi, Pyszczynski, Maxfield, & Luszczynska, 2011; Chatard et al., 2012; Kesebir, Luszczynska, Pyszczynski, & Benight, 2011) has revealed that PTSD-inflicted individuals do not respond to death reminders with the typical worldview defense or death-thought suppression that psychologically healthier individuals with functional anxiety buffers do, and that this disruption of anxiety-buffer functioning plays an important role in the onset and maintenance of PTSD symptoms.

As a whole, these studies highlight the role that mismanagement of existential anxiety plays in the development and maintenance of psychopathology, and how crucial it is to have an intact buffer against existential dread. Because self-esteem is one such powerful buffer, it is intimately associated with healthy human functioning. Attesting to self-esteem's fundamental protective function for the psyche, Routledge and colleagues (2010) have shown that the salience of death thoughts decreases satisfaction with life, subjective vitality, meaning in life, and exploration, and increases negative affect, state anxiety, and socially avoidant behavior – but only for participants who have low self-esteem, and not for those who have high self-esteem. The picture emerging from their program of research is that self-esteem's capacity to insulate existential anxiety frees up the psychological resources necessary for people to grow and flourish. We turn now to an existential analysis of the role of self-esteem in promoting growth, self-expansion, and the optimization of an individual's capacities.

Self-esteem and self-expansion

A long tradition of theorists, including Otto Rank (1936), Jean Piaget (1952), Robert White (1959), Carl Rogers (1961), Abraham Maslow (1970), and Mihaly Csikszentmihalyi (1980), have argued that people are intrinsically motivated to expand their understandings and capacities. Fredrickson's (e.g., 2001) broaden-and-build theory of positive emotions helps elucidate the processes that motivate such growth, suggesting that positive emotions *broaden* people's momentary thought-action repertoires, which helps *build* their physical, intellectual, social, and psychological resources. She argues that positive emotions make people want to expand their capacities by incorporating new information and capacities into their selves, and reviews studies showing that positive affect leads to thinking that is flexible, creative, integrative, and open-minded (e.g., Isen, Daubman, & Nowicki, 1987). As we have seen, high self-esteem is robustly associated with positive affect, and low self-esteem with negative affect. As such, it stands to reason that high self-esteem can energize people and provide them with the necessary psychological resources from which to "broaden and build" their potentials. Thus, self-esteem encourages achievement-oriented behavior, creativity, exploration, and growth. The heightened positive affect and exhilaration resulting from such self-expansive behavior can act as an incentive for one to approach challenging tasks in the future and as a reinforcer for such engagement once it has occurred.

In addition, most (but not all) cultures place a high value on creativity and the development of new capacities. Creative activity enables us to meet these standards and thus provides self-esteem, which from the TMT perspective, functions to control anxiety. Thus activities involving creativity, exploration, and growth can be motivated both by the intrinsic sense of exhilaration that such activities can produce and by the extrinsic sense of personal value that comes from success in such endeavors. Interestingly, Stipek (2001) has shown that young children enjoy tasks for their own sake, but that as they mature, they focus more on pride in achievements. Thus the initial intrinsically motivated power of interesting activities is often usurped by the anxiety-reducing self-esteem that success at these tasks can produce.

We posit that anxiety *must* be controlled for people to be willing to engage in activities that promote growth and expansion of their capacities (Pyszczynski, Greenberg, & Arndt, 2011). The finding that human infants cling to their caregivers when anxious and use them as a secure base from which to explore (Bowlby, 1988) is consistent with this proposition. Similarly, adults with secure attachment styles have less need for cognitive closure and are more likely to rely on new information in making social judgments than either anxious-ambivalent or avoidant individuals (Mikulincer, 1997). Other studies have found that anxiety leads to defensiveness, which is antithetical to growth. Finally, Elliot, Sheldon, and Church (1997) showed that individuals high in neuroticism tend to pursue avoidance-oriented rather than approach-oriented goals. This is consistent with Maslow's (1970) idea that deficit motives must be met before being motives can be pursued. Existential anxiety must be controlled by an intact anxiety-buffering mechanism in order for people to be able to afford self-expansion.

The central point of our analysis is that the integrity of their cultural anxiety buffer affects how people respond to information that challenges their existing conceptions of self and world. The more secure these structures and the more they embrace diversity of beliefs, the more open and unbiased the integrative processing is likely to be. But there is a paradox here. Although the security provided by self-esteem and faith in their cultural worldview is needed for integrative processing to occur in an open and unbiased way, people typically control anxiety by clinging to their conceptions of self and world, and defending them against threats. Such clinging to the status quo and the sense of self-esteem derived from it is, of course, antithetical to the integrative processing through which growth occurs. Thus people are often left between the metaphorical "rock and a hard place," struggling to control their anxieties so that they can be open to new experiences by clinging to their existing conceptions of self and world. Although controlling anxiety could open the doors for creative growth and change, clinging to existing conceptions slams those very doors shut. The more tentative is an individual's basis of security, the more rigid and biased his or her integrative processing is likely to be, and the more he or she is likely to reject new information in favor of early introjects. When there is extreme instability in existing worldviews or self-views, an individual may abandon the existing structures and introject new ideals and values with minimal integration. Dramatic cases of religious conversion, cult affiliation, or counter-cultural identification are examples of this.

Ultimately, it is through this interaction of intrinsically motivated growth-producing integrative processing of new information and the defensive needs for security provided by our pre-existing anxiety-buffering conceptions of self and world that the individual carves out his or her own individualized version of the cultural worldview. It is this individualized structure that provides protection from existential fears. Perhaps, it is possible to fashion an individualized worldview that more strongly encourages creative thinking as a better way to manage existential fears. Although the lack of a status quo on which to rely may render this a more precarious strategy, it may also facilitate more open and integrative processing of ideas and people that present alternatives to mainstream cultural views. Such an approach would be less vulnerable to anxiety to the extent that it is highly valued by one's culture. Accordingly, Routledge and colleagues (Routledge & Arndt, 2009; Routledge, Arndt, & Sheldon, 2004) have found that when creativity is primed after mortality salience, to the extent that creativity is not perceived as threatening social bonds and is instead culturally embraced, it leads to less defensiveness toward those who derogate national identities, and more interest in exposing oneself to alternative cultural views. Such effects, it seems, may be fostered by more deeply connecting creative expression to a sense of social cohesion that might otherwise be undermined by expressing oneself in novel and unique ways.

To sum up, a positive sense of self-worth acts as an existential resource by keeping anxiety and other types of negative affect (e.g., depression, pessimism, loneliness, hostility) farther away from consciousness, thus freeing people to concern themselves more with actualizing possibilities than protecting against threats. An authentic sense of positive self-worth turns the self, to the extent that it is possible, into a non-issue and in so doing frees up psychic energy that is needed for achievement and innovation. The energy not directed toward grappling with anxieties can in turn facilitate self-regulation and effective pursuit of goals. We might say that "the curse of the self" (Leary, 2004) is lighter for people with authentic, secure self-esteem, resulting in a less intrusive self, and possibly less frequent attempts to escape the self through potentially destructive means (Baumeister, 1991).

The phenomenology of low self-esteem – feeling incompetent and unworthy, unfit for life – inevitably translates into experiencing existence as frightening and futile. This turns life for the person lacking in self-esteem into a chronic emergency: that person is psychologically in a constant state of danger, surrounded by a feeling of impending disaster and a sense of helplessness. Suffering from low self-esteem thus involves having one's consciousness ruled by fear, which sabotages clarity and efficiency (Branden, 1985). The main goal for such a person is to keep the anxieties, insecurities, and self-doubts at bay, at whatever cost that may come. On the other hand, a person with a satisfying degree of self-respect, whose central motivation is not fear, can afford to rejoice in being alive, and view existence as a more exciting than threatening affair. As Dillon notes,

> individuals who are blessed with a confident respect for themselves have something that is vital to living a satisfying, meaningful, flourishing life, while those condemned to live without it or with damaged or fragile self-respect are thereby condemned to live constricted, deformed, frustrating lives, cut off from possibilities for self-realization, self-fulfillment, and happiness.
>
> (Dillon, 1997, p. 226)

Conclusion

Self-esteem is a psychological variable with profound and wide-ranging effects on behavior and emotions; it is of vital importance to the course and quality of one's life. As such, it has a long and voluminous history within psychology. In this chapter, we attempted to add to this by examining self-esteem's functions from an existential perspective. Building on insights from terror management theory and research, we have discussed what self-esteem is, why it is needed, how it is obtained, how it relates to psychological well-being and dysfunction, and the role it plays in the growth and expansion of the individual's capacities and potentials. Self-esteem is determined by and determines our relationship to existence. If it is a truth universally acknowledged that people want to feel good about themselves, this has much to do with the fact that we are self-aware animals for whom death is and always will be an unavoidable fact of life.

References

Abdollahi, A., Pyszczynski, T., Maxfield, M., & Luszczynska, A. (2011). Posttraumatic stress reactions as a disruption in anxiety-buffer functioning: Dissociation and responses to mortality salience as predictors of severity of post-traumatic symptoms. *Psychological Trauma: Theory, Research, Practice, and Policy, 3*, 329–341.

American Psychiatric Association. (2000). *Diagnostic and statistical manual of mental disorders* (4th edn, Text Revision). Washington, DC: American Psychiatric Association.

Arbona, C., & Power, T. (2003). Parental attachment, self-esteem, and antisocial behaviors among African American, European American, & Mexican American adolescents. *Journal of Counseling Psychology, 50*, 40–51.

Armsden, G. C., & Greenberg, M. T. (1987). The inventory of parent and peer attachment: Individual differences and their relationship to psychological well-being in adolescence. *Journal of Youth and Adolescence, 16*, 427–454.

Arndt, J. (in press). A significant contributor to a meaningful cultural drama: Terror management research on the functions and implications of self-esteem. In M. Mikulincer & P. R. Shaver (eds.), *The social psychology of meaning, mortality, and choice*. Washington, DC: APA Press.

Arndt, J., Greenberg, J., Schimel, J., Pyszczynski, T., & Solomon, S. (2002). To belong or not to belong, that is the question: Terror management and identification with gender and ethnicity. *Journal of Personality and Social Psychology, 83*, 26–43.

Arndt, J., Greenberg, J., Solomon, S., Pyszczynski, T., & Schimel, J. (1999). Creativity and terror management: The effects of creative activity on guilt and social projection following mortality salience. *Journal of Personality and Social Psychology, 77*, 19–32.

Arndt, J., Routledge, C., Cox, C. R., & Goldenberg, J. L. (2005). The worm at the core: A terror management perspective on the roots of psychological dysfunction. *Applied and Preventative Psychology, 11*, 191–213.

Arndt, J., & Solomon, S. (2003). The control of death and the death of control: The effects of mortality salience, neuroticism, and worldview threat on the desire for control. *Journal of Research in Personality, 37*, 1–22.

Baumeister, R. F. (1991). *Escaping the self: Alcoholism, spirituality, masochism, and other flights from the burden of selfhood*. New York, NY: Basic Books.

Baumeister, R. F., Campbell, J. D., Krueger, J. I., & Vohs, K. D. (2003). Does high self-esteem cause better performance, interpersonal success, happiness, or healthier lifestyles? *Psychological Science in the Public Interest, 4*, 1–44.

Becker, E. (1971). The *birth and death of meaning*. New York, NY: Free Press.

Becker, E. (1973). *The denial of death*. New York, NY: Free Press.

Becker, E. (1975). *Escape from evil*. New York, NY: Free Press.

Bosson, J. K., & Swann, W. B., Jr. (2009). Self-esteem. In M. R. Leary & R. H. Hoyle (eds.), *Handbook of individual differences in social behavior* (pp. 527–546). New York, NY: Guilford Press.

Bowlby, J. (1988). *A secure base*. New York, NY: Basic Books.

Branden, N. (1985). *Honoring the self*. New York, NY: Bantam Books.

Buhrmester, M. D., Blanton, H., & Swann, W. B., Jr. (2011). Implicit self-esteem: Nature, measurement and a new way forward. *Journal of Personality and Social Psychology, 100*, 365–385.

Carver, C. S., & Scheier, M. F. (1981). *Attention and self-regulation: A control-theory approach to human behavior*. New York, NY: Springer-Verlag.

Carver, C. S., & Scheier, M. F. (2002). Control processes and self-organization as complementary principles underlying behavior. *Personality and Social Psychology Review, 6*, 304–315.

Cassidy, J. (1988) Child-mother attachment and the self in six-year-olds. *Child Development, 59*, 121–34.

Castano, E., Yzerbyt, V., Paladino, M.-P., & Sacchi, S. (2002). I belong, therefore, I exist: Ingroup identification, ingroup entitativity, and ingroup bias. *Personality and Social Psychology Bulletin, 28*, 135–143.

Chatard, A., Pyszczynski, T., Arndt, J., Selimbegović, L., Konan, P., & Van der Linden, M. (2012). Extent of trauma exposure and PTSD symptom severity as predictors of anxiety-buffer functioning. *Psychological Trauma: Theory, Research, Practice, and Policy, 4*, 47–55.

Chatard, A., Selimbegović, L., & Konan, P. (2009). Self-esteem and suicide rates in 55 nations. *European Journal of Personality, 23*, 19–32.

Cox, C. R., & Arndt, J. (in press). How sweet it is to be loved by you: The role of perceived regard in the terror management of close relationships. *Journal of Personality and Social Psychology*.

Cox, C. R., Arndt, J., Pyszczynski, T., Greenberg, J., Abdollahi, A., & Solomon, S. (2008). Terror management and adults' attachment to their parents: The safe haven remains. *Journal of Personality and Social Psychology, 94*, 696–717.

Cox, C. R., Cooper, D. P., Vess, M., Arndt, J., Goldenberg, J. L., & Routledge, C. (2009). Bronze is beautiful but pale can be pretty: The effects of appearance standards and mortality salience on tanning outcomes. *Health Psychology, 28*, 746–752.

Crocker, J., & Park, L. E. (2004). The costly pursuit of self-esteem. *Psychological Bulletin, 130*, 392–414.

Csikszentmihalyi, M. (1980). Love and the dynamics of personal growth. In K. S. Pope (ed.), *On love and loving* (pp. 306–326). San Francisco, CA: Jossey-Bass.

Dechesne, M., Greenberg, J., Arndt, J., & Schimel, J. (2000). Terror management and the vicissitudes of sports fan affiliation: The effects of mortality salience on optimism and fan identification. *European Journal of Social Psychology, 30*, 813–835.

Dillon, R. S. (1997). Self-respect: Moral, emotional, political. *Ethics, 107*, 226–249.

Donnellan, B., Trzesniewski, K., Robins, R., Moffitt, T., & Caspi, A. (2005). Low self-esteem is related to aggression, antisocial behavior, and delinquency. *Psychological Science, 16*, 328–335.

Elliot, A. J., Sheldon, K. M., & Church, M. A. (1997). Avoidance personal goals and subjective well-being. *Personality and Social Psychology Bulletin, 23*, 915–927.

Epstein, S. (1979). The ecological study of emotions in humans. In K. Blankstein (ed.), *Advances in the study of communications and affect* (pp. 47–83). New York, NY: Plenum.

Epstein, S. (1980). The self-concept: A review and the proposal of an integrated theory of personality. In E. Straub (ed.), *Personality: Basic aspects and current research* (pp. 83–131). Englewood Cliffs, NJ: Prentice Hall.

Florian, V., Mikulincer, M., & Hirschberger, G. (2002). The anxiety-buffering function of close relationships: Evidence that relationship commitment acts as a terror management mechanism. *Journal of Personality and Social Psychology, 82*, 527–542.

Frazier, P. H., & Foss-Goodman, D. (1988). Death anxiety and personality: Are they truly related? *Omega: Journal of Death and Dying, 19*, 265–274.

Fredrickson, B. L. (2001). The role of positive emotions in positive psychology: The broaden-and-build theory of positive emotions. *American Psychologist, 56*, 218–226.

Gecas, V. (1982). The self-concept. *Annual Review of Sociology, 8*, 1–33.

Goldenberg, J. L., & Arndt, J. (2008). The implications of death for health: A terror management health model for behavioral health promotion. *Psychological Review, 115,* 1032–1053.

Goldenberg, J. L., McCoy, S. K., Pyszczynski, T., Greenberg, J., & Solomon, S. (2000). The body as a source of self-esteem: The effect of mortality salience on identification with one's body, interest in sex, and appearance monitoring. *Journal of Personality and Social Psychology, 79,* 118–130.

Goldenberg, J. L., Pyszczynski, T., McCoy, S. K., Greenberg, J., & Solomon, S. (1999). Death, sex, love, and neuroticism: Why is sex such a problem? *Journal of Personality and Social Psychology, 77,* 1173–1187.

Goldenberg, J. L., Routledge, C., & Arndt, J. (2009). Mammograms and the management of existential discomfort: Threats associated with the physicality of the body and neuroticism. *Psychology and Health, 24,* 563–581.

Greenberg, J. (2008). Understanding the vital human quest for self-esteem. *Perspectives on Psychological Science, 3,* 48–55.

Greenberg, J., Kosloff, S., Solomon, S., Cohen, F., & Landau, M. J. (2010). Toward understanding the fame game: The effect of mortality salience on the appeal of fame. *Self and Identity, 9,* 1–18.

Greenberg, J., Pyszczynski, T., & Solomon, S. (1986). The causes and consequences of a need for self-esteem: A terror management theory. In R. F. Baumeister (ed.), *Public self and private self* (pp. 189–212). New York, NY: Springer-Verlag.

Greenberg, J., Pyszczynski, T., Solomon, S., Pinel, E., Simon, L., & Jordan, K. (1993). Effects of self-esteem on vulnerability-denying defensive distortions: Further evidence of an anxiety-buffering function of self-esteem. *Journal of Experimental Social Psychology, 29,* 229–251.

Greenberg, J., Pyszczynski, T., Solomon, S., Rosenblatt, A., Veeder, M., Kirkland, S., & Lyon, D. (1990). Evidence for terror management II: The effects of mortality salience on reactions to those who threaten or bolster the cultural worldview. *Journal of Personality and Social Psychology, 58,* 308–318.

Greenberg, J., Solomon, S., & Arndt, J. (2008). A basic but uniquely human motivation: Terror management. In J. Y. Shah, W. L. Gardner (eds.), *Handbook of motivation science* (pp. 114–134). New York, NY: Guilford Press.

Greenberg, J., Solomon, S., Pyszczynski, T., Rosenblatt, A., Burling, J., Lyon, D., et al. (1992). Why do people need self-esteem? Converging evidence that self-esteem serves an anxiety-buffering function. *Journal of Personality and Social Psychology, 63,* 913–922.

Gruber, J., Oveis, C., Keltner, D., & Johnson, S. L., (2011). A discrete emotions approach to positive emotion disturbance in depression. *Cognition & Emotion, 25,* 40–52.

Haney, P., & Durlak, J. A. (1998). Changing self-esteem in children and adolescents: A meta-analytic review. *Journal of Clinical Child Psychology, 27,* 423–433.

Hansen, J., Winzeler, S., & Topolinski, S. (2010). When death makes you smoke: A terror management perspective on the effectiveness of cigarette on-pack warnings. *Journal of Experimental Social Psychology, 46,* 226–228.

Harmon-Jones, E., Simon, L., Greenberg, J., Pyszczynski, T., Solomon, S., & McGregor, H. (1997). Terror management theory and self-esteem: Evidence that increased self-esteem reduces mortality salience effects. *Journal of Personality and Social Psychology, 72,* 24–36.

Harter, S. (1999). *The construction of the self: A developmental perspective.* New York, NY: Guilford.

Hayes, J., Schimel, J., Faucher, E. H., & Williams, T. J. (2008). Evidence for the death thought accessibility hypothesis II: Threatening self-esteem increases the accessibility of death thoughts. *Journal of Experimental Social Psychology, 44*, 600–613.

Hewitt, J. P. (2009). Self-esteem. In Shane Lopez (ed.), *Encyclopedia of Positive Psychology*. New York, NY: Wiley-Blackwell.

Higgins, E. T., Tykocinsky, O., & Vookles, J. (1990). Patterns of self-beliefs: The psychological significance of relations among the actual, ideal, ought, can, and future selves. In J. M. Olson & M. P. Zanna (eds.), *Self-inference processes: The Ontario Symposium* (Vol. 6, pp. 148–180). Hillsdale, NJ: Erlbaum.

Isen, A. M., Daubman, K. A., & Nowicki, G. P. (1987). Positive affect facilitates creative problem solving. *Journal of Personality and Social Psychology, 52*, 1122–1131.

James, W. J. (1890/1950). *Principles of psychology*. Oxford: Dover Publications.

Judge, T. A., Erez, A., Bono, J. E., & Thoresen, C. J. (2002). Are measures of self-esteem, neuroticism, locus of control, and generalized self-efficacy indicators of a common core construct? *Journal of Personality and Social Psychology, 83*, 693–710.

Kesebir, P., Luszczynska, A., Pyszczynski, T., & Benight, C. (2011). Posttraumatic stress disorder involves disrupted anxiety-buffer mechanisms. *Journal of Social and Clinical Psychology, 30*, 819–841.

Kesebir, P., & Pyszczynski, T. (2012). The role of death in life: Existential aspects of human motivation. In R. Ryan (ed.), *The Oxford handbook of human motivation* (pp. 43–64). New York, NY: Oxford University Press.

Kosloff, S., & Greenberg, J. (2009). Pearls in the desert: Death reminders provoke immediate derogation of extrinsic goals, but delayed inflation. *Journal of Experimental Social Psychology, 45*, 197–203.

Landau, M. J., Greenberg, J., & Sullivan, D. (2009). Managing terror when self-worth and worldviews collide: Evidence that mortality salience increases reluctance to self-enhance beyond authorities. *Journal of Experimental Social Psychology, 45*, 68–79.

Leary, M. R. (2004). *The curse of the self: Self-awareness, egotism, and the quality of human life*. New York, NY: Oxford University Press.

Leary, M. R., & MacDonald, G. (2003). Individual differences in self-esteem: A review and theoretical integration. In M. R. Leary & J. P. Tangney (eds.), *Handbook of self and identity* (pp. 401–418). New York, NY: Guilford Press.

Lifton, R. J. (1979). *The broken connection: On death and the continuity of life*. New York, NY: Simon & Schuster.

Malouff, J. M., Thorsteinsson, E. B., & Schutte, N. S. (2005). The relationship between the five-factor model of personality and symptoms of clinical disorders: A meta-analysis. *Journal of Psychopathology and Behavioral Assessment, 27*, 101–114.

Maslow, A. (1970). *Motivation and personality* (2nd edn). New York, NY: Harper & Row.

McGregor, H. A., Lieberman, J. D., Greenberg, J., Solomon, S. Arndt, J., Simon, L. et al. (1998). Terror management and aggression: Evidence that mortality salience motivates aggression against worldview-threatening others. *Journal of Personality and Social Psychology, 74*, 590–605.

McGuire, S., Manke, B., Saudino, K., Reiss, D., Hetherington, E. M., & Plomin, R. (1999). Perceived competence and self-worth during adolescence: A longitudinal behavioral genetic study. *Child Development, 70*, 1283–1296.

Mikulincer, M. (1997). Adult attachment style and information processing: Individual differences in curiosity and cognitive closure. *Journal of Personality and Social Psychology, 72*, 1217–1230.

Mikulincer, M., & Florian, V. (2000). Exploring individual differences in reactions to mortality salience: Does attachment style regulate terror management mechanisms? *Journal of Personality and Social Psychology, 79*, 260–273.

Mikulincer, M., & Florian, V. (2002). The effect of mortality salience on self-serving attributions: Evidence for the function of self-esteem as a terror management mechanism. *Basic and Applied Social Psychology, 24*, 261–271.

Mikulincer, M., Florian, V., & Hirschberger, G. (2003). The existential function of close relationships: Introducing death into the science of love. *Personality and Social Psychology Review, 7*, 20–40.

Mikulincer, M., Florian, V., & Tolmacz, R. (1990). Attachment styles and fear of personal death: A case study of affect regulation. *Journal of Personality and Social Psychology, 58*, 273–280.

Mruk, C. J. (2006). *Self-esteem research, theory, and practice: Toward a positive psychology of self-esteem* (3rd edn). New York, NY: Springer.

O'Brien, E. J., Bartoletti, M., & Leitzel, J. D. (2006). Self-esteem, psychopathology, and psychotherapy. In M. H. Kernis (ed.), *Self-esteem issues and answers: A source book of current perspectives* (pp. 306–315). New York, NY: Psychology Press.

O'Connor, B. P., & Vallerand, R. J. (1998). Psychosocial adjustment variables as predictors of mortality among nursing home residents. *Psychology and Aging, 13*, 368–374.

Ogilvie, D. M., Cohen, F., & Solomon, S. (2008). The undesired self: Deadly connotations. *Journal of Research in Personality, 42*, 564–576.

Peters, H. J., Greenberg, J., & Williams, J. M. (2005). Applying terror management theory to performance: Can reminding individuals of their mortality increase strength output? *Journal of Sport and Exercise Psychology, 27*, 111–116.

Piaget, J. (1952). *The origins of intelligence in children* (trans. M. Cook). New York, NY: International Universities Press.

Pyszczynski, T., Greenberg, J., & Arndt, J. (2011). Freedom vs. fear revisited: An integrative analysis of the defense and growth of self. In M. Leary & J. Tangney (eds.), *Handbook of self and identity* (2nd edn). New York, NY: Guilford.

Pyszczynski, T., Greenberg, J., Solomon, S., Arndt, J., & Schimel, J. (2004). Why do people need self-esteem? A theoretical and empirical review. *Psychological Bulletin, 130*, 435–468.

Pyszczynski, T., & Kesebir, P. (2011). Anxiety buffer disruption theory: A terror management account of posttraumatic stress disorder. *Anxiety, Stress, & Coping, 24*, 3–26.

Rank, O. (1936). *Will therapy and truth and reality*. New York, NY: Knopf.

Rogers, C. R. (1961). *On becoming a person*. Boston, MA: Houghton-Mifflin.

Rosenberg, M. (1965). *Society and the adolescent self-image*. Princeton, NJ: Princeton University Press.

Rosenberg, M., Schooler, C., Schoenbach, C., & Rosenberg, F. (1995). Global self-esteem and specific self-esteem: Different concepts and different outcomes. *American Sociological Review, 60*, 141–156.

Routledge, C., & Arndt, J. (2009). Creative terror management: Creativity as a facilitator of cultural exploration after mortality salience. *Personality and Social Psychology Bulletin, 35*, 493–505.

Routledge, C., Arndt, J., & Sheldon, K. M. (2004). Task engagement after mortality salience: The effects of creativity, conformity, and connectedness on worldview defense. *European Journal of Social Psychology, 34*, 477–487.

Routledge, C., Ostafin, B., Juhl, J., Sedikides, C., Cathey, C., & Liao, J. (2010). Adjusting to death: The effects of mortality salience and self-esteem on psychological well-being, growth motivation, and maladaptive behavior. *Journal of Personality and Social Psychology, 99*, 897–916.

Roy, M. A., Neale, M. C., & Kendler, K. S. (1995). The genetic epidemiology of self-esteem. *British Journal of Psychiatry, 166*, 813–820.

Schimel, J., Hayes, J., Williams, T., & Jahrig, J. (2007). Is death really the worm at the core? Converging evidence that worldview threat increases death-thought accessibility. *Journal of Personality and Social Psychology, 92*, 789–803.

Schmeichel, B. J., Gailliot, M. T., Filardo, E. McGregor, I., Gitter, S., & Baumeister, R. F. (2009). Terror management theory and self-esteem revisited: The roles of implicit and explicit self-esteem in mortality salience effects. *Journal of Personality and Social Psychology, 96*, 1077–1087.

Solomon, S. (2006). Self-esteem is central to human well-being. In M. H. Kernis (ed.), *Self-esteem, issues and answers. A sourcebook of current perspectives* (pp. 254–260). New York, NY: Psychology Press.

Stipek, D. J. (2001). Classroom context effects on young children's motivation. In F. Salili, C. Chiu, & Y. Hong (eds.), *Student motivation: The culture and context of learning* (pp. 273–292). New York, NY: Plenum Press.

Strachan, E., Schimel, J., Arndt, J., Williams, T., Solomon, S., Pyszczynski, T., & Greenberg, J. (2007). Terror mismanagement: Evidence that mortality salience exacerbates phobic and compulsive behaviors. *Personality and Social Psychology Bulletin, 33*, 1137–1151.

Strauman, T. J., Lemieux, A. M., & Coe, C. L. (1993). Self-discrepancy and natural killer cell activity: Immunological consequences of negative self-evaluation. *Journal of Personality and Social Psychology, 64*, 1042–1052.

Swann, W. B., Jr, Chang-Schneider, C., & McClarty, K. (2007). Do our self-views matter? Self-concept and self-esteem in everyday life. *American Psychologist, 62*, 84–94.

Swann, W. B., Jr, Chang-Schneider, C., & McClarty, K. (2008). Yes, cavalier attitudes can have pernicious consequences: A reply to Krueger, Vohs, & Baumeister. *American Psychologist, 63*, 65–66.

Tafarodi, R. W., & Swann, W. B., Jr. (1995). Self-competence and self-liking as dimensions of global self-esteem: Initial validation of a measure. *Journal of Personality Assessment, 65*, 322–342.

Tajfel, H., & Turner, J. (1979). An integrative theory of intergroup conflict. In W. G. Austin & S. Worchel (eds.), *The social psychology of intergroup relations* (pp. 33–47). Monterey, CA: Brooks/Cole.

Taubman Ben-Ari, O., Florian, V., & Mikulincer, M. (1999). The impact of mortality salience on reckless driving: A test of terror management mechanisms. *Journal of Personality and Social Psychology, 76*, 35–45.

Trzesniewski, K., Donnellan, B., Moffitt, T., Robins, R., Poulton, R., & Caspi, A. (2006). Low self-esteem during adolescence predicts poor health, criminal behavior, and limited economic prospects during adulthood. *Developmental Psychology, 42*, 381–390.

Trope, Y., & Lieberman, N. (2010). Construal level theory of psychological distance. *Psychological Review, 117*, 440–463.

Twenge, J. M., & Campbell, W. K. (2009). *The narcissism epidemic: Living in the age of entitlement*. New York, NY: Free Press.

Vallacher, R. R., & Wegner, D. M. (1987). What do people think they're doing? Action identification and human behavior. *Psychological Review, 94*, 3–15.

Vess, M., & Arndt, J. (2008). The nature of death and the death of nature: The impact of mortality salience on environmental concern. *Journal of Research in Personality, 42,* 1376–1380.

Watson, D., Suls, J., & Haig, J. (2002). Global self-esteem in relation to structural models of personality and affectivity. *Journal of Personality and Social Psychology, 83,* 185–197.

Werner, E. E., & Smith, R. S. (1992). *Overcoming the odds: High risk children from birth to adulthood.* Ithaca, NY: Cornell University Press.

White, R. W. (1959). Motivation reconsidered: The concept of competence. *Psychological Review, 66,* 297–331.

Yalom, I. (1980). *Existential psychotherapy.* New York, NY: Basic Books.

8 Badge of honor or mark of shame

Self-esteem as an interpersonal signal

Jessica Cameron, Jennifer MacGregor, and Tracy Kwang

Self-esteem has captured the public interest like no other psychological construct (Twenge, 2006), and that interest seems to be growing. A recent Google search (October 17, 2011) on the term "self-esteem" resulted in over 50 million hits. This number has risen dramatically since 2003, when the same search retrieved just below 3 million hits (Solomon, 2006). But what is self-esteem in the eyes of the public? The overarching perspective expressed in the public media is that high self-esteem is a cure-all, a panacea of joy and success, whereas low self-esteem is a fault that needs to be corrected. Not surprisingly, interest in self-esteem programs has also risen dramatically. In a recent Google search (October 17, 2011) the number of hits retrieved for the search term "self-esteem program" was over 70,000, whereas in 2003 the same search resulted in only 2,430 hits (Koch, 2006). Given the growing cultural fascination with self-esteem, it stands to reason that possessing, or perhaps simply appearing to possess, self-esteem means something on the social playing field. In other words, self-esteem is not simply a psychological state experienced by an individual, but a social identity that can function as an interpersonal signal.

In the current chapter, we will review the burgeoning research detailing what social information is conveyed by perceived levels of self-esteem. Research exploring lay theories of self-esteem and the stereotypes of those low and high in self-esteem convincingly demonstrate that self-esteem is indeed an interpersonal signal. We then turn our discussion to the implications of being perceived as having low or high self-esteem, focusing on a variety of potential consequences. An underlying issue throughout the chapter is how accurately people detect others' self-esteem and how people convey their self-esteem to others, whether those attempts are intentional or not. Lastly, we will suggest directions for future research.

Self-esteem: the intra- and inter-personal

Generally speaking, self-esteem refers to the degree to which an individual favorably evaluates himself or herself (Baumeister, Smart, & Boden, 1996). This global evaluation is conceptualized by some as more cognitive (e.g., Cooper-smith, 1967) and by others as more affective (Brown, 1993), but regardless of which camp one ascribes to, self-esteem is traditionally seen as an intrapersonal experience. Although much of the research on self-esteem has focused on associated internal experiences, there is a long history of accounting for self-esteem's interpersonal influences. Writings concerning the nature of the self that are more than a century old refer to the interpersonal nature of feelings toward the self (e.g., Cooley, 1902). From these perspectives, how an individual believes that he or she is viewed in the eyes of others (i.e., reflected appraisals) is critical in forming feelings toward the self. More recently, Leary and colleagues have argued that self-esteem functions as a gauge of a person's relational value (Leary & Baumeister, 2000; Leary & Downs, 1995); for example, Jill's sense of self-worth is based on how accepted she feels by Jack. This gauge, termed the "sociometer," alerts the individual with feelings of distress (lowered state self-esteem) when a person is (or feels) devalued by others. The discomfort of lowered state self-esteem motivates a person to take measures to re-establish his or her interpersonal value (Richman & Leary, 2009). Zeigler-Hill, Besser, Myers, Southard, and Malkin (in press) have referred to this monitoring of interpersonal value as the "status-tracking" function of self-esteem. From an evolutionary standpoint, this process is critical to social life, and consequently survival, because it helps people avoid social exclusion (Tooby & Cosmides, 1996). Indeed, ample evidence demonstrates that self-esteem is associated with actual and perceived social acceptance (e.g., Leary, Tambor, Terdal, & Downs, 1995; Stinson et al., 2008), and that acute drops in self-esteem lead people to take steps to increase their value to others (see Williams, 2007).

Although past research has emphasized how social environments are *internalized* to shape self-views, researchers are increasingly interested in how self-views are *externalized* to shape one's social environment. From the externalized perspective, people will use information about another's self-esteem as a gauge of that person's worth (Cameron, MacGregor, Hole, & Holmes, 2012; Zeigler-Hill et al., in press); so, for example, Jack decides on how acceptable Jill is based on whether he thinks she has relatively high or low self-esteem. Thus, self-esteem does not only have a "status-tracking" or "sociometer" function, but also serves as an interpersonal signal. This interpersonal signal is then interpreted by others as an indicator of worth.

Why might the self-esteem of *others* be socially relevant information? What purpose could perceptions of others' self-esteem serve? Zeigler-Hill and colleagues (in press) argue that self-esteem serves a "status-signaling" function that complements the status-tracking function outlined by sociometer theory. From this perspective, self-esteem influences one's self-presentational behavior, which in turn influences how others view the self. This status-signaling system in humans should work much like the status-signaling models developed in non-human animals (e.g., feather coloration signals dominance in birds; see Senar, 2006). Ultimately, these status signals have important evolutionary outcomes, such as access to mates and consequent reproductive success. In essence, self-esteem signals important status-related information to others in one's social world. Although we will touch on *how* people convey self-esteem to others later in the present chapter, the basic notion here is that conveying high (or low) self-esteem provides social information to others.

Lay theories about self-esteem

In an effort to understand their social world, people form lay theories about the world around them. These lay theories consist of information about how characteristics covary within individuals (Uleman, Saribay, & Gonzalez, 2008). The concept of lay theories overlaps with that of stereotypes (Ashmore & Del Boca, 1979), as both pertain to ascribing characteristics to individuals on the basis of a social identity or group membership. Do people hold lay theories and stereotypes about self-esteem? Given the propensity for people to form generalizations about others and the prominence of self-esteem in the social media, it is perhaps not surprising that participants, regardless of their own self-esteem level, are quick to judge others on the basis of the label "low self-esteem" or "high self-esteem" (Cameron, MacGregor, et al., 2012; Zeigler-Hill et al., in press) and on the presence of self-esteem cues (e.g., slogans on T-shirts; Zeigler-Hill et al., in press).

What conclusions do people draw about those labeled as low or high in self-esteem? Research on the status-signaling function of self-esteem (Zeigler-Hill et al., in press) and on self-esteem stereotypes (Cameron, MacGregor, et al., 2012) report a consistent positive bias in the impressions formed about high self-esteem individuals and a consistent negative bias about those with low self-esteem. In several studies conducted by Cameron and her colleagues (Cameron, MacGregor, et al., 2012; Cameron, Hole, & Cornelius, 2012), when Canadian and American participants were asked to rate how the average person would describe a high self-esteem individual, they universally reported that higher self-esteem people were attractive, intelligent, warm, competent, emotionally stable, extraverted, open to experience, conscientious, and agreeable. Basically, on all characteristics in the rating list, high self-esteem people were described as superior. Importantly, when a new sample of participants was given the opportunity to provide an open-ended description of high self-esteem individuals, they again described high self-esteem individuals as possessing a variety of virtues.

Whereas people sing the praises of high self-esteem, low self-esteem is viewed as a "fatal flaw." In the same set of studies, Cameron and her colleagues (Cameron, MacGregor, et al., 2012; Cameron, Hole, & Cornelius, 2012) found that participants attributed negative characteristics to low self-esteem individuals. Across all of the characteristics assessed, low self-esteem people were seen as inferior. They were described as less attractive, less intelligent, less warm, less competent, less sociable, and so forth. The only time that the stereotypes of low self-esteem individuals were rated as "more" than the group of high self-esteem individuals was on negative characteristics, such as experiencing more negative moods and possessing more interpersonally disadvantageous characteristics (e.g., jealousy). Again, these responses were evident in both the close-ended ratings and the open-ended questions. Granted, low self-esteem individuals were seen more negatively than were people with high self-esteem, but were the stereotypes about low self-esteem really negative? In one study, Cameron and colleagues compared the closed-ended ratings about low and high self-esteem individuals to that of known stigmatized groups (Cameron, Mac-Gregor, et al., 2012). The results were startling: low self-esteem individuals were seen just as negatively as welfare recipients and mentally ill people on most characteristics, two groups consistently viewed so negatively that they've been termed the "parasites of society" (Fiske, Cuddy, Glick, & Xu, 2002). Furthermore, low self-esteem people were viewed even more negatively on some characteristics than other stigmatized groups (e.g., obese people).

Cameron and colleagues (Cameron, MacGregor, et al., 2012; Cameron, Hole, & Cornelius, 2012) have looked at broad judgments about low and high self-esteem individuals at a group level. However, research examining how people react to specific individuals labeled with low and high self-esteem confirms the notion that low self-esteem is generally undesirable. Zeigler-Hill and his colleagues (in press; see also Zeigler-Hill & Myers, 2011) presented participants with a single target, identified as low self-esteem or high self-esteem, and asked for their evaluations of the target. Whether the target was identified as low self-esteem by an explicit label (Study 3), a self-deprecating slogan on a T-shirt (Study 4), or their email address (Study 5, e.g., sadeyes@), participants rated an opposite-sex low self-esteem target as less romantically desirable than a high self-esteem target (Zeigler-Hill & Myers, 2011). However, ascribing negative characteristics to low self-esteem individuals is not just limited to decisions about an opposite-sex target. Zeigler-Hill and colleagues demonstrated that, regardless of match or mismatch of perceiver-target gender, when people thought a target had lower self-esteem they were more likely to ascribe negative traits to him or her, such as being lower in conscientiousness and openness to experience.

Overall, people are apt to assume that people with low self-esteem possess negative characteristics, whereas those with high self-esteem possess positive characteristics. Such assumptions are made at the group level (Cameron, MacGregor, et al., 2012; Cameron, Hole, & Cornelius, 2012) and at the individual level (Zeigler-Hill & Myers, 2011; Zeigler-Hill et al., in press). But are the characteristics ascribed to low and high self-esteem individuals so diametrically opposite? Although for the most part it is low self-esteem that people associate with negative qualities, there is a dark side to being labeled as having high self-esteem. People who are believed to have high self-esteem are seen as more narcissistic (Zeigler-Hill & Myers, 2011), self-absorbed, and egotistical (Cameron, MacGregor, et al., 2012; Cameron, Hole, & Cornelius, 2012) than those believed to possess low self-esteem. Moreover, the benefits of being seen as high self-esteem may be moderated by gender. When rating an opposite-sex target, men were often more positive toward female targets with moderate self-esteem than those with high self-esteem (Zeigler-Hill & Myers, 2011), suggesting that expressing high self-esteem may be disadvantageous at times. It is possible that group membership in other social categories may moderate how self-esteem shapes the impression one has on others, a question for future research.

Is there a light side to being labeled with low self-esteem? Unfortunately, the answer to this question seems to be no. According to Cameron and colleagues (Cameron, MacGregor, et al., 2012; Cameron, Hole, & Cornelius, 2012), fewer than 1% of the sample ascribed *any* positive characteristics to people with low self-esteem when asked to give open-ended descriptions. Furthermore, on the overwhelming majority of characteristics assessed, low self-esteem individuals were rated more negatively than high self-esteem individuals (Cameron, MacGregor, et al., 2012; Cameron, Hole, & Cornelius, 2012; Zeigler-Hill & Myers, 2011). Given the consistency and the extremity of the negativity toward those with low self-esteem, it appears that low self-esteem should be considered a stigma. A stigma is a "mark" of a devalued social identity (Crocker, Major, & Steele, 1998; Goffman, 1963) and the research discussed above confirms that people, at least in North America, devalue the social identity of "low self-esteem." Importantly, people believe that low self-esteem individuals may "contaminate" uncontrollable events, and thus including low self-esteem individuals in self-relevant events seems to "sour" future prospects (MacGregor & Gaucher, 2012). For example, participants thought they were less likely to win big when they imagined that a low, rather than a high, self-esteem person, had purchased the lottery ticket. Likewise, participants thought they were more likely to get sunburn if a low self-esteem individual had been responsible for planning the trip to the beach. We turn next to discussing the consequences of the low self-esteem stigma and the benefits of being labeled with high self-esteem.

Implications of self-esteem stereotypes

Those possessing a devalued social identity, like low self-esteem, are vulnerable to a host of negative consequences, such as discrimination. Discrimination may be especially likely for those identified as having low self-esteem because of the status-signaling function of self-esteem (Zeigler-Hill et al., in press). Such a finding would be unfortunate, but certainly consistent with a large literature documenting discrimination against low-status individuals (Dovidio, Brigham, Johnson, & Gaertner, 1996).

Research on discriminatory actions toward low self-esteem individuals is very much in its infancy. However, the evidence to date suggests that people do discriminate against those with low self-esteem. In two studies, Zeigler-Hill and Myers (2009) found that people were generally less willing to consider voting for political candidates who were assumed to have low self-esteem (Study 1) and who were explicitly labeled as low self-esteem (Study 2) as compared to high self-esteem candidates. A study by MacGregor, Cameron, and Holmes (2010) also suggests people may discriminate against low self-esteem people in hiring situations. Participants read a resumé and reference letter of a data analyst job applicant. The reference either contained a line suggesting the referee thought the applicant lacked self-confidence (low self-esteem condition) or this line was omitted (control condition). To make the skills required by the job relevant to the self-esteem of the applicant, the job was either described as requiring excellent social skills or no such information was provided. Previous research suggests that people perceive low self-esteem individuals as less socially skilled in general (Furr & Funder, 1998), and low self-esteem individuals are less prosocial when the situation is considered high risk (Cameron, Stinson, Gaetz, & Balchen, 2010). Participants then evaluated the job applicant. Unfortunately, high self-esteem individuals judged the low self-esteem applicant harshly without cause – they judged the low self-esteem applicant as less well suited to the job than the high self-esteem applicant even when the position required nothing that low self-esteem individuals might conceivably lack. On the other hand, low self-esteem individuals were particularly harsh (i.e., suggested a lower starting wage) with the low self-esteem candidate only when the job required social skill, indicating they may have special insight into the situations that elicit poor social responding among low self-esteem individuals. Although these results indicate that low self-esteem individuals may experience discrimination under some circumstances, to our knowledge no research to date has demonstrated discriminatory *behavior* against low self-esteem individuals.

Implications for close relationships

Not only might perceptions of others' self-esteem influence interactions among relative strangers, but they may also be particularly important in close relationships. Ample evidence demonstrates that a friend or partner's self-esteem can have actual relational consequences (Wood, Hogle, & McClellan, 2009). Relationships involving low self-esteem people tend to be less satisfying and less committed (Robinson & Cameron, in press), due at least in part to low self-esteem people's tendency to engage in defensive, self-protective behavior and their enhanced expectations of rejection (Bellavia & Murray, 2003; Murray, Bellavia, Rose, & Griffin, 2003). Mounting evidence suggests that people can intuit these disadvantages, and thus use self-esteem as an interpersonal signal. Indeed, people's lay theories about self-esteem contain negative expectations for relationships with low self-esteem partners. Research by MacGregor and Holmes (2007) suggests that people expect to be less satisfied in a romantic relationship with a low self-esteem partner than a high self-esteem partner, directly blaming low self-esteem individuals for relationship mishaps.

Given the generally negative expectations people have regarding low self-esteem individuals, it is perhaps not surprising that people may prefer to form relationships with more secure people (Latty-Mann & Davis, 1996). Indeed, it appears that people use self-esteem as a signal to indicate desirability as a mate: People report themselves as less likely to date or have sex with those explicitly labeled as having "low self-esteem" compared to those labeled as having "high self-esteem" (Zeigler-Hill & Myers, 2011).[1] Even when considering friendships, low self-esteem individuals are rated less socially appealing based on their email addresses (Chang & Swann, 2009) and Facebook updates (Forest & Wood, in press). In general, it appears that low self-esteem individuals are viewed as less-than-ideal relationship partners.

Despite people's explicit aversion to forming social bonds with low self-esteem individuals, those with low self-esteem do form close relationships. Nevertheless, even these established relationships may suffer when one person detects another's low self-esteem. For example, people believe that interactions with low self-esteem friends or family members are more exhausting and require more work than interactions with high self-esteem friends and family (Mac-Gregor & Holmes, 2007). In the context of romantic relationships, Lemay and Dudley's (2011) findings confirm the notion that relationships with low self-esteem individuals require extra relationship maintenance (or "work") as people attempt to "regulate" their romantic partner's insecurities. Specifically, participants who detected their partner's low self-esteem tended to exaggerate affection for their partner and conceal negative sentiments, likely in an effort to maintain harmony in their relationship. Unfortunately, this inauthenticity was actually associated with decreased relationship satisfaction for the regulating partner over time.

MacGregor and colleagues (MacGregor & Holmes, 2011; MacGregor, Fitzsimons, & Holmes, 2012) have explored a different type of communication in close relationships. Their focus was on capitalization, which is the disclosure of positive personal experiences to others (Gable, Reis, Impett, & Asher, 2004). In two experiments (MacGregor & Holmes, 2011), participants who were led to believe that their close other had low self-esteem capitalized less positively (i.e., enthusiastically) compared to control participants. The effect was consistent across the mode of disclosure (verbal or written) and relationship type (friendship or dating), and was not moderated by the discloser's own self-esteem. Moreover, in a study involving friend dyads, participants reported capitalizing less frequently with their friend to the extent they perceived him or her as having low self-esteem (MacGregor & Holmes, 2011; MacGregor, Fitzsimons, & Holmes, 2012). Furthermore, this pattern held in a dyadic interaction study, in which people capitalized less positively with their partner when they believed he or she had low, rather than high, self-esteem (MacGregor & Holmes, 2011; MacGregor, Fitzsimons, & Holmes, 2012). However, evidence from this study demonstrates that low self-esteem individuals are actually no less responsive to others' capitalization attempts than are high self-esteem partners. Despite this fact, MacGregor and Holmes (2011) found that people are reluctant to capitalize with low self-esteem individuals precisely because they expect them to be less responsive than high self-esteem partners. Thus people appear to be holding back from low self-esteem individuals unnecessarily. Nevertheless, the consequences may be very real given that capitalization is a process associated with personal and interpersonal benefits (Gable & Reis, 2010). Indeed, disclosers who were less enthusiastic while discussing their positive experiences in the lab interaction were more likely to experience decreased relationship satisfaction six weeks later (particularly for women; see MacGregor & Holmes, 2011; Mac-Gregor, Fitzsimons, & Holmes, 2012). More research is needed to examine other types of communication that may be influenced by perceptions of others' self-esteem.

Conveying and detecting self-esteem

Given that people negatively judge low self-esteem individuals and may even treat them poorly, are people motivated to convey or conceal their self-esteem? Answering this question is not as straightforward as it might first appear. First, low and high self-esteem individuals may be influenced by different motivations. High self-esteem individuals should feel unabated in conveying their self-esteem. Indeed, if their self-esteem is obvious to others, this should only have positive ramifications.[2] However, low self-esteem individuals may experience competing motivations. On the one hand, they may want to achieve acceptance and thus try to convey a high self-esteem image, or at least hide their low self-esteem status. Although people in general try to conceal their flaws and vulnerabilities from others (Baxter & Wilmot, 1985; DePaulo, Kashy, Kirkendol, Wyer, & Epstein, 1996), low self-esteem individuals are especially apt to conceal their deficiencies (e.g., Wood, Giordano-Beech, Taylor, Michela, & Gaus, 1994). By trying to appear to have higher self-esteem than they actually do, low self-esteem individuals may be trying to avoid the negative outcomes associated with looking like a low self-esteem person in Western society. On the other hand, low self-esteem individuals may want authentically to express who they are, seeking understanding and acceptance from significant others, a possibility we return to later in this section.

So, do low self-esteem individuals want to conceal their self-esteem? In the first two parts of the chapter, we have reviewed mounting evidence that people hold negative stereotypes about people with low self-esteem and that these low self-esteem individuals may experience discrimination based solely on their low self-esteem status. Moreover, low self-esteem individuals are aware of self-esteem stereotypes (Cameron, MacGregor, et al, 2012; Cameron, Hole, & Cornelius, 2012). Given that low self-esteem individuals are also hyper-vigilant to rejection (Downey & Feldman, 1996) and highly concerned with achieving acceptance from others (Leary & Baumeister, 2000), they may be particularly apt to conceal their low self-esteem from others in an attempt to procure acceptance. There is some evidence that this is indeed the case. Cameron (2010) asked participants to indicate how much they tried to conceal or reveal their self-feelings and insecurities with significant others (best friends, romantic partners, and parents). Those with lower self-esteem reported attempting to conceal their insecurities and self-doubts to a greater degree than those with higher self-esteem. Thus, even in close relationships, low self-esteem individuals appear to see the benefit of hiding their self-esteem.

Cameron, Hole, and Cornelius (2012) further investigated whether concealing self-esteem was linked with relational benefits for those with low self-esteem. In several studies, participants were asked to report their own self-esteem and then to provide their "self-esteem image", or what level of self-esteem they thought they had conveyed to their significant others. Participants then indicated their relationship quality (e.g., satisfaction, commitment, trust). Across all studies and across all relationship types studied (friends, romantic partners, and parents), people reporting a higher self-esteem image, regardless of their own self-esteem level, reported greater relationship quality. To bolster these correlational findings further, Cameron and colleagues conducted experiments wherein participants were led to believe that their self-esteem was either transparent to a friend or romantic partner or concealed from this person. In both studies, when low self-esteem participants believed their self-esteem was concealed, they reported greater relationship quality than when low self-esteem individuals believed their self-esteem was obvious. The converse was true for high self-esteem participants: when they believed their self-esteem was concealed, they suffered detriments in relationship quality compared to when they thought their self-esteem was obvious to their friend or partner. In other words, people reaped greater relational benefits when they believed a socially desirable quality (i.e., high self-esteem) had been conveyed. These results attest to the notion that low and high self-esteem individuals may have different motivations towards self-presenting their actual self-esteem, and ultimately there are different consequences for their true self-esteem being detected by others. However, both low and high self-esteem individuals benefit from believing that a high self-esteem image has been conveyed, though this experience may feel "inauthentic" for low self-esteem people.

Is it possible that low self-esteem individuals want to reveal their self-esteem? Although they try to conceal their low self-esteem and try to "pass" as a high self-esteem individual, there may also be motivations for low self-esteem individuals to reveal their low self-esteem to others. First, if self-esteem is an interpersonal signal, much like status signals in other animal species (see Zeigler-Hill et al., in press), then there may be costs associated with producing false signals (see Hurd & Enquist, 2005). For example, people with low self-esteem who successfully deceive others by presenting a high self-esteem image may be vulnerable to higher expectations from others, which they fear they cannot fulfill. Such social pressure should rouse anxiety (Wood, Heimpel, Newby-Clark, & Ross, 2005). Moreover, low self-esteem individuals may fear being discovered as high self-esteem "imposters," and suffering social rejection as a result. Thus, for low self-esteem individuals, exaggerating their self-esteem may not always seem worth the risk.

A second reason low self-esteem individuals may prefer to present an authentic self-esteem image is that people seem driven to confirm or verify their pre-existing self-views (e.g., self-verification theory; see Swann, 1983). Such self-verification affirms an individual's self-views and thus serves both the epistemic function of affirming people's sense of reality and the pragmatic function of guiding behavior in interpersonal interactions, as it lays out clear expectations and boundaries of how someone might behave in social situations. From this perspective, both low and high self-esteem individuals may hope to been seen as they truly are by their close others. Despite this drive, low self-esteem individuals do not always want to be seen as negatively as they see themselves. Both married and dating partners experience relational benefits when their partners view them positively, regardless of their self-esteem (Neff & Karney, 2002;

Swann, De La Ronde, & Hixon, 1994). In a recent meta-analysis, Kwang and Swann (2010) proposed that individuals desire verification *unless* there is a high risk for rejection. Thus, those with negative self-views may desire to be viewed positively, but only if being seen negatively jeopardizes their relationship. From this perspective, romantic partners should signal high self-esteem during courtship, job applicants should signal high self-esteem to potential bosses, and politicians should signal high self-esteem to their voters. Once the relationship has been cemented (and the potential for rejection has been reduced), however, people should desire to be seen as they are. Importantly, the results of the meta-analysis supported this proposal. While this boundary condition has shed some light on this debate, more research is needed to understand fully under what contexts people are motivated to communicate either positive or negative self-views.

So far, our discussion of conveying self-esteem has assumed that individuals have a choice in what image they present to others. In some cases, people may be simply unaware of the image they convey. In other cases, people may not be able to self-present continuously. Self-presentation is effortful and may actually exhaust low self-esteem individuals, leaving them vulnerable to self-regulation failure (see Vohs, Baumeister, & Ciarocco, 2005). Perhaps it is not surprising, then, that when the salience of rejection is low (as proposed by Kwang & Swann, 2010), such as disclosing on Facebook, those with low self-esteem present a more negative image to others (Forest & Wood, in press).

Self-esteem signals

How do people convey and detect self-esteem? Although there have been only a few studies investigating this question, self-esteem signals appear in many forms, ranging from public appearance to body stance, and even email addresses. Naumann, Vazire, Rentfrow, and Gosling (2009) photographed targets who had previously reported their own self-esteem, and had perceivers estimate the self-esteem of the targets. Self-rated self-esteem was positively associated with a healthier (vs sickly) appearance, smiling, energetic (vs tired) stance, and standing with arms behind the back (vs crossed arms). Furthermore, these cues were also associated with observer ratings of target self-esteem, suggesting that observers were able to pick up on self-esteem signals simply by viewing a photograph. Furthermore, Chang and Swann (2009) found self-esteem differences in the self-created email addresses that students provided their university for official purposes (e.g., "superstar@", "awkward_turtle@").[3] Specifically, self-rated self-esteem was positively associated with judges' ratings of email handles, indicating that self-esteem influenced self-presentation through email communication. Although the effects were relatively small, together these two studies suggest that people use appropriate cues to detect self-esteem. That is, people who present themselves in a self-enhancing manner – whether through physical cues or email addresses – are indeed more likely to have self-reported high self-esteem.

However, not all research suggests that people use appropriate cues to infer self-esteem. Cameron and her colleagues (Cameron, MacGregor, et al., 2012; Cameron, Hole, & Cornelius, 2012) found that participants were more likely to ascribe low self-esteem to targets possessing any single negative trait (e.g., cold, shy) and high self-esteem to targets possessing any single positive trait (e.g., attractiveness, intelligence, sociability). Importantly, participants did not discriminate between traits actually related to self-esteem (e.g., neuroticism and sociability, see Furr & Funder, 1998, or negative emotionality, see Murrell, Meeks, & Walker, 1991) and those unrelated to self-esteem (e.g., attractiveness, see Feingold, 1992, or intelligence, see Gabriel, Critelli, & Ee, 1994). Thus, it appears that people's judgments of others' self-esteem are partly well informed, yet also based on inaccurate stereotypes about characteristics not actually linked to self-esteem.

Accuracy in perceptions of self-esteem

If people use appropriate and inappropriate cues to detect self-esteem, do they form accurate impressions? Accurately detecting self-esteem should be a particularly difficult task relative to other social judgments people make. Traits that do not readily manifest in behavior, or are low in observability, should be more difficult to detect accurately (see Funder & Dobroth, 1987). Self-esteem is one of these "low-observability" traits (Vazire, 2010). A trait like extraversion, on the other hand, would be high in observability, because extraversion (e.g., talkativeness, enthusiasm) is easy to observe in others. Although the operationalization of accuracy is tricky (e.g., see Kenny & Albright, 1987), it does appear that people are somewhat accurate in their impressions of self-esteem. For example, Vazire (2010) found that a target's self-rated self-esteem and a close friend's judgment of the target's self-esteem were correlated with observed behaviors theorized to indicate self-esteem. Furthermore, research from various laboratories indicates that both friends (MacGregor et al., 2012; Watson, Hubbard, & Wiese, 2000; Watson, Suls, & Haig, 2002; Vazire, 2010; Zeigler-Hill et al., in press) and romantic partners (MacGregor et al., 2012; Swann & Gill, 1997; Watson, Hubbard, & Wiese, 2000) are fairly accurate in judging each other's self-esteem.

Self-esteem projection

Thus far, we have discussed the different cues (e.g., appearances, behaviors, email addresses, etc.) that people use to determine others' self-esteem. However, people may also use information that has nothing to do with the appearances or behaviors of target. Instead, people may make judgements about another's personality traits based on how they perceive their own traits (Hoch, 1987). In other words, people tend to project their own characteristics onto others (Lee et al., 2009; Murray, Holmes, Bellavia, Griffin, & Dolderman, 2002). Self-esteem judgments appear to be no different in this respect. People's ratings of others' self-esteem tend to be correlated with their own, be it for friends or romantic partners (Cameron, Hole & Cornelius, 2012; MacGregor et al., 2012; Mac-Gregor & Holmes, 2011). Given that some evidence demonstrates a small correlation between romantic partners' actual self-esteem (MacGregor et al., 2012; Robinson & Cameron, in press) and that people more generally tend to prefer to associate with those who are similar to themselves (Condon & Crano, 1988), using one's own self-esteem to determine that of a close other may be somewhat justifiable. Projection may indeed be more likely for a trait like self-esteem: given its low observability, people may have to rely on their own self-esteem to fill in the gaps about their knowledge of others. Overall, these results highlight the importance of controlling for a participant's own self-esteem when examining self-esteem impressions.

Future research

Although research exploring self-esteem as an interpersonal signal is growing, there are many open questions for future research. Perhaps the most glaring void in the research to date pertains to cross-cultural differences. All cultures do not view self-esteem in the same way. In East Asian cultures, for example, the term "self-esteem" is not commonly used, and when it is used it is viewed much differently than in Western cultures (Heine, Lehman, Markus, & Kityama, 1999). There is some evidence to suggest that East Asian cultures link high self-esteem with more negative qualities (Miller, Wang, Sandel, & Cho, 2002), and thus the implications of conveying a high self-esteem image in such cultures would be very different. Future research should aim to explore these cultural differences.

A second fruitful avenue for future research is to explore the source of self-esteem lay theories. Research to date identifies three potential sources: evolutionary status-based communication, social media, and just-world beliefs. First, high self-esteem may convey high social status and conveying such information would be evolutionarily adaptive. In this manner, self-esteem may be an inherent signal, designed to convey desirability as a mate (Zeigler-Hill et al., in press). Second, social media in North American culture may be contributing to self-esteem stereotypes. In the beginning of this chapter, we described the explosion of social interest in self-esteem. This interest is not confined to the internet; policies have been adopted by the public school system to enhance self-esteem (see Mecca, Smelser, & Vasconcellos, 1989), there is a national association created to enhance self-esteem (NASE), and even high-powered media icons like Oprah Winfrey have declared that "lack of self-esteem is the root of all the problems in the world" (see Harrison, 1999). The message in the social media seems abundantly clear: high self-esteem is a virtue, a badge of honor; and low self-esteem is a flaw, a mark of shame. A third potential source is that stereotypes about self-esteem are constructed to reinforce a just-world belief system. In a just world (Lerner, 1980), people who have low self-esteem should have a just reason for feeling bad about themselves, whereas people with high self-esteem should have a just reason for feeling good about themselves. From this perspective, the logical conclusion for the average person to make is that low self-esteem individuals are indeed bad people and high self-esteem individuals are indeed good people. Future research aimed at examining these three potential sources of self-esteem lay theories may illustrate how each process functions, and perhaps how these different sources may interact or reinforce each other.

A third potential area for future research is to explore the consequences of being labeled as low or high in self-esteem more carefully. Research by Cameron and her colleagues (Cameron, MacGregor, et al, 2012; Cameron, Hole, & Cornelius, 2012) suggests that being labeled as having low self-esteem has negative connotations, whereas being labeled as having high self-esteem has positive associations. However, research by Zeigler-Hill and his colleagues (in press) suggests that the positive connotations of high self-esteem may have its limits: women labeled with high self-esteem were seen less positively than women labeled as moderate in self-esteem by men. Thus, there may be other social identities or social contexts where a high self-esteem image is not as beneficial as it first appears. Are there social contexts where being seen as possessing low self-esteem is more advantageous? Further research investigating the discriminatory reactions of others to low self-esteem individuals may clarify the boundaries of the stigma of low self-esteem. Indeed, Cameron is building upon the foundation of stigma research by exploring how attributions of controllability (see Weiner, Perry, & Magnusson, 1988) of self-esteem might mitigate some of the negative effects of the low self-esteem stigma.

Finally, future researchers would benefit by investigating the process of self-esteem signaling and perception in more naturalistic dynamic interactions. Only a handful of studies have addressed this question, and the contexts wherein self-esteem can be conveyed far outnumber those that have been assessed already. We have highlighted here only a few of the possible avenues for research in this rich and growing area.

Conclusions and synthesis

Self-esteem is not only an internal experience but one that acts as an interpersonal signal in our social world. The self-esteem image that one presents to the world, or perhaps the self-esteem that one is labeled with, impacts how others evaluate and treat one. The research conducted in this area to date has illustrated that being branded as having low self-esteem has negative repercussions for impressions both related and unrelated to actual self-esteem (Cameron, MacGregor, et al, 2012; Cameron, Hole, & Cornelius, 2012; Zeigler-Hill & Myers, 2011). Furthermore, being branded as having low self-esteem may negatively impact the likelihood of being asked out on a date (Zeigler-Hill & Myers, 2011), hired for a job (MacGregor et al., 2010), or voted for as a political candidate (Zeigler-Hill & Myers, 2009). On the flip side, being seen as possessing high self-esteem can have positive consequences in all of these same domains. Although such findings might discourage those who possess low self-esteem, the research on accurately detecting self-esteem in others might actually be encouraging. Research on self-esteem detection suggests that people are not entirely accurate in detecting other's self-esteem, and so if people are inclined to hide their low self-esteem they may well be successful.

Notes

1 Low self-esteem individuals have many qualities that make them attractive partners, and recent work suggests they are able to advertise these qualities in some dating contexts (Brumbaugh & Fraley, 2010; but also see McClure, Lydon, Baccus, & Baldwin, 2010).
2 Except for high self-esteem women when trying to attract a male romantic partner (Zeigler-Hill & Myers, 2011).
3 To preserve participants' anonymity, these email addresses have been changed slightly.

References

Ashmore, R. D., & Del Beco, F. K. (1979). Sex stereotypes and implicit personality theory: Toward a cognitive-social psychological conceptualization. *Sex Roles, 5*, 219–248.

Baumeister, R. F., Smart, L., & Boden, J. M. (1996). Relation of threatened egotism to violence and aggression: The dark side of self-esteem. *Psychological Review, 103*, 5–33.

Baxter, L. A., & Wilmot, W. W. (1985). Taboo topics in close relationships. *Journal of Social and Personal Relationships, 2*, 253–269.

Bellavia, G., & Murray, S. (2003). Did I do that? Self-esteem-related differences in reactions to romantic partner's mood. *Personal Relationships, 10*, 77–95.

Brown, J. D. (1993). Self-esteem and self-evaluation: Feeling is believing. In J. Suls (ed.), *Psychological perspectives on the self* (Vol. 4, pp. 27–58). Hillsdale, NJ: Erlbaum.

Brumbaugh, C. C. & Fraley, R. C. (2010). Adult attachment and dating strategies: How do insecure people attract mates? *Personal Relationships, 17*, 599–614.

Cameron, J. J. (2010, June). *A Blessing or a Curse? The Consequences of Exaggerated Metaperceptions in Close Relationships*. Paper presented at the 71st Annual Convention for the Canadian Psychology Association, Winnipeg, Manitoba.

Cameron, J. J., Hole, C., & Cornelius, L. (2012). *Projecting a (false) sense of security: Self-esteem and the impact of beliefs about transparency of self-esteem in close relationships*. Manuscript in preparation.

Cameron, J. J., MacGregor, J. C. D., Hole, C., & Holmes, J. G. (2012). *The stigma of low self-esteem: Pervasive and extreme*. Manuscript in preparation.

Cameron, J. J., Stinson, D. A., Gaetz, R., & Balchen, S. (2010). Acceptance is in the eye of the beholder: Self-esteem and motivated perceptions of acceptance from the opposite sex. *Journal of Personality and Social Psychology, 99*, 513–529.

Chang, C. S., & Swann, W. B. (2009). *Wearing self-esteem like a flag: Conveying our high and low self-esteem to others*. Unpublished manuscript.

Condon, J. W., & Crano, W. D. (1988). Inferred evaluation and the relation between attitude similarity and interpersonal attraction. *Journal of Personality and Social Psychology, 54*, 789–797.

Cooley, C. H. (1902). *Human nature and the social order*. New York, NY: Scribner.

Coopersmith, S. (1967). *The antecedents of self-esteem*. San Francisco, CA: W. H. Freeman.

Crocker, J., Major, B., & Steele, C. M. (1998). Social stigma. In D. Gilbert, S. T. Fiske,

& G. Lindzey (eds.), *The handbook of social psychology* (4th edn). Boston, MA: McGraw-Hill.

DePaulo, B. M., Kashy, D. A., Kirkendol, S. E., Wyer, M. M., & Epstein, J. A. (1996). Lying in everyday life. *Journal of Personality and Social Psychology, 70*, 979–995.

Dovidio, J. F., Brigham, J. C., Johnson, B. T., & Gaertner, S. L. (1996). Stereotyping, prejudice, and discrimination: Another look. In N. Macrae, C. Stangor, & M. Hewstone (eds.), *Stereotypes and stereotyping* (pp. 276–319). New York, NY: Guilford Press.

Downey, G., & Feldman, S. I. (1996). Implications of rejection sensitivity for intimate relationships. *Journal of Personality and Social Psychology, 70*, 1327–1343.

Feingold, A. (1992). Good-looking people are not what we think. *Psychological Bulletin, 111*, 304–341.

Fiske, S. T., Cuddy, A. J. C., Glick, P., & Xu, J. (2002). A model of (often mixed) stereotype content: Competence and warmth respectively follow from perceived status and competition. *Journal of Personality and Social Psychology, 82* (6), 878–902.

Forest, A. L., & Wood, J. V. (in press). When social networking is not working: Individuals with low self-esteem recognize but do not reap the benefits of self-disclosing on Facebook. *Psychological Science*.

Funder, D. C., & Dobroth, K. M. (1987). Differences between traits: Properties associated with interjudge agreement. *Journal of Personality and Social Psychology, 52*, 409–418.

Furr, R. M., & Funder, D. C. (1998). A multimodal analysis of personal negativity. *Journal of Personality and Social Psychology, 74*, 1580–1591.

Gable, S. L., & Reis, H. T. (2010). Good news! Capitalizing on positive events in an interpersonal context. In M. L. Zanna (ed.), *Advances in experimental social psychology* (Vol. 42, pp. 195–257). New York, NY: Elsevier.

Gable, S. L., Reis, H. T., Impett, E. A., & Asher, E. R. (2004). What do you do when things go right? The intrapersonal and interpersonal benefits of sharing positive events. *Journal of Personality and Social Psychology, 87*, 228–245.

Gabriel, M. T., Critelli, J. W., & Ee, J. S. (1994). Narcissistic illusions in self-evaluations of intelligence and attractiveness. *Journal of Personality, 62*, 143–155.

Goffman, E. (1963). *Stigma: Notes on the management of spoiled identity.* Englewood Cliffs, NJ: Prentice-Hall.

Harrison, E. (1999). The importance of being Oprah. In J. Harris, J. Rosen, & G. Calpas (eds.), *Media journal reading and writing in popular culture* (2nd edn, pp. 187–201). Boston, MA: Allyn & Bacon.

Heine, S. J., Lehman, D. R., Markus, H. R., & Kitayama, S. (1999). Is there a universal need for positive self-regard? *Psychological Review, 106*, 766–794.

Hoch, S. J. (1987). Perceived consensus and predictive accuracy. The pros and cons of projection. *Journal of Personality and Social Psychology, 53*, 221–234.

Hurd, P. L., & Enquist, M. (2005). A strategic taxonomy of biological communication. *Animal Behaviour, 70*, 1155–1170.

Kenny, D. A., & Albright, L. (1987). Accuracy in interpersonal perception: A social relations analysis. *Psychological Bulletin, 102*, 390–402.

Koch, E. J. (2006). Examining the role of self-esteem in psychological functioning and well-being. In M. H. Kernis (ed.), *Self-esteem: Issues and answers* (pp. 260–266). New York, NY: Psychology Press.

Kwang, T., & Swann, W. B., Jr. (2010). Do people embrace praise even when they feel unworthy? A review of critical tests of self-enhancement versus self-verification. *Personality and Social Psychology Review, 14*, 263–280.

Latty-Mann, H., & Davis, K. E. (1996). Attachment theory and partner choice: Preference and actuality. *Journal of Social and Personal Relationships, 13*, 5–23.

Leary, M. R., & Baumeister, R. F. (2000). The nature and function of self-esteem: Sociometer theory. In M. P. Zanna (ed.), *Advances in experimental social psychology* (Vol. 32, pp. 1–62). New York, NY: Academic Press.

Leary, M. R., & Downs, D. L. (1995). Interpersonal functions of the self-esteem motive: The self-esteem system as a sociometer. In M. Kernis (ed.), *Efficacy, agency, and self-esteem* (pp. 123–144). New York, NY: Plenum.

Leary, M. R., Tambor, E., Terdal, S., & Downs, D. L. (1995). Self-esteem as an interpersonal monitor: The sociometer hypothesis. *Journal of Personality and Social Psychology, 68*, 518–530.

Lee, K., Ashton, M. C., Pozzebon, J. A., Visser, B. A., Bourdage, J. S., & Ogunfowora, B. (2009). Similarity and assumed similarity in personality reports of well-acquainted persons. *Journal of Personality and Social Psychology, 96*, 460–472.

Lemay, E. P., & Dudley, K. L. (2011). Caution: Fragile! Regulating the interpersonal security of chronically insecure partners. *Journal of Personality and Social Psychology, 100*, 681–702.

Lerner, M. (1980). *The belief in a just world: A fundamental delusion*. New York, NY: Plenum Press.

MacGregor, J. C. D., Cameron, J. J., & Holmes, J. G. (2010, February). *Discriminating against people with low self-esteem: Are low self-esteem individuals each others' worst enemy?* Poster presented at the annual meeting of the Society for Personality and Social Psychology, Las Vegas, NV.

MacGregor, J. C. D., Fitzsimons, G. M., & Holmes, J. G. (2012). *Stifling success stories: Perceiving low self-esteem in close others impedes capitalization*. Manuscript in preparation.

MacGregor, J. C. D., & Gaucher, D. (2012, January). *Sunny days and lottery winnings: Associations with low self-esteem people taint judgments about uncontrollable events*. Poster accepted for presentation at the 13th Annual Conference of the Society for Personality and Social Psychology, San Diego, CA.

MacGregor, J. C. D., & Holmes, J. G. (2011). Rain on my parade: Perceiving low self-esteem in close others hinders positive self-disclosure. *Social Psychological and Personality Science, 2*, 523–530.

MacGregor, J. C. D., & Holmes, J. G. (2007). *Self-esteem awareness first study*. Unpublished raw data.

McClure, M. J., Lydon, J. E., Baccus, J. R., & Baldwin, M. W. (2010). A signal detection analysis of chronic attachment anxiety at speed dating: Being unpopular is only the first part of the problem. *Personality and Social Psychology Bulletin, 36*, 1024–1036.

Mecca, A. W., Smelser, N. J., & Vasconcellos, J. (1989). *The social importance of self-esteem*. Berkeley, CA: University of California Press.

Miller, P. J., Wang, S., Sandel, T., & Cho, G. E. (2002). Self-esteem as folk theory: A comparison of European, American and Taiwanese mothers' beliefs. *Parenting: Science and Practice, 2*, 209–239.

Murray, S. L., Bellavia, G. M., Rose, P., & Griffin, D. W. (2003). Once hurt, twice hurtful: How perceived regard regulates daily marital interactions. *Journal of Personality and Social Psychology, 84*, 126–147.

Murray, S. L., Holmes, J. G., Bellavia, G., Griffin, D. W., & Dolderman, D. (2002). Kindred spirits? The benefits of egocentrism in close relationships. *Journal of Personality and Social Psychology, 82* (4), 563–581.

Murrell, S. A., Meeks, S., & Walker, J. (1991). Protective functions of health and self-esteem against depression in older adults facing illness or bereavement. *Psychology and Aging, 6*, 352–360.

Naumann, L. P., Vazire, S., Rentfrow, P. J., & Gosling, S. D. (2009). Personality judgments based on physical appearance. *Personality and Social Psychology Bulletin, 35*, 1661–1671.

Neff, L. A., & Karney, B. R. (2002). Judgments of a relationship partner: Specific accuracy but global enhancement. *Journal of Personality, 70*, 1079–1112.

Richman, L. S., & Leary, M. (2009). Reactions to discrimination, stigmatization, ostracism, and other forms of interpersonal rejection: A dynamic multi-motive model. *Psychological Review, 116*, 365–383.

Robinson, K. J., & Cameron, J. J. (in press). Self-esteem is a shared relationship resource: Additive effects of dating partners' self-esteem levels predict relationship quality. *Journal of Research in Personality.*

Senar, J. C. (2006). Bird colors as intrasexual signals of aggression and dominance. In G. E. Hill & K. J. McGraw (eds.), *Bird coloration: Vol. 2. Function and evolution* (pp. 125–193). Cambridge, MA: Harvard University Press.

Solomon, S. (2006). Self-esteem is central to human well-being. In M. H. Kernis (ed.), *Self-esteem: Issues and answers* (pp. 254–259). New York, NY: Psychology Press.

Stinson, D. A., Logel, C., Zanna, M. P., Holmes, J. G., Cameron, J. J., Wood, J. V., & Spencer, S. J. (2008). The cost of lower self-esteem: Testing a self- and social-bonds model of health. *Journal of Personality and Social Psychology, 94*, 412–428.

Swann, W. B., Jr. (1983). Self-verification: Bringing social reality into harmony with the self. In J. Suls & A. G. Greenwald (eds.), *Social psychological perspectives on the self* (Vol. 2, pp. 33–66). Hillsdale, NJ: Erlbaum.

Swann, W. B., Jr, De La Ronde, C., & Hixon, J. G. (1994). Authenticity and positivity strivings in marriage and courtship. *Journal of Personality and Social Psychology, 66*, 857–869.

Swann, W. B., Jr, & Gill, M. J. (1997). Confidence and accuracy in person perception: Do we know what we think we know about our relationship partners? *Journal of Personality and Social Psychology, 73*, 747–757.

Tooby, J., & Cosmides, L. (1996). Friendship and the banker's paradox: Other pathways to the evolution of adaptations for altruism. *Proceedings of the British Academy, 88*, 119–143.

Twenge, J. M. (2006). *Generation me: Why today's young Americans are more confident, assertive, entitled – and more miserable than ever before.* New York, NY: Free Press.

Uleman, J. S., Saribay, S. A., & Gonzalez, C. M. (2008). Spontaneous inferences, implicit impressions, and implicit theories. *Annual Review of Psychology, 59*, 329–360.

Watson, D., Hubbard, B., & Wiese, D. (2000). Self-other agreement in personality and affectivity: The acquaintanceship, trait visibility, and assumed similarity. *Journal of Personality and Social Psychology, 78*, 546–558.

Watson, D., Suls, J., & Haig, J. (2002). Global self-esteem in relation to structural models of personality and affectivity. *Journal of Personality and Social Psychology, 83*, 185–197.

Weiner, B., Perry, R. P., & Magnusson, J. (1988). An attributional analysis of reactions to stigmas. *Journal of Personality and Social Psychology, 55*, 738–748.

Williams, K. D. (2007). Ostracism. *Annual Review of Psychology, 58*, 425–452.

Wood, J. V., Giordano-Beech, M., Taylor, K. L., Michela, J. L., & Gaus, V. (1994). Strategies of social comparison among people with low self-esteem: Self-protection and self-enhancement. *Journal of Personality and Social Psychology, 67*, 713–731.

Wood, J. V., Heimpel, S. A., Newby-Clark, I. R., & Ross, M. (2005). Snatching defeat from the jaws of victory: Self-esteem differences in the experience and anticipation of success. *Journal of Personality and Social Psychology, 89*, 764–780.

Wood, J. V., Hogle, A., & McClellan, J. C. D. (2009). Self-esteem and relationships. In H. Reis & S. Sprecher (eds.), *Encyclopedia of Human Relationships* (Vol. 3, pp. 1422–1425). Thousand Oaks, CA: Sage.

Vazire, S. (2010). Who knows what about a person? The self-other knowledge asymmetry (SOKA) model. *Journal of Personality and Social Psychology, 98*, 281–300.

Vohs, K. D., Baumeister, R. F., & Ciarocco, N. J. (2005). Self-regulation and self-presentation: Regulatory resource depletion impairs impression management and effortful self-presentation. *Journal of Personality and Social Psychology, 88*, 632–657.

Zeigler-Hill, V., Besser, A., Myers, E. M., Southard, A. C., & Malkin, M. L. (in press). The status-signaling property of self-esteem: The role of self-reported self-esteem and perceived self-esteem in personality judgments. *Journal of Personality*.

Zeigler-Hill, V., & Myers, E. M. (2009). Is high self-esteem a path to the White House? The implicit theory of self-esteem and the willingness to vote for presidential candidates. *Personality and Individual Differences, 46*, 14–19.

Zeigler-Hill, V., & Myers, E. M. (2011). An implicit theory of self-esteem: The consequences of perceived self-esteem for romantic desirability. *Evolutionary Psychology, 9*, 147–180.

9 Changing self-esteem through competence and worthiness training

A positive therapy

Christopher J. Mruk and Edward J. O'Brien

There are at least three good reasons anyone interested in self-esteem would do well to begin by defining how the term is to be used in a given work. For one thing, operational definitions are an important part of the scientific method because specifying how one is employing a concept avoids unnecessary confusion. For another, areas of research often involve multiple or competing definitions of basic terms, a condition that necessitates identifying one's position from the outset. Finally, setting the stage in this way establishes solid foundations for the entire body of a particular work. Consequently, this look at self-esteem begins by first defining what is meant by that term and then describes a highly structured psychoeducational program called competence and worthiness training (CWT) that has been shown to enhance self-esteem. Also, CWT emphasizes expanding experiences and increasing behaviors that result in authentic or healthy self-esteem instead of focusing on more problematic ones. Thus, it is shown that CWT may also stand as a form of positive therapy.

Although John Milton is generally credited with coining the term "self-esteem" in 1642 (Patrides, 1985), the concept was introduced to American psychology by William James in 1890. Thus, this topic is one of the oldest and most heavily researched themes in the discipline. Indeed, even a cursory search of the PsycINFO database reveals that the term is used in the title of over 8,300 articles, chapters, and books, and occurs as an identified subject in over 17,200 works. Similarly, Rhodewalt & Tragakis (2003) reported that self-esteem is the third-most frequently occurring theme in personality and social psychology, following gender and negative affectivity. During this time, three definitions appear to have given rise to relatively consistent schools of thought, research, and findings concerning self-esteem.

James' original work on self-esteem defined it as a ratio of a person's successes divided by the number of failures in areas of life that matter to the individual in regard to personal identity. As he said,

> So our self-feeling in this world depends entirely on what we *back* ourselves to be and do. It is determined by the ratio of our actualities to our supposed potentialities; a fraction of which our pretensions are the denominator and the numerator our success: thus, Self-esteem = Success/Pretensions. Such a

fraction may be increased as well by diminishing the denominator as by increasing the numerator.

(James, 1890/1983, p. 296)

The careful reader will notice that there are several crucial dimensions of this definition to appreciate. In particular, by emphasizing the word "back" in italics, James views self-esteem in terms of a particular type of action, ability, or behavior that in today's parlance is probably best captured by the word "competence."

This approach to self-esteem results in a very rich stream of work beginning with psychodynamic theories, such as seen in Adler's (1927) notion of a need to compensate for an innate sense of inferiority by demonstrating one's individual superiority. Bandura's (1997) idea of self-efficacy, which emphasizes beliefs about one's abilities and likelihood of success, may stand as a more contemporary manifestation. Another aspect of this definition worth noting is that it is the basis for the discrepancy model of self-esteem, which focuses on the difference between one's "real" or actual self and one's so-called "ideal self" (Pope, McHale, & Craighead, 1988). Finally, James' original definition also included something that is particularly germane to this chapter, namely the dynamic nature of self-esteem, especially how to change it. In other words, by defining self-esteem as a ratio, James also offered a key to altering it. Self-esteem may be increased by helping people to become more competent in areas of life that are meaningful to them, helping them to reduce failures in those areas, or both.

Unfortunately, the weaknesses associated with defining self-esteem largely in terms of competence are also substantial. One obvious difficulty is that it is possible to be very competent at very negative forms of behavior. Such proficiencies as the ability to lie, skill in manipulating others, and the willingness to intimidate or even harm people in order to succeed are seldom associated with genuine, healthy self-esteem. Yet, being good at bad things, so to speak, would satisfy a definition of self-esteem based on success. Clearly, neither Milton nor James originally intended to make such a proposal. A deeper look at the problem reveals that tying self-esteem to success has the unfortunate consequence of making failure almost as important. Such contingent self-esteem, as it is now becoming called (Crocker & Park, 2004), means that people who base their sense of self on success may also be highly vulnerable to its other side: potential failures. The results of such a condition are, of course, a greater sensitivity to failure, becoming vigilant concerning that possibility, and developing costly ways of avoiding failure or defending against its meaning when failure occurs. Research based on this way of understanding self-esteem, for example, often ties it to many types of psychological and social problems, including low self-esteem, perfectionism, and eating disorders. Indeed, there is an entire literature on what is known as "defensive" self-esteem based on similar notions (Coopersmith, 1967; O'Brien & Epstein, 1983, 1988; Mruk, 2006).

Although psychologists first defined self-esteem in relation to competence, this approach is not the one utilized most often in social science. Instead, the distinction goes to Rosenberg's (1965) approach, which is based on understanding self-esteem as an attitude or affect concerning personal worth, especially the degree to which one feels good about oneself. As he said, "High self-esteem ... expresses the feeling that one is 'good enough.' The individual simply feels that he is a person of worth; he respects himself for what he is" (Rosenberg, 1965, p. 31). One advantage of this definition is that focusing on one's attitude or feelings lends itself to the development of fairly basic self-report measures. Such scales or inventories make research much easier to conduct than attempting to assess actual levels of skill and their meaning for a given individual, which is important for competence-based definitions. Consequently, Rosenberg's ten-item Self-Esteem Inventory (1965) is so widely used in the field that nearly one-quarter of all the research done on self-esteem is reported to involve this instrument (Tafarodi & Swann, 1996). A second advantage is that earlier research on self-esteem was largely limited to clinical and social psychology. However, defining self-esteem in terms of worth and creating easy-to-use measurements for it became popular in the educational and legislative arenas of the late 1980s. This development played an important role in the popularization of self-esteem and the so-called "self-esteem movement" of the early 1990s in which self-esteem was seen as a "social antidote" for a host of personal and social problems (Mruk, 2006).

Defining self-esteem largely in terms of a sense of worth or worthiness also involves serious limitations. First, such a definition emphasizes feeling good about oneself over actually earning a good experience, for example through honest work, real accomplishments, or actual ability. Second, having a sense of worth without evidence to support the position creates a certain danger sometimes referred to as the "dark side" of self-esteem (Baumeister, Smart, & Boden, 1996). For instance, developing this type of self-esteem as a child may lead to unrealistic expectations of what to expect in adult life, an inflated sense of worth based on overestimating the value of one's abilities or accomplishments, and, much more seriously, the development of clinically significant phenomena such as narcissism or violent behavior (Baumeister, Smart, & Boden, 1996).

It is important to note that the one thing each of these two major definitions of self-esteem holds in common is that it is founded on a single factor, namely either competence or worthiness. By contrast, the third approach defines self-esteem as a relationship between these two variables, which is why it is most commonly referred to as a two-factor approach (Tafarodi & Swann, 1995). One of the chief advantages to this definition is that it avoids the pitfalls of the others. For example, from this vantage point, self-esteem can never be based on feelings of worth alone, because such affect must be warranted by corresponding meritorious characteristics or actions as well. In the same fashion, competence alone cannot provide a legitimate basis for self-esteem because not all forms of success are worthy. In other words, self-esteem is more than just praise or success: in all cases, genuine, healthy self-esteem is earned by the quality of one's choices and actions, especially when facing the challenges of living.

Like the others, this more existential definition of self-esteem also gives rise to a body of empirically supported research demonstrating its value. For example, Gecas (1971) began thinking in terms of two factors when he noticed that Rosenberg's scale is more effective in accounting for various adolescent phenomena only after the test items are broken down into those that assess competence and those that measure worthiness, rather than a simple combined score. Kernis (2003) found that making authentic choices based on one's own intrinsic values and motivations is associated more with healthy (i.e., stable and non-defensive) self-esteem than its unstable or defensive forms. Epstein (1979), Jackson (1984), and Mruk (1983) found both factors to be involved in what may be called self-esteem moments, which are times of life associated with facing certain challenges of living, such as establishing healthy relationships, standing up for one's intrinsic values, or responding to losses and setbacks with integrity. Finally, one major self-esteem measure, namely the Multidimensional Self-Esteem Inventory or MSEI (O'Brien & Epstein, 1983, 1988), happens to be based on assessing both competence and worthiness. Not so coincidentally, this test is one of the few that includes a scale capable of differentiating authentic self-esteem from its defensive forms.

Enhancing authentic (healthy) self-esteem

As we just saw, definitions make an important difference when dealing with the theory of self-esteem or research concerning it. However, defining what one means may be even more important at the applied or clinical levels, because this affects the lives of real human beings. Thus it is important to note that CWT is a self-esteem enhancement program based on helping people identify strengths and weaknesses in the two areas of life that affect self-esteem: competence and worthiness. In addition, the program rests upon three sets of findings. The first concerns the general features that most standard self-esteem programs have in common, such as a structured format that includes specific stages, some sort of assessment of individual self-esteem, and a series of experiential, cognitive, or behavioral activities aimed at fostering self-esteem (Mruk, 2006). Next, CWT emerges from qualitative research that involved examining self-esteem moments, or times in life when one faces a challenge of living that has a positive or negative impact on one's competence and worthiness, and therefore self-esteem as defined by the two-factor approach. Third, the program consists of well-established standard therapeutic techniques, such as cognitive restructuring and problem-solving methods, and can be empirically validated through pre- and post-testing (Mruk, 2006).

The program is a well-structured set of five progressively related two-hour group sessions that are typically offered over five weeks at the rate of a single two-hour session per week. Each session consists of a set of specific goals, activities, and handouts that guide participants and clinicians throughout the process. In respective order, the sessions focus on: (1) understanding self-esteem in terms of competence and worthiness; (2) identifying self-esteem strengths and weaknesses for each participant through the MSEI; (3) providing activities designed to enhance one's sense of worth as a person; (4) offering opportunities to develop greater competence; and (5) ending by helping participants to develop a way of continuing to enhance self-esteem on their own once the program is completed. CWT has been used with various clinical populations, including those working on such issues as anxiety or depression, as well as non-clinical groups interested in personal growth and development. The MSEI is used to assess self-esteem strengths and weaknesses as well as to validate the program, so it makes good sense to present the nature of the instrument and how it is compatible with the two-factor approach before examining each step in some detail.

The Multidimensional Self-Esteem Inventory (MSEI)

The MSEI was developed from previous theories of self-esteem and self-esteem sources, along with gathering thousands of incidents that participants reported as impacting on their self-esteem (O'Brien & Epstein, 1988). Participants reported incidents affecting their self-esteem over periods of time ranging from a day, to a week, a month, a year, or over the participant's entire life. Categorizing these incidents led to the identification of eight specific areas of life experience that impact on overall self-esteem. These eight categories allowed correct classification of 96.3% of nearly 3,000 self-esteem diary incidents (O'Brien & Epstein, 1988). Four of these categories of self-esteem can be construed as corresponding to worthiness issues in which the source of self-esteem is more dependent on acceptance and worth: lovability, likability, moral self-approval, and body appearance. These categories have in common that they are based in part on a judgment of acceptance and value as a person (worthiness), rather than on competence. Four categories can likewise be related to competence issues: competence, personal power, self-control, and body functioning. Each of these categories involves issues of effectance (Bakan, 1966) or being able to act in a way that impacts on the world.

In addition to the eight specific areas or components of self-esteem, the MSEI includes a global measure of self-esteem (global self-esteem), a global measure of having a secure sense of identity (identity integration), and a measure of defensiveness (defensive self-enhancement). The two global measures provide an overall view of feelings of worthiness and sense of security in one's identity and purpose in life. The defensiveness scale provides a way to differentiate between secure vs insecure self-esteem, with high scores representing biased self-presentations that deny weaknesses and claim strengths that may not correspond to genuine self-evaluations. Extensive validity evidence can be found in studies that have utilized the MSEI in research and clinical work (O'Brien, 2010).

From a self-esteem change perspective, the MSEI provides a number of important areas that can be targeted to increase self-esteem related to worthiness and competence. Global measures of self-esteem (including the global self-esteem scale in the MSEI) are useful, but may not provide sufficient specificity to know how a particular client might initiate self-esteem change. Measures that are too specific are also problematic, as noted earlier in the William James definition of self-esteem, in that a specific competency like athletic success will be meaningless to someone whose competence is attached to musical rather than athletic performance. The eight components of self-esteem identified above have the advantage that they are each strongly related to overall self-esteem, and thus changes in these component areas can be expected to have an impact on overall self-appraisal. The mid-level specificity of these scales provides direction as to how one might both build on one's strengths and overcome weaknesses. Consider, for example, two commonly observed profiles: the first profile describes people who view themselves as extremely competent (strength) while doubting their ability to create and maintain close love relationships (weakness); the second profile describes people who feel very popular and liked by peers, but doubt their abilities to succeed in a career (doubts about competence). Interventions that recognize and build on individuals' strengths while addressing their perceived weaknesses are more likely to succeed than more generalized interventions based only on global self-esteem (e.g., Rosenberg, 1965). There are many other possible MSEI profile variations that allow the MSEI to have considerable flexibility in accounting for various client patterns of worthiness and competence.

Defensiveness is a critical element in evaluating self-esteem. Some individuals present themselves as having positive self-esteem, but this image may be part of a broader negative pattern of underlying negativity, instability, contingent, and/or narcissistic self-evaluations. The MSEI approach to dealing with such defensiveness involves evaluating a social desirability bias in which individuals claim rare virtues (e.g., gladly accepting criticism) and deny common human weaknesses (e.g., never trying to avoid unpleasant responsibilities). Evaluating defensiveness scores on the MSEI allows insight into likely biases in self-appraisal. For example, consider the example of a client in an adolescent outpatient clinic who was in serious jeopardy of being imprisoned for failure to follow through with court-mandated drug treatment after being caught dealing drugs to support his heroin habit. This person reported near "perfect" self-esteem in all MSEI self-esteem scales, but also scored near "perfect" on the defensiveness scale. The score on the defensiveness scale allowed a more accurate consideration of this client's other self-evaluations as being part of a pattern of denial that had led the client to such a precarious life situation. Addressing client defensiveness in treatment requires considerable therapist skill, without which clients are at risk of dropping out of treatment (for example, if challenged too directly) or of not benefiting from treatment (for example, if clients maintain their defensive self-evaluation).

Interesting research findings have led to other considerations regarding how positive self-evaluations might have a dark side. For example, Kernis and others showed that some individuals who rate themselves positively also had considerable variability in their overall feelings of worthiness, and such instability was associated with some of the "dark" sides of high self-esteem, such as narcissism and aggression when goals are frustrated (see Kernis, 2003, for a review). Unfortunately, this work has not led to clinical assessment or intervention approaches that provide norms or strategies for addressing this concern. Likewise, contingent self-esteem studies (e.g., Crocker & Park, 2004; Crocker, Brook, Niiya, & Villacorta, 2006) have suggested another dark side of positive self-appraisal in which individuals become vulnerable due to their dependence on external validation for their self-esteem. General principles from this work may be useful for clinical consideration, but no specific implications have yet been developed or tested for assessing or intervening clinically to address contingent self-esteem.

There has been a voluminous outpouring of research in the area of narcissism, with PsycINFO identifying over 3,000 publications related to either "narcissism" or "narcissistic personality disorder" since 1990. Much of this research has relied on the Narcissistic Personality Inventory (NPI; see Raskin & Terry, 1988), which purports to measure a single dimension of narcissism in normal individuals but which has repeatedly been shown to be a multidimensional measure that includes some maladaptive elements (e.g., entitlement) along with other adaptive elements (e.g., leadership qualities). This has led to discriminant validity problems for the NPI in which some elements of scores are related to problematic functioning while other elements are related to adaptive functioning. While it is true that narcissists seek out leadership roles, it is not the case that leaders are necessarily high in narcissism; seeking leadership roles is thus perhaps a correlate of narcissism but should not be included in the measurement of narcissism in order to avoid confounding the measure. Such confounding is no doubt partly responsible for the controversies surrounding research in this area (Ackerman et al., 2011). It is important, regardless of the controversies in the narcissism literature, clinically to assess and treat narcissistic trends as one attempts to raise self-esteem. In one clinical trials outcome study of CWT (Bartoletti, 2008) it was found that implementing the CWT program led to increases in self-esteem without leading to increases in narcissism.

The importance of changing self-esteem in the direction of authentic positive self-esteem seems obvious to most clinicians, but given the controversies in this field (e.g., Baumeister, Campbell, Krueger, & Vohs, 2003) it is perhaps worth making the case as to why most clinicians emphasize the importance of seeking authentic high self-esteem. First, self-esteem is intimately tied to other global markers of adjustment and well-being, such as optimism, life satisfaction, or depression (e.g., low self-esteem is a specific criterion for diagnosing depression). The strength of the association among these markers of global adjustment has led some to argue that creation of an overall aggregate index of adjustment may produce more robust findings than are obtained by the individual elements of this index (Judge, Erez, Bono, & Thoresen, 2002). Most clinicians would argue that there is value in these global adjustment markers in terms of assessment and treatment, even if none of these markers shows strong prediction to specific behavioral criteria. For example, it is often found that markers such as global self-esteem show correlations with school performance that are in the .20 to .30 range (Baumeister et al., 2003; O'Brien, Bartoletti, Leitzel, & O'Brien, 2006).

Second, links between global adjustment and specific performance indicators should be expected to be low because of differences in the bandwidth or generality of such measures. That is, global self-esteem and depression are aggregate indicators of a broad range of life-event judgments, whereas specific performance measures may not be equally relevant for different individuals. For some, school performance is of central importance, whereas for others school may be of little importance compared to sporting events, social activities, or musical involvements. It is useful to recall that no global marker of adjustment (e.g., optimism, life satisfaction, depression, or self-esteem) shows strong links to specific performance measures such as school performance (O'Brien et al., 2006). A recent example in the depression literature found that depression scores in adolescents correlated −.18 with school performance (Li & Lerner, 2011). These findings do not mean that depression, optimism, life satisfaction, or self-esteem is unimportant nor do they mean that school performance is unimportant. These findings *do* mean that life adjustment is at a different level of integration or centrality than school performance, since the former variables integrate school, social, familial, and socio-cultural factors into a broad bandwidth measure, whereas the latter is more specific. Consistent with findings of strong relationships between self-esteem and other global measures of adjustment Bartoletti (2008) found that successful change in self-esteem was associated with increases in optimism (Peterson, Buchanan, & Seligman, 1995) and constructive thinking (Epstein, 2001).

Promotion of authentic positive self-esteem is one way to promote overall psychological adjustment. Such increases in self-esteem and adjustment are important in their own right, since having positive self-esteem, being optimistic, finding constructive ways to cope with life problems, and being free of depression are worthy goals in and of themselves. In certain cases such broad markers of adjustment can also be relevant to specific problems of living, such as drug abuse or poor school performance, even if global adjustment measures show only modest correlations with such specific behavioral problems in the general population. In some cases drug use and abuse can be, at least in part, a self-medication for depression, and poor school performance can be understood as a product of a negative self-view, pessimism, depression, and poor constructive thinking. Interventions to address drug abuse or poor school performance need to take into account multiple factors related to these problems (peer group influences, family problems, academic preparation, etc.), and such interventions should typically be multimodal, including self-esteem change along with other components (e.g., tutoring to promote realistic performance in school, family interventions to promote appropriate supports for school performance). Treatments that focused only on improving school performance while ignoring global adjustment would be problematic, as it would be nonsensical to conduct treatments that allow people to do well in school while continuing to be depressed and self-loathing. There are certainly many students who perform well in school and yet are severely depressed and lacking in self-esteem. The CWT program aims to address both competence and worthiness issues in a more comprehensive approach to promote positive adjustment.

The program

Each of the five steps that constitute the standard offering of CWT includes a number of procedures, activities, handouts, and commentary that are found in the third edition of the book, *Self-Esteem Research, Theory, and Practice: Toward a Positive Psychology of Self-Esteem* (Mruk, 2006), and subsequent editions. Although it is not possible to duplicate all of that information here, it is reasonable to provide readers with an overview of the program in order to understand how it works and why it may be regarded as a form of positive psychotherapy (Mruk, 2006).

Step 1: the focusing phase

This step is designed to achieve three goals. The first is to introduce participants to the idea of working on enhancing self-esteem, especially as a group. After all, some participants may be unfamiliar with the concept of group work and others may have issues that make group work frightening. In order to address these concerns, participants are provided with a simple handout that lists each of the five steps and very briefly describes what is to occur in each one. This "road map" of the program and group eases some anxiety and provides the foundation for a good working or the clinical contract for the rest of the meetings.

The next part of the session consists of common icebreaker activities, such as describing the facilitator's professional background, introducing individuals to each other, and so forth. It is also important to help people understand self-esteem in terms of competence and worthiness. This goal is achieved through an exercise that involves presenting both parts of the definition and then giving people the opportunity to "existentialize" their understanding of these two factors and how they pertain to self-esteem. Typically, participants are given a handout that asks them to write a description of two experiences. One involves a time they demonstrated competence at dealing with a challenge, and the other a time when they felt worthwhile as a person. Depending on how comfortable the group seems to feel with self-disclosure, participants may be asked to share what they wrote with the rest of the group. The group is then instructed to start a self-esteem journal by tracking such positive (but not negative, as they already do too much of that) self-esteem-related moments until the next meeting.

Finally, we end the first session by administering the MSEI. It usually takes approximately 20–30 minutes for most individuals to complete the 116-question instrument, as its questions are fairly straightforward. However, people read at different rates, and presenting the test at the end of the session allows individuals to stay past the two hours allotted for the first meeting if necessary. Another advantage of ending the first session on this note is that people are generally curious about themselves and may become more motivated to return to the second meeting in order to receive their results.

Step 2: the awareness phase

The goal of this session is to help participants develop a greater awareness of the various types of self-esteem and how they manifest themselves behaviorally and experientially. A handout describing the basic types of self-esteem is covered, but special attention is paid to low self-esteem because it is so common in these groups. In addition, some attention is given to defensive self-esteem and its more common manifestations, such as hypersensitivity to criticism, a sense of fragility, the tendency to be highly critical of self and others, and so forth. Some mention is also made of medium self-esteem because it is the most common type, and because, for many, getting to that level is often a major achievement in itself. Finally, healthy authentic self-esteem is discussed as a final goal.

The second half of the session is dedicated to helping participants understand the results of their individual self-esteem profiles, which are scored between the first and second session to save time. Although the MSEI's 11 clinical scales are important, going over all of them is avoided for two reasons. First, such detailed coverage takes too much time with 10–12 people in a group, not to mention that many of them would not have the psychological background necessary to understand all of the information available through the instrument. Second, since the program is a practical one, it is much more useful simply to inform each individual about their highest and lowest scores for the scales that measure competence, and then for those that assess worthiness. This information is conveyed on a form given to each participant individually, so that it is personalized. The facilitator then explains all eight of the scales, so that everyone can understand what the MSEI may be telling them about their particular self-esteem profiles.

The step ends with a review of four major sources of self-esteem that have been identified in the literature (personal achievement, having the ability to influence one's environment, acceptance, and virtuous behavior). Special attention is given to the ideas that achievement and influence are tied to competence, as well as how acceptance and virtue are connected to worthiness, so that participants can see how the sources of self-esteem correspond to both of its definitional factors. Finally, participants are asked to add another theme to their journals. In addition to tracking new self-esteem moments where they found themselves being competent or worthy or both, they are now asked to start paying attention to the sources of self-esteem that seem most available in their own lives.

Step 3: the enhancing phase (increasing worthiness)

The lack of self-acceptance and engaging in self-demeaning cognitive behaviors often decrease sense of worth. Several fairly standard activities can be used to address this basic self-esteem problem, focusing especially on changing negative, irrational, or dysfunctional thinking patterns. Most clinicians today are familiar with this well-established therapeutic technique. Whether based on Ellis and Harper (1977), Burns (1980), or others, the basic idea is that mental habits that detract from one's sense of dignity as a person and can result in a loss of esteem for oneself may be connected to such things as depression, anxiety, or poor relationships. The rationale underlying the technique is that breaking these destructive cognitive habits and replacing them with more rational, functional, or positive ones also changes affect and behavior in the desired direction. Indeed, there is so much evidence supporting cognitive therapy today that we do not need to reference its clinical efficacy. However, research also shows that five cognitive distortions, such as overgeneralizing or personalizing events, are common to most of the major lists of negative thinking patterns proposed by leading cognitive therapists (Mruk, 2006). Thus, CWT focuses on helping participants to understand and identify these. Handouts are offered in this regard, and the facilitator illustrates the process of cognitive restructuring by offering an example from his or her own life. He or she then asks for a volunteer to offer an instance for the group to process. Identifying and correcting irrational thinking patterns is then assigned as homework for the next week, which is to be recorded in the self-esteem journal.

Step 4: enhancing phase (increasing competence)

Many authors point out that merely helping people feel good about themselves does little good in the long run, and may do some harm. For example, Damon (1995) discusses how such "feel-good" self-esteem programs offered in the educational setting may facilitate believing that one's academic abilities are sufficient, when in fact they are not. As the title of one popular article on such programming described the problem, it is one of "Feeling Good, Doing Bad" (Leo, 1990). Fortunately, the two-factor approach helps us avoid such pitfalls by always providing a counterpoint, namely earning the feeling of being worthy through meritorious actions and behaviors, or, to paraphrase, "Doing Good, Feeling Good."

One especially powerful way of experiencing a sense of worth as a person is to face a life challenge competently. Such challenges can range from the routine (e.g., dealing with ordinary developmental issues, such as becoming an adult) to the heroic (e.g., facing one's own limitations in an authentic fashion, such as confronting a personal fear). Facing personal and interpersonal existential challenges with integrity, which is to say in ways that reflect competence *and* worthiness, creates the very type of experiences and moments that enhance self-esteem because they involve both of its factors. Similarly, failing to face them in earnest lessens self-esteem for the same reason. Thus, CWT includes a variation of another well-established therapeutic technique that fosters competence, namely increasing one's ability to solve problems effectively.

As with cognitive therapy, there are many variations of this technique from which to choose. CWT employs a modification of the problem-solving method developed by D'Zurilla and Goldfried (1971). The session begins by reviewing a handout that explains the basic concepts involved in solving problems effectively, especially learning how to recognize a problem when it is still in its early stages by paying better attention to feelings. The handout also includes a step-by-step problem-solving method that is examined in detail. Next, the facilitator selects a problem in his or her own life that is real but not excessively personal and uses it to work through the steps, asking the participants to assist in the process. After being shown how the method may be applied to a real-life problem through this demonstration, participants are then asked to volunteer to do the same. This time, the facilitator and the group help the individual to develop a good plan. "Good" is defined as reasonable, realistic, and responsible. Finally, participants are assigned the homework of identifying a problem they would like to work on in their own lives, develop a step-by-step plan for it, and track their progress in the journal over the next week.

Step 5: the management phase (maintaining self-esteem)

The last step is extremely important for two reasons. One concerns the usual issues associated with "termination" or, to use a gentler term, "transitioning." Most clinicians and facilitators are familiar with this process so there is no need to detail it. However, the other set of issues deserves more explicit attention because after this session participants go back to managing their self-esteem largely on their own. Also, because self-esteem is an existential issue, managing it is a life-long process we all must deal with, even under the most ideal conditions (Harter, 1999; Trzesniewski, Robins, Roberts, & Caspi, 2004). Therefore, in addition to equipping people for maintaining the gains associated with the program, it is also important for them to learn how to manage self-esteem in the future.

The session begins with discussing two things: the fact that people have had self-esteem problems for many years, which means that permanent change takes time, and the notion that self-esteem is a life-long issue because challenges of living will always meet us down the road. Next, the focus shifts to understanding how each such challenge actually constitutes a positive self-esteem opportunity that we can use to our advantage, providing we understand what is at stake in the situation and do our best to respond to it authentically. In order to create a sense of how to manage self-esteem effectively, participants are then asked to create an individual self-esteem action plan that is based on the results of the MSEI and the enhancing skills taught in the program.

They begin by examining their own MSEI results, which had been given to them earlier and consisted of their highest and lowest scores out of eight competence- or worthiness-based domains of self-esteem covered by the instrument. The four competence-related scales include competence, personal power, self-control, and bodily functioning. The four worthiness-based scales consist of lovability, likability, moral self-approval, and bodily appearance. Usually, individuals have sufficient levels of self-esteem that they are best served by working on lower or more problematic areas in order to raise them. However, sometimes people are in such poor self-esteem shape that risking failure is too much to ask, and they are advised to work on increasing strengths to higher levels before taking on a weakness. Either way, participants are asked to select an area in which they would like to improve and are then shown how to design a program for the targeted domain.

The plan involves identifying whether the domain they selected to work on is tied primarily to competence or to worthiness, in order to understand which sources of self-esteem are most likely to be helpful. Participants are then asked to use the problem-solving method to design a step-by-step strategy aimed at turning the challenges of living that emerge in the targeted domain into positive self-esteem moments. For example, if someone suffers from a lack of competence in a domain of life that he or she feels is important, then he or she may elect to develop a plan aimed at increasing skills relevant to that area. If someone suffers from a lack of acceptance, then selecting a volunteer activity of interest might increase his or her sense of worth. Naturally, participants are asked to continue their self-esteem journals to whatever degree they find helpful, as journal writing is another established therapeutic tool.

One final comment is necessary before moving on to the last section of this chapter. It is extremely important to understand that although CWT is a highly structured program that can be "manualized," such a description would miss two very important dimensions concerning the role of the therapist or facilitator. First, as with all effective therapies, there are certain aspects of the process that these key individuals bring into play. Such "common factors," as they are often called (Prochaska & Norcross, 1994), are the intangible interpersonal qualities necessary to create a nurturing and transformative environment. For example, all such programs work better if the leader is genuine, respectful, compassionate, and offers hope, for example, while interacting with participants. Second, in this program the facilitator is as much a teacher as a therapist and, like much good teaching, being a positive role model is an important part of the process. Offering personal examples of cognitive restructuring and problem solving is one valuable way to help people build healthy behavior. Although it is always important to be mindful of the pitfalls of self-disclosure, transference, and countertransference, it is usually beneficial to remember that teaching by showing and doing are important parts of the learning process.

CWT, validity, and positive psychology

Fortunately, CWT is characterized by several features that facilitate researching its clinical efficacy, something that is increasingly important in the era of evidence-based therapy. First, CWT is founded on a clear operational definition that is consistently used throughout the program. For example, each step is based on the two factors found in the definition and specifically addresses them in a systematic fashion. Next, the major clinical activities of journal writing, homework, cognitive restructuring, and problem-solving are all standard techniques that have their own bodies of supportive literature. In addition, the program is highly structured in a stepwise fashion. This characteristic increases reliability and allows researchers to replicate the process. Finally, the fact that CWT includes a good measure of self-esteem is important. Not only is the MSEI used early in the program but it can also be employed at its end, meaning that setting up a pre- and post-test design is a straightforward process that can be readily employed by researchers.

Consequently, the program has been used in a number of community mental health and college counseling center settings, some of which have also been researched with published results (Hunt, 2010). For example, CWT was initially evaluated in a community mental health setting by Hakim-Larson and Mruk (1997). Mruk ran the program with several clinical groups suffering from anxiety or depression, as well as with a non-clinical group as a control. Hakim-Larson independently analyzed the data generated by pre- and post-testing with the MSEI. In another study, CWT was offered in a community mental health setting, a college counseling setting, and also included a control group (Bartoletti & O'Brien, 2003). More recently, a larger-scale study that applied CWT to healthy populations to assess its power as a form of positive psychology has been conducted in conjunction with the Institute of Positive Psychology in Denmark (Haringsma, 2011). All three studies found positive change in the expected direction – an increase in self-esteem – as indicated by the MSEI. Moreover, the size effect for the clinical groups was large. While smaller for the "normal" group, the increase was still moderate which is as it should be if clinical groups suffer greater problems with self-esteem than non-clinical or normal populations.

Finally, there is good reason to believe that CWT may be regarded as a "positive therapy." Positive therapy is an applied dimension of the new positive psychology that emerged at the end of the twentieth century. Although clearly preceded by humanistic psychology, the goals of positive psychology focus on researching and facilitating positive or healthy experiences, positive or admirable characteristics, and positive or prosocial behavior (Seligman & Csikszentmihalyi, 2000). Thus, positive therapy is distinguished by focusing on such things as expanding periods of well-being in a person's life and increasing individual strengths rather than concentrating on problems or weakness, though those are dealt with as well. However, unlike humanistic therapies, positive therapy also insists upon traditional empirical evidence (Seligman, Steen, Park, & Peterson, 2005). Thus, most positive therapies are also systematic, time-limited, often manualized, and always evidence-based.

CWT appears to meet these criteria. Instead of focusing on negative self-esteem moments, for example, the self-esteem journal asks participants to describe positive ones. Rather than talking about failures, the program aims at successfully dealing with life's challenges. Similarly, CWT emphasizes self-esteem strengths as well as weaknesses. In addition, the program is standardized, time-limited, and accompanied by enough independent empirical research to stand as evidence based. In short, CWT is an existentially based form of positive therapy that has been shown to enhance self-esteem in both clinical and general-population settings. Thus it is hoped that the approach continues to receive research attention in the future. For example, new areas of research could include investigating whether or not CWT can be modified for clinical populations beyond those that involve depression and anxiety, such as for those who suffer from schizophrenic or bipolar disorders. Similarly, some educators expressed interest in this model and its psychoeducational approach (Jindal-Snape & Miller, 2008), prompting questions concerning the possibility of modifying it for use with children, adolescents, and adults in educational settings.

References

Ackerman, R. A., Witt, E. A., Donnellan, M. B., Trzesniewski, K. H., Robins, R. W., & Kashy, D. A. (2011). What does the Narcissistic Personality Inventory really measure? *Assessment, 18*, 67–87.

Adler, A. (1927). *Understanding human nature*. New York, NY: Fawcett.

Bakan, D. (1966). *The duality of human existence*. Chicago, IL: Rand McNally.

Bandura, A. (1997). *Self-efficacy: The exercise of control*. New York, NY: W. H. Freeman & Co.

Bartoletti, M., & O'Brien, E. J. (2003, August). *Self-esteem, coping and immunocompetence: A correlational study*. Poster session presented at the annual meeting of the American Psychological Association, Toronto.

Bartoletti, M. (2008). Effectiveness of Mruk's self-esteem change program on psychological and physiological measures of well-being. *Dissertation Abstracts International: Section B: The Sciences and Engineering, 68* (8-B), p. 5557.

Baumeister, R. F., Campbell, J. D., Krueger, J. I., & Vohs, K. D. (2003). Does high self-esteem cause better performance, interpersonal success, happiness, or healthier lifestyles? *Psychological Science in the Public Interest, 4*, 1–44.

Baumeister, R., Smart, L., & Boden, J. (1996). Relation of threatened egotism to violence and aggression: The dark side of self-esteem. *Psychological Review, 103*, 5–33.

Burns, D. (1980). *Feeling good: The new mood therapy*. New York, NY: Signet.

Coopersmith, S. (1967). *The antecedents of self-esteem*. San Francisco, CA: Freeman.

Crocker, J., Brook, A. T., Niiya, Y., & Villacorta, M. (2006). The pursuit of self-esteem: Contingencies of self-worth and self-regulation. *Journal of Personality, 74*, 1749–1771.

Crocker, J., & Park, L. E. (2004). The costly pursuit of self-esteem. *Psychological Bulletin, 130*, 392–414.

Damon, W. (1995). *Great expectations: Overcoming the culture of indulgence in our homes and schools*. New York, NY: Free Press.

D'Zurilla, T. J., & Goldfried, M. R. (1971). Problem solving and behavior modification. *Journal of Abnormal Psychology, 78*, 107–126.

Epstein, S. (1979). The ecological study of emotions in humans. In K. Blankstein (ed.), *Advances in the study of communications and affect* (pp. 47–83). New York, NY: Plenum.

Epstein, S. (2001). *CTI: Constructive thinking inventory*. Odessa, FL: Psychological Assessment Resources, Inc.

Ellis, A., & Harper, R. (1977). *A new guide to rational living*. North Hollywood, CA: Wilshire Book Company.

Gecas, V. (1971). Parental behavior and dimensions of adolescent self-evaluation. *Sociometry, 34*, 466–482.

Hakim-Larson, J., & Mruk, C. (1997). Enhancing self-esteem in a community mental health setting. *American Journal of Orthopsychiatry, 67*, 655–659.

Haringsma, R. C. (2011). Competence and worthiness training as a positive psychological intervention to enhance self-esteem: A randomized trial. VU University, Denmark.

Harter, S. (1999). *The construction of the self: A developmental perspective.* New York, NY: Guilford.

Hunt, B. (2010). Women and self-esteem. In M. Guindon (ed.), *Self-esteem across the lifespan* (pp. 191–204). New York, NY: Routledge.

Jackson, M. (1984). *Self-esteem and meaning: A life historical investigation.* Albany, NY: State University of New York.

James, W. (1890/1983). *The principles of psychology.* Cambridge, MA: Harvard University Press.

Jindal-Snape, D., & Miller, D. J. (2008). A challenge of living? Understanding the psycho-social processes of the child during primary-secondary transition through resilience and self-esteem theories. *Education Psychological Review, 20,* 217–236.

Judge, T. A., Erez, A., Bono, J. E., & Thoresen, C. J. (2002). Are measures of self-esteem, neuroticism, locus of control, and generalized self-efficacy indicators of a common core construct? *Journal of Personality and Social Psychology, 83,* 693–710.

Kernis, M. H. (2003). Optimal self-esteem and authenticity: Separating fantasy from reality. *Psychological Inquiry, 14,* 83–89.

Leo, J. (1990, May 18). Damn, I'm good! *U.S. News and World Report,* p. 21.

Li, Y., & Lerner, R. M. (2011). Trajectories of school engagement during adolescence: Implications for grades, depression, delinquency, and substance use. *Developmental Psychology, 47,* 233–247.

Mruk, C. (1983). Toward a phenomenology of self-esteem. In A. Giorgi, A. Barton, & C. Maes (eds.), *Duquesne studies in phenomenological psychology* (Vol. 4, pp. 137–148). Pittsburgh, PA: Duquesne University Press.

Mruk, C. (2006). *Self-esteem research, theory, and practice: Toward a positive psychology of self-esteem* (3rd edn). New York, NY: Springer Publishing Co.

O'Brien, E. J. (2010). Bibliography of references to the Multidimensional Self-Esteem Inventory (MSEI). Odessa, FL: Psychological Assessment Resources.

O'Brien, E. J., Bartoletti, M., Leitzel, J., & O'Brien, J. P. (2006). Global self-esteem: Divergent and convergent validity issues. In M. Kernis (ed.), *Self-esteem: Issues and answers* (pp. 26–35). New York, NY: Psychology Press.

O'Brien, E., & Epstein, S. (1983). Manual for the sources of self-esteem inventory. Unpublished manuscript, Bucknall University, Lewisburg, PA.

O'Brien, E., & Epstein, S. (1988). *MSEI: The multidimensional self-esteem inventory.* Odessa, FL: Psychological Assessment Resources.

Patrides, C. A., II. (1985). *John Milton: Selected prose.* Columbia, MS: University of Missouri Press.

Peterson, C., Buchanan, G. M., & Seligman, M. E. P. (1995). Explanatory style: History and evolution of the field. In. G. M. Buchanan & M. E. P. Seligman (eds.), *Explanatory style* (pp. 1–20). Mahwah, NJ: Lawrence Erlbaum Associates.

Pope, A., McHale, S., & Craighead, E. (1988). *Self-esteem enhancement with children and adolescents.* New York, NY: Pergamon Press.

Prochaska, J. O., & Norcross, J. C. (1994). *Systems of psychotherapy: A transtheoretical analysis* (3rd edn). Pacific Grove, CA: Brooks/Cole.

Raskin, R., & Hall, C. S. (1979). A narcissistic personality inventory. *Psychological Reports, 45,* 590.

Raskin, R., & Terry, H. (1988). A principal-components analysis of the Narcissistic

Personality Inventory and further evidence of its construct validity. *Journal of Personality and Social Psychology, 54*, 890–902.

Rhodewalt, F., & Tragakis, M. W. (2003). Self-esteem and self-regulation: Toward optimal studies of self-esteem. *Psychological Inquiry, 14*, 66–70.

Rosenberg, M. (1965). *Society and the adolescent self-image.* Princeton, NJ: Princeton University Press.

Seligman, M. E. P., & Csikszentmihalyi, M. (2000). Positive psychology: An introduction. *American Psychologist, 55*, 5–14.

Seligman, M. E. P., Steen, T. A., Park, N., & Peterson, C. (2005). Positive psychology progress: Empirical validation of interventions. *American Psychologist, 5*, 410–421.

Tafarodi, T. W., & Milne, A. B. (2002). Decomposing global self-esteem. *Journal of Personality, 70*, 443–483.

Tafarodi, R. W., & Swann, W. B., Jr. (1995). Self-liking and self-competence as dimensions of global self-esteem: Initial validation of a measure. *Journal of Personality Assessment, 65*, 322–342.

Tafarodi, R. W., & Swann, W. B., Jr. (1996). Individualism-collectivism and global self-esteem: Evidence for a cultural trade-off. *Journal of Cross-Cultural Psychology, 27*, 651–672.

Trzesniewski, K. H., Robins, R. W., Roberts, B. W., & Caspi, A. (2004). Personality and self-esteem development across the life span. In P. T. Costa & I. C. Siegler (eds.), *Psychology of Aging* (pp. 163–185). Amsterdam: Elsevier Science.

Index

Page numbers in *italics* denote tables, those in **bold** denote figures.